'This fantastic book marks a significant addition to the conceptual and theoretical tools for analysing contemporary human mobility. Through an analysis of migration/movement and labour/active life, Tataryn explores how our coming together in a shared world is not only governed but shaped through nation states, markets, and law. She demonstrates how labour migration helps us better understand and imagine contemporary socialities and goes beyond critique to open up new possibilities for imagining ways of being together in the world. Migration needs new thinking, and this is what this book gives us.'

– **Bridget Anderson,** *Professor of Migration, Mobilities and Citizenship, University of Bristol, UK*

'A new light is shed on labour migration with this book. Through Jean Luc Nancy's work on ecotechnics, Tataryn links the political dimension of migration with geopolitical, technological, legal, philosophical, and broadly understood ecological concepts, and allows us to imagine a new material and embodied way of conceptualising migration and thereby resisting easy neoliberal constructions. It shows how migration is not an isolated phenomenon but the inescapable sense of our ontological condition. This is a profoundly topical book, unapologetically putting labour migration at the forefront of the contemporary global political move to the right, and offering strategies of resistance that question the usual preponderance of the market, the nation-state, and the law. Migration is no longer a problem to be solved but an onto-epistemic plurality of flows.'

– **Andreas Philippopoulos-Mihalopoulos,** *Professor of Law & Theory, University of Westminster, UK*

Law, Migration and Precarious Labour

Providing a radical new approach to labour migration, this book challenges the prevailing legal and political construction of the figure of the irregular migrant labourer, whilst at the same time reimagining this irregularity as the basis of an alternative, post-capitalist, sociality.

The text draws on the work of contemporary philosopher Jean-Luc Nancy, and more specifically his term 'ecotechnics', in order to examine how economic, political, and juridical norms deny the full legal status of certain people who are deemed to be irregular. This ostensible irregularity is revealed as a regular feature of labour market practice, and a necessary support for the conceptual foundations of capitalist legality. As this book shows, however, this legality – and with it, the technological subordination of life to the circulation of capital as if this were the only possibility for our being in the world – is not insurmountable. The book's consideration of the figure of the irregular migrant labourer comes to provide an alternative basis for reimagining our relationships not only with migration and with labour itself, but ultimately with each other.

This powerful analysis of contemporary labour migration is of considerable interest to legal and political theorists, philosophers, labour lawyers, migration experts, and others with theoretical, political, or policy interests in this area.

Anastasia Tataryn is an Assistant Professor at St. Jerome's University of Waterloo, Canada.

Law, Migration and Precarious Labour

Ecotechnics of the Social

Anastasia Tataryn

Routledge
Taylor & Francis Group
LONDON AND NEW YORK

First published 2021
by Routledge
2 Park Square, Milton Park, Abingdon, Oxon OX14 4RN

and by Routledge
605 Third Avenue, New York, NY 10017

First issued in paperback 2022

Routledge is an imprint of the Taylor & Francis Group, an informa business

British Library Cataloguing-in-Publication Data
A catalogue record for this book is available from the British Library

Library of Congress Cataloging-in-Publication Data
A catalog record for this book has been requested

ISBN: 978-0-367-62166-7 (pbk)
ISBN: 978-1-138-70049-9 (hbk)
ISBN: 978-1-315-20467-3 (ebk)

DOI: 10.4324/9781315204673

Typeset in Bembo
by Apex CoVantage, LLC

To the movement, that keeps us all in love.

Contents

Acknowledgements

The initial premise of this book was conceived during my years as a PhD student at the Birkbeck School of Law, under the guidance of Peter Fitzpatrick. I am indebted to the liveliness of intellectual life, dynamism, generosity and thoughtfulness of my friends and colleagues that I met during my years in London. You all continue to inspire, challenge and shape me as a thinker. Thank you. Thank you especially to Stephen Connolly, Stacy Douglas and Dan Matthews, who at crucial moments during the writing of this book provided much-needed conversations and comments on chapter drafts, in spite of us now being scattered around the world. To Colin Perrin, thank you for all the thought-provoking conversations and support as an editor and a friend.

The work and writings of so many brilliant thinkers (critical theorists, migration and labour law scholars), researchers and investigative journalists nurtured me as I developed this book, most of whom are cited throughout the text and bibliography. In particular, I continuously returned to Jean-Luc Nancy's philosophy, Aníbal Quijano's critique and Bridget Anderson's research for guidance and energy. Thank you.

Thank you to the University of Liverpool Department of Law for institutional support during a year-long research leave, without which completing this would not have been possible.

It would be remiss of me not to extend a big thank you to the wonderful participants and hosts of the Garsdale creative writing retreat in Yorkshire. In addition to creating a comfortable, inspirational and delicious environment for writing, as non-academic writers you gave me the space I needed to open my thinking and graciously put up with me trying to explain ecotechnics during the early stages of articulation. And thank you to Jane Kite for permission to reprint Styx.

My parents, Maria and Myroslaw, painstakingly read through multiple drafts and tirelessly offered comments, discussions and encouragement across distances and time zones. Your patience, support and faith in me is truly infinite. And thank you too to Aleksandra and Myroslava for perspective, and constant love.

To Seán Columb, thank you for challenging me to write and communicate more clearly. As a colleague, your intellectual bravery and courageous research will forever push me to root my thinking in experience, and to listen to the narratives of those on the ground, however uncomfortable, risky and frame-breaking these may be. Thank you for the hours you spent reading and providing thoughtful comments to this manuscript and the ideas behind it. As a companion, and most of all, thank you for the time you were living *home* with me.

I dedicate this book to the movement, that keeps us all in love.

Styx

but there must be

you took my wad of notes
you're supposed to give me
an authority to travel
that I can fold safe and neat
into a partitioned purse
or curl through my fingers for a while
or even slip into the pouch of photographs
i have taped to my heart

a ticket is proof
that you will take me to the other side
and life will go on
don't cheat me
a voucher chit or stamp is evidence
to the authorities
that I'm going somewhere
I am legitimate
proves i don't ride reckless

step in you say
the inflatable is near brim full

Jane Kite
janekite.co.uk

1 The ecotechnics of immigration and employment law

In this book, I address situations that have become new normals in migration (movement across territorial boundaries) and conditions of work (labour). As new norms, current practices and discourses of migration and labour expose a deeper 'crisis' of politics, economics and law. Each day, news headlines, reported events and soundbites from politicians seem to reach new levels of catastrophe and disbelief. News fatigue is not limited to being exhausted by horrific events, for instance people dying by the hundreds at sea along migrant routes; villages being attacked by Daesh fighters or Boko Haram or Russian or American or Saudi or British-backed military jets; children being shot at in schools and shopping malls; islands and coastal villages being decimated by extreme weather or earthquakes; wildfires ravaging forests and ecosystem; coral reefs bleached, icebergs melting, ocean levels rising and desertification spreading. We are exhausted by the deferral of responsibility (Medland et al. 2019), the short-sightedness and the obfuscation of reality guiding politicians, political conduct and debate around the world (Trilling 2018).

Humanity, in its mess, is hurtling towards drastic ecological change caused by resource extraction, industrialisation, contamination, poisoning of water systems and the widespread destruction of biodiversity. Technology expels its residue both materially and in the breakdown of empathetic relationality through the reification of the 'social'. This new social is an ephemeral space, where Tweets replace political expertise, debate and diplomacy, and insecurities about everything from physical appearance to opinions on political matters are loudly filtered, edited, judged, and indiscriminately circulated. The rapid pace of technological development and infiltration into every minutia of our lives: sourcing and consuming calories (food), digesting, moving, sleeping, communicating, choosing friends, partners, reproducing, prolonging life, and selecting life, is unprecedented. Life is being outsourced, physically and mentally, for the benefit of capital accumulation favouring a fragment of the world's population (Anderson 2017, 1534). We experience this, and yet as plural and diverse people we have yet to develop pluralistic and contextualised understandings of this infiltration. In the meantime, attempts to remedy or resolve the increasingly common experiences of insecurity and precarity originate in the modern liberal political-economic-legal system. The historically and culturally specific onto-epistemological framework of this system may or may not have ever successfully addressed challenges to social, political, economic and cultural experience. Yet, as seemingly the only option available, this paradigm continues to frame our understanding and experience of twenty-first-century technological life.

Joining other scholars and writing that looks towards 'plural, ethicopolitical' rethinking, reimagining and reimbodiments (see Kothari et al. 2019, xxviii; Thomas-Pellicer and De Lucia 2016, 10; Grear in Thomas-Pellicer and De Lucia 2016, 2; Philippopoulos-Mihalopoulos 2015, 11; Viveiros De Castro 2004, 484), I put forward ecotechnics as an onto-epistemological challenge to explore, disrupt and exceed normative categories in migration and labour law. Ecotechnics, a term drawn from Jean-Luc Nancy, provides a diagnosis as well as a deconstructive possibility. In this introductory chapter, I will first sketch my understanding and use of the term ecotechnics. Second, I will demonstrate how ecotechnics can be applied to being, migration and labour, and why ecotechnics is a helpful onto-epistemological challenge through which to understand the technologies, legal and otherwise, associated with migration and labour. Third, I will provide a chapter outline of the subsequent chapters, to conclude with a summary of the overarching themes of the book.

Ecotechnics – what?

In the introduction to her book on Judith Butler's work, Moya Lloyd comments on Butler's writing style: Butler poses questions in the place of normative assertions, 'to open a field rather than close it' (Lloyd 2007, 22). Butler identifies and questions the normative violence where contingent foundations categorise bodies – people – as corporeal ontologies in a particular way. The normative categories imposed through this violence are the focus of political projects that seek recognition and agency for persons or groups marginalised by the mainstream. Paradoxically, there is on the one hand, a political fight for subjugated identities, for persons (bodies) to be recognised and not discriminated against within the existing system of categories and norms. On the other hand, the norms are based on contingent foundations, grounded by a particular conceptualisation of being (ontology) that has created a system that constructs, and subjugates, difference. Within this Western, modern, liberal paradigm, the autonomous individual 'I' is privileged in what Mignolo (2010) refers to as 'ego-logics'. The recognition of persons who do not conform to the ego-logical norm will always be insufficient and limited. Juridical systems of power assign categories and align subjectivities according to normative categories that are assumed to be necessary and natural and, moreover, the only possibility for recognition (see Marks 2011). The norm is affirmed constantly through language, discourses and popular culture including media, news and social media. Failure to conform to the norm renders persons abnormal, sub-citizen, or irregular. Furthermore, the fault of not conforming is attributed to the failure of the marginalised individual, not to the system allocating recognition.

Where persons are identified as 'irregular' and 'migrant' and 'worker', these labels serve a purpose in the circulation of political, juridical, economic and technical processes. These categories, and the bodies interpreted into these labels, are part of the world that is ecotechnical. Nancy (2012) asserts that our world is now ecotechnical. Moreover, there is nothing outside the ecotechnical circulation of being. The normative violence of contingent foundations identified by Butler is part of an ecotechnical reality. But what is ecotechnics? The term ecotechnics links the *eco*, home, environment (from οικος, meaning dwelling, and used in eco-nomic and eco-logy), with *technē* (from τέχνη, meaning 'craft' or 'art', and used in techn-ology, techn-ique), the technical structure that orders and 'makes sense of' the interruptive, incoherent and incommensurable (see Miller 2012). Thus, ecotechnics refers to the circulation of techne, technologies, of capital, of law, of intelligibility, that circulate at the same time as we are existing in eco-: the sense that sustains and maintains being in the world. To diagnose the world as ecotechnical is to say that everything, everyone, every being, moves as techne (overwhelmingly experienced as capital) and eco – this is how we create, how we live and how we give meaning to our reality.

Etymologically linked with 'economy' and 'ecology', ecotechnics is distinct from both. Yet, at the same time, it is intricately connected to the former two terms. In ecology, oikos is joined with logos (λόγος), meaning form, or ground. Ecology is the form of dwelling or habitating in the world. Ecology refers to the form that our environment exists in and assumes. In economy, oikos joins with nomos (νόμος), meaning order or law: the law or order of dwelling. Distinctly, ecotechnics is oikos with *technē* (τέχνη), the craft or technique of dwelling. Towards the conclusion of this book, I offer a fourth term which moves towards the possibility of opening thought to 'eco', by not denying, but existing in spite of ecotechne: the term *ecosociality*, which joins oikos + social (*socialis*) meaning allied, common, to explore dwelling in common.

As a term, ecotechnics recognises both environment/home (dwelling/eco) and craft (techne/technology) when referring to the capital circulation in the world that affects the circulation of sense. *Sense* refers to the circulation of life that exceeds containment into techne (Hutchens 2005, 141). Ecotechnics diagnoses a circulation of life that has been dominated by processes of neoliberalisation, including current key market values such as flexibility, casualisation and mobility reinforced within the nation-state. These processes of neoliberalisation technologise the reproduction of being through the coming together of singular beings in a plural (eco), which happens in spite of neoliberalisation (Nancy 2000). Our being is, from Nancy (2000), singular plural. What this means is that we are singular beings in this world only because of and in a plural. In other words, we only ever know ourselves ('I' know 'myself') through the plurality of other singularities. And the plurality of other singularities is not limited to human or animal singularities, but all things. Being singular plural, therefore, identifies being in the world – which is the world *happening* – as the plurality of beings that know their own singularity only because the world exists, *we exist*, in a plurality.

In Nancy's words, 'being' is an action that is 'neither negative nor positive but the mode of being-together or being-with' (2000, 13). Moreover, the plurality of singular beings – the world *happening* – is an ongoing site of sociality. For Nancy, this is an 'originary sociality'.[1] It is originary because in every instance of an alterity, a difference, between the singular and the plural (i.e. another singular), the sociality that happens is original. The coming together of being singular plural, as an originary sociality, forms a limit (being singular plural) that is potentially unique each time. This limit is original to that sociality because it – the coming together of that singular plural – is an originary response to the singular plural. This limit is the need for and the existence of law.

Law is a techne that concretises at the limit of a sociality. However, beyond or before law as a juridical infrastructure, the singular plural is an ethical imperative. The ethical imperative is an imperative to respond, to be response-*able*, in/to that originary sociality. The originary sociality which is open and potentially new every time (Chapter 4 and 5). The singular plural, as it is happening, goes beyond a predetermined structure that would aim to determine what is the being that takes place in a sociality. For instance, the coming together of singular beings to be plural in any given territory is happening. Interactions take place that determine certain basic needs or relationships, for instance requiring shelter, food, water, work or care. Technologies of intelligibility, order and

1 Nancy writes of the 'originary sociality' in the *The Inoperative Community* (Nancy 1991, 28). Originary sociality is similar to Derrida's originary sociability. Sociability, in Derrida's originary sociability, is 'prior to all *determined* law, *qua* natural law or positive law, but not prior to law *in general*' (Derrida 2006, 231). This 'law in general', has been understood by Peter Fitzpatrick to be a form empty of universal claim. It is preceded by a sense of 'pre-legal' justice. According to Peter Fitzpatrick, law depends on what is excluded from it – the excluded provides content to what is included. In other words, the community that is the originary sociability, 'as a continuate being-with cannot be contained within any existent realisation of it [determined law] . . . it must ever extend receptively beyond present existence, otherwise it will not be able to continue "in being"' (Fitzpatrick 2008, 289). Thus, law is both determinate and responsive, meaning that it has the capacity-within-law to be something other than what it purports to 'be'. The question that is debated and discussed about Derrida's writing on law via Fitzpatrick's work concerns how to understand the exteriority of law and the boundaries or limits of sociability as a negative/negated law (see Fitzpatrick 2012, 2009, 2008). This particular discussion of Fitzpatrick's work is beyond the focus of this work; nevertheless, the concerns about law as both a limit and extending beyond a prescribed, determined limit are relevant. Here, rather than discuss Derrida and Fitzpatrick's work, I refer to Nancy's reference to 'originary sociality' in order to discuss the alterity that is the sense or 'eco' circulation. This differs from Fitzpatrick's and Derrida's respective works because my analysis is not focused primarily on the quality or 'being' of law, rather it is concerned more with how ecotechnics opens onto approaching sociality beyond legally reinforced practices of citizenship and subjectivity in irregular migration and labour. I provide a more detailed discussion of ecotechnics in relation to law in Chapter 4.

capital identify beings according to nationality, skills and abilities, legalities and economic value. These technologies determine the experience of a sociality, but not at the expense of the sociality happening. As ecotechnical, our interactions, relationships, experiences, happen both as a consequence of technologies providing form and structure, and world-creating sense, which holds the possibility of being originary (unique) every time. Given current migration discourses, labour and employment 'crises', populist politics, 'global' market economics, protectionist nation-states and embedded legal regimes, openness to *sense* through originary sociality may not seem a satisfactory resolution or alternative. But it does not claim to be. Openness is a onto-epistemological challenge to be explored and to expand paradigms of thought; what comes after is unknown.

Within ecotechnics, and nothing is external or outside this circulation, *sense* is ontological – it refers to the very basic element of space, or exposure, that constitutes our being in the world. Again, referring to 'our' being is inclusive of all living beings, nature and its products. *Sense* is touching, not assimilating, the difference of another singularity be it a human, an animal, an object, a city. According to Morin, singularities are everything that exists (2012, 3). The coming together as singular plural creates *sense* as the excess of the being singular plural. This excess is not transcendence. There is no metaphysical heavenly bliss produced because there is no outside; excess is absolute immanence, grounded, here and now. It is what happens and what is *happening*, 'with the question of ethical and political violence already inscribed' (Morin 2012, 2). The openness to being that is *sense* creates the possibility for a world that is creative, creating and originary every time. The possibility of such world emerges because the originary element of this sense creating is the difference, the alterity, within the plurality of singular being. In Nancy's words, the origin is not 'that from which the world comes' but 'the coming of each presence of the world, each time singular' (2000, 15).

Where Butler refers to the power authoring categories as normative violence, through ecotechnics we can identify the violence of the technical seizure of life through capital circulation and accumulation. Techne, as capital, threatens to overwhelm all possibilities of creative dwelling. This violence is obscured through technologies of intelligibility that are rarely questioned, such that the categories (i.e. legal status, citizenship, employment) themselves become the goal or the political aim for advocacy groups, thereby reaffirming the violence. Along a similar vein, the continuing existence of 'irregular' 'migrant' labourers benefits the function of national and supranational economic markets. Categories delimiting regular versus irregular immigration and work statuses, migrant versus citizen, aid a particular constitution of the nation-state and citizenship, which facilitates the circulation of capital, embedding processes of neoliberalisation. The techne of borders, legal categories such as legal versus illegal, employed versus self-employed, citizen versus noncitizen, and discourses such as dependent versus independent, marketised versus non-marketised, deserving versus opportunistic, can appear to be all consuming such that we are without recognition and status if we do not conform. At the same time, the circulation of beings in the world exceeds techne – we exist, we dwell, in spite of, not because of, the categories and legal-political systems and structures that uphold them. Techne does not make or sustain life in its entirety. Indeed, techne is impossible without *eco*. And *eco* is made intelligible and concretised through techne.

To diagnose labour and migration as ecotechnical is different from a deep critique of neoliberalisation. Identifying the phenomenon of migration and labour as ecotechnical is not only about analysing an ideological manifestation of capital and state. In neoliberalism, the state, and its role in organising populations, is captured and redeployed (Peck 2019, 249). In neoliberalism, and processes of neoliberalisation, the state is reformed to 'foster and bolster the market as an ongoing political creation' while deferring social responsibility (and 'society') onto individuals, encouraging commodification and implementing disciplinary social policy (Wacquant 2012). Migration discourses, in particular policies and punitive legal measures controlling labour migration and legally excluding precarious workers, illustrate these processes and procedures of neoliberalism. Yet neoliberalism 'is never the only causal presence' (Peck 2013, 150). In focusing on neoliberalism as a cause and effect, the explanatory framework and the reason, critical studies can participate in the production of neoliberalism's, and neoliberalisation's, totalising presence. Ecotechnics relating to labour migration is therefore not a synonym for neoliberalism and processes of neoliberalisation. To see our world as ecotechnical is to simultaneously open onto a micro and meta level: we are at once concerned with the microscopic circulation of life in an ecosystem and the circulation of capital in a market economy. But all as it relates to sense: the *happening* of singular beings in a plurality.

For example, the 'irregular' acts as a foil to the 'regular' citizen by responding to actual labour market opportunities that the ideal citizen aspires to reject. For instance, working in waste disposal, recycling facilities, food processing, factory labour, elderly care or supporting people with disabilities. In spite of linguistic dichotomies that terms construct, such as regular/irregular, legal/illegal, marketised/nonmarketised, there is no separate or different economy. The irregular worker is a condition of the formal labour market reproduced within the nation-state, its legal system and the globalised market economy just as the sub-citizen or irregular is a product of restrictive categories of citizenship. Precarious, 'low-skilled', workers and people considered 'migrant' exist in shared spaces of irregularity juxtaposed to the 'regular' citizen-worker subject. All within the same ecotechnical circulation of being. Precarious employment and income, precarious migration status, precarious housing and precarious access to health care are all experiences marginalised from the ideal, legally recognised standard of employment and citizenship. While 'irregular' or 'precarious' experiences are a consequence of government (nation-state) priorities to bolster short-term financial capital growth at the expense of social welfare support, they are also living realities of survival and being. The techne of categories of recognition enforce marginalisation while the sense exceeds technologisation. This excessive sense furthermore reveals a common, shared experience of being, as precarious to the dominant system, not limited to migrants or irregular migration.

Persons are moving, migrating, and working, in spite of, and as a condition of, the technologies of citizenship and employment. These technologies, however, do not only discriminate according to passport and actual immigration status in the way that one might assume (i.e. at the physical border of a country). Labour migration, and labour migrants in irregular situations, is not a distinct category or experience of persons who are exclusively moving or migrating for employment. The complexities of migration and migration discourses in the UK and Europe together with the precaritisation of the labour force has broadened the scope of who may be considered a migrant labourer or a labour migrant, and how these workers are included in the technologies of the state and capital as excluded. Thus, this book is concerned not with labour migrants as a legal category per se, but with the people at work at the nexus of labour and migration as exemplary of ecotechnics of the social. This is the space where economies and ecologies of being are concretised as labour market and citizenship participation in the nation-state, embedded within capital and law. This ecotechnical juncture is the crux of contemporary political, economic and social upheaval. It is here that concepts and practices of value, belonging and home are exposed. Value, belonging and home are not found in the concretised techne of the ostensibly global marketised economic system, nation-state and citizenship alone. Rather, that which exists, happens, beyond and in spite of the technological seizure of life, begs us to rethink value, belonging and home. Rethinking, through ecotechnics, leads us to consider a plural, pluriversal, embodied being that is ecological and ecosocial.

Ecotechnics – how?

The diagnosis of our world as ecotechnical moves attention away from solely focusing on the modern legal system and the marketised 'global' economy within a nation-state framework. Even when we draw attention to the gaps of the law in immigration or employment, for example, the predominance of our faith in the nation-state, modern law and economic market suggests that if the law were constructed better or differently (notwithstanding the framework), the gaps would not exist. Especially when considering labour in a sociality, a lot *happens* beyond the ambit of formal legal structures that continues unrecognised when searching for legal, institutional, solutions. On such a grounded level, before predetermined community and structures, we do not have to necessarily turn to focus on empirical data and narrative analysis. Rather, to disentangle our thinking from a fixation on the nation-state, this book engages in a theoretical and philosophical exploration of how we may think of our world as ecotechnical through the global movement of persons for work, in an era where globalised technologies increasingly seize every aspect of life. Migration (discourses) and labour (law and practice), therefore, are understood as primary techniques that frame the world, our being and movement. Currently, the technologies of normative categories deny any broader sense of movement and work, scapegoating 'migrant' crises and 'un/employment' fears in attempts to bolster a historically and culturally specific, modern epistemological frame.

My analysis of the techniques involved in what has become known as 'irregular migrant labour' begins from the following observations:

1 Low-waged, low-skilled labour migration operates within a new normal where the 'irregular' is 'regular'. Both the formal and informal economy is technologised, concretised according to categories of intelligibility that support the nation-state, capital and as such, processes of neoliberalisation. Both irregular migration and irregular (precarious, non-standard) work have become normalised because of difficulties accessing immigration status and the deregulation of employment which has resulted in a declining number of standard protected employment contracts in favour of short-term, atypical work arrangements.
2 The preservation of legally constructed 'irregularity' benefits the ostensibly global market economy by prioritising capital growth and bolstering a fantasy of citizenship-belonging within the nation-state.
3 Law does not hold the weight we, especially as legal scholars, may presume. Twentieth-century employment law, for instance, grounded itself with the aim of reducing the inequality of bargaining power between employers and employees. Currently, with the decline of trade unions and organised labour sectors in the United Kingdom (UK), many workers in need of bargaining power are not recognised as 'employees' under the Employment Rights Act 1996 and are shut out of collective and individual employment law protections. Immigration laws have bolstered hard borders and a 'hostile environment' while internationally agreed refugee protocols are systematically ignored or denied, and vulnerable migrants seeking a livelihood through their work are criminalised rather than protected. Nevertheless, the idea of law provides us with a ground. The idea of law provides a foundation for our sociality. We not only need law, but 'we *need* the law to be considered universal and abstract in order for us to carry on believing in its possibility of delivering justice' (Philippopoulos-Mihalopoulos 2015, 31).

While 'migration' triggers difference against a fantastical panacea of citizenship and bounded national territory, the order promised by the aspiration of Liberalism, which can be traced back to the consolidation of nation-states under the League of Nations and the post-war United Nations (see Forrester 2019), is un-ordered. The social welfare state espoused by post-war governments, as will be discussed in the subsequent chapters, promised a 'society' supported by the state. These nation-states are now burdened by inequality, exclusions and judgements of who is deserving or 'undeserving'. The rise of populism, divisive politics and brazen individualism bears down on volatile communities.

Labour migration, examined through the onto-epistemological challenge of ecotechnics, reveals that the crises of migration and employment in the UK are more than simply issues of border control and labour market opportunities (Chapter 2). Labour migration, moreover, illuminates the ecotechnical nature of our sociality, a sociality which has been limited epistemologically to the frame of the nation-state and modern conceptualisation of the individual-as-citizen-worker, in both migration and labour law (Chapter 2 and 3). The impact of immigration and labour laws and policies in the UK is obscured by the discursive panic around 'migration'. This panic draws attention away from legally enacted responses to labour market shifts and widespread precaritisation of work towards a consolidation of citizenship and national borders. The discourses of migration confuse both the experiences in the circulation of sense in sociality, and the technologisation of capital exploitation that benefits from a precarious, fragmented (i.e. lacking in collective solidarity and organisation) and low-waged labour force. Consequently, responses to the conditions of irregularity and precarity in migration and labour are limited in their capacity to think of, identify, and explore alternatives. Labour migration is examined only through a particular onto-epistemological frame: modern law and the nation-state. This frame facilitates neoliberalisation. Ecotechnics, however, as both techne and eco, forces our analyses to rethink deeply our relationship within/as law, embodied (*happening*) and ecological (Chapter 4).

Migration discourses in Europe have, at least since the mid-2010s, been captivated by the 'migrant crisis'. This 'crisis' is characterised by daily accounts of thousands of people committing to perilous journeys across the Mediterranean Sea to reach the shores of the European Union, fleeing violence, poverty and environmental catastrophe. The migrant spectre is often portrayed as the figure of a black, presumably Muslim, body propelled by desperation, crossing the sea to 'drain' the resources of a European Union built by hard-working, likeminded (i.e. Christian) taxpayers (see De Genova 2018). This threat, in spite of being imbued with historically embedded racist and xenophobic fantasies, is publicly deemed a 'migrant-refugee' threat, deracialised and 'ostensibly race neutral' (De Genova 2018, 1777). The administrative and bureaucratic veneer of deracialised migration and refugee policies obscure the clear juxtaposition that these bodies posed to notions of Europeanness – i.e. whiteness, Christianity (more in Chapter 5). Notwithstanding that the migrant crisis on the Mediterranean Sea has been attributed not only to U.S. and European intervention in the Middle East (Iraq, Afghanistan, Libya, Syria) spurring intensified violence and war in the region, the build-up of physical and technical borders around the

EU have made it nearly impossible to escape violence in North Africa and the Middle East through formal, legal, immigration or refugee resettlement channels (Columb 2020; Guild and Ansems de Vries 2019; Trilling 2018). The new normal for people crossing territorial borders and searching for work is that they must break laws in order to survive. Consequently, when entering Europe, 'people are illegalised having been denied the right to ask for protection' (Guild and Ansems de Vries 2019, 6).

Simultaneously, the impact of government-led austerity measures forced onto European citizens manifest in precarious jobs, the gig economy, insecurity in employment, lack of access to pension funds, sick pay, continuity of employment, and, in the UK in particular, an underfunded National Health Service, and a neglected education and benefits system. Terms such as 'in-work poverty' and 'working poor' characterise more and more of the UK population. Indeed, insecurity and precarity are no longer experiences reserved for 'non-British' migrant (foreign) workers. As Anderson illuminated in 2013, the vulnerability and lack of security that characterised the migrant labour force, who were hitherto accused of drawing down wages and consenting to 'work for less', are conditions any 'Good Citizen' could slip into at any moment. This slippage is not the consequence of immigrant laws and policies, but neoliberalism where the nation-state is redeployed for capital gain (Peck 2019).[2]

Migration, as Anderson argues, must be considered in line with the global movement of labour and capital. We cannot think of immigration policies or law in isolation (Anderson 2017). Moreover, migration does not only concern or affect people moving across borders and entering into a territory where they are not recognised as a citizen-national. Anderson (2017) uses 'migration' as a lens and a site of analysis to expose inequalities both inside and outside the nation-state. Migration challenges concepts of citizenship and exposes the 'breakdown within the fantasy of citizenship'; a breakdown of the idea that citizenship and the state provide security, equality and freedom (Anderson 2015, 196). Migration discourses trouble and affect everyone, whether those crossing borders and moving, or those who stay put. Detention centres, deportation lists, refusal of entry to asylum seekers, refusal of refugee claims, tent cities under motorways, near ferry ports, in agricultural fields (Trilling 2018) have become normal in many European cities (and throughout Central and North America, North Africa and beyond). Meanwhile, emotional responses to migration and

2 Between 2013–2018, cuts to social spending in the UK were estimated to be around £1 billion; by 2021, it is estimated that £37 billion will have been cut (P. Butler 2018). Particularly targeted in government and political rhetoric are 'benefit scroungers' and cutting down on 'welfare dependency'. Meanwhile, where individuals can even have access to state support, these cuts most harshly impact persons dependent on disability support payments (Slater 2014; Grice 2013). Neoliberalisation connects to the breakdown of the social welfare state beginning with economic shifts as early as the 1970s, responding to the oil crisis and the internationalisation or globalisation of markets.

labour, advertised and encouraged by populist leaders, captivate voters who seek meaning and stability in increasingly fragmented, globalised life.[3]

Media, social media, news, entertainment, community centres and spaces, have radically transformed communication, with the proliferation of technologies including on demand, 24-hour media and personal communication. Vocabularies identifying 'precarity', 'fragmentation', 'disconnection', 'breakdown', 'crisis', 'dislocation', 'isolation' and 'vulnerability' abound, with the irregular migrant labourer embodying a spectre to be targeted and blamed. The fixation on migration and its ostensible threat to employment and labour market opportunities defies evidence and experience (Dustman and Preston 2019; Dustman and Frattini 2014). Nevertheless, the profound emotional anxiety to globalisation roused by the notion of migration and employment in 'crisis' reverberates as support for nationalist leaders fortressing belonging within the nation-state (Trilling 2019). Such reinforcement of territorial borders to create and sustain an imaginary organisation of citizens and nations creates a sociality that is technologised, concretised and consolidated as a polis, a nation and a governing state. Meanwhile the sociality, meaning the people coming together in this space, exceed the technology that tries to contain citizenship as a bounded unified population in a nation-state: it is ecotechnical. Relying on disciplinary distinctions of economics, law, labour, politics and society as discursive tools and distinct categories obscures material experiences of being in the world. Being in the world is more than the cold circulation of capital; the world is not, and cannot be, reduced to a technological monad functioning as if it were a natural phenomenon.

Ecotechnics concerns relationality: how singularities exist with the plural. Ecotechnics is happening, inclusive of all beings singular plural; there is no external body or force acting upon beings. When 'the world has become ecotechnical' the seemingly total technologisation of life – through the capitalisation of being – gives us no choice but to be open to existence of *sense* (eco): we are not yet robots. This openness is pluriversal, originary and creative/creation. Openness is *happening* because the techne is not the same as originary sociality. As mentioned previously, there is no definitive project that comes from this openness, but I refer to the gesture, the anarchic openness of sense as a possible opening from ecotechnical diagnosis. Ecotechnics leaves us with an imperative to deconstruct the nation-state, ideas of home and grounding,

3 The popularity of leaders such as Donald Trump, Boris Johnson, Nigel Farage, Marine Le Pen, Jair Bolsonaro and Viktor Orban, demonstrates that their discourses disparaging of 'elites', 'experts', 'media', 'judges' resonates with populations of people who feel like their ground, or their sense of the world, has been lost. The lasting, perhaps even growing, concern for migration feeds into this fear that 'home' is no longer ones' own home, but open to anyone and everyone. The Brexit leave campaign in 2016 successfully seized on a fear of migration to win the referendum. Similarly, in the 2019 European parliamentary elections many right-wing parties across Europe gained significant support, undeniably due to their vociferous anti-immigrant rhetoric.

to suggest where an anarchic openness may open onto: pluriversal, ecological relational being.

The relationality of ecotechnics, for example, can be the cup of coffee next to me, which is singular plural: its contents historically, politically and economically rich. Coffee, me drinking it now, is a result of trade and coffee's popularisation in England in the sixteenth century. Coffee was part of the plantation complex of goods and persons, slaves, controlled by imperial powers throughout the colonial era (see Wild 2005). This coffee that I am drinking, singularly planted in Peru, roasted in East London, packaged, transported to Liverpool, ground with a grinder powered by energy provided by a solar farm in Monmouthshire, prepared with water from the water systems in urban Liverpool, heated with electrical energy, poured into a mug, another singular being in the plural, and so on. My drinking it as I type brings calories, nutrients, water and caffeine that I metabolise. It also gives me warmth, energy, comfort and even a feeling of security. My eco-technical relationship with my mug of coffee precedes signification at the same time that the techne grounds a reality of technological innovation (transport, processing, production) and historical specificity. This does not change the eco, which is the alterity, me and my coffee share out a meaning that exists: metabolisation and an emotional response that *happens*, even before ecotechnics inevitably creates meaning, which is then signified through my being 'a writer that drinks coffee', or my being a consumer that is part of the chain of labour, production and consumption that sustains a multi- and transnational coffee industry. My coffee mug and I are presence, singular plural – immanent, finite and creative – and techne.[4]

It may seem that persons migrating for work, into situations of precarious labour, experience the technologisation of life and capital seizure of life with little else. Yet the actions and interactions that (a) cause people to cross territorial borders and travel for work, in the hopes of securing a better income and employment opportunities and (b) that identify persons as 'migration labourers' or 'irregular migrants at work' are deeply relational and exceed being totally consumed by techne. What sustains and maintains migration and work, in particular where either or both of these experiences are the most dangerous, dehumanising and difficult, is ecotechnical: a craft of dwelling. Trilling (2018) documented stories of men, women, children and families who travelled on perilous journeys with the hope of securing a better future for themselves and their families in Europe. Giving names and voice to what otherwise are anonymously referred to as 'irregular migration' or 'refugee experiences', these narratives communicate both collective, shared experiences of tragedy (including violence and exploitation) and individual personality and contexts, which

4 Thank you to Chris O'Connor for sparking this conversation and explanation over mugs of coffee at the Garsdale Creative Writing Retreat in June 2019.

are personal and specific. A person arriving to the shores of Europe – whether in Lampedusa, or Samos, Kos, Lesbos, or Dover – is singular plural. As a singularity, for instance Zainab (Trilling 2018) has a history, a story, a personality and a purpose. Her arrival from Iraq with her three children to the UK, via Turkey (Izmir), Athens, Italy, and France (Calais) is politically, economically, socially, culturally and historically interpreted and understood within a broader 'irregular migrant' journey. But simultaneously, Zainab's years trying to get to the UK, and the reasons why she left her middle-class, comfortable life in Iraq (fleeing ISIS occupation), individually happened because of their singularity and her singular actions and interactions. Her movement, departure and arrival, continuing or settling, precedes signification in the moment of its occurrence. Zainab sought out the services offered by people smugglers. These 'smugglers' were people Zainab met as fellow refugees fleeing their home country, distinguished by their opportunistic or entrepreneurial (depending on the person and their motivations, or one's interpretation of their actions) role capitalising on the need for people to facilitate illicit movement across territorial borders. Zainab's capacity to communicate in Arabic, Kurdish and Farsi with Sudanese, Iraqi, Kurdish and Egyptian migrants allowed her to navigate tensions and violence in unique ways in the camps where Zainab and her children waited. At various times during her harrowing journey with her children, Zainab trusted people who let her down, stole from her, or were themselves manipulated or misinformed by others. Zainab was able to pay people in attempts to secure her and her children's safety, yet her actions were motivated by her particular desperation and fear for her children's lives. But this does not mean that she has suffered more or less than others or was more or less culpable for actions that are deemed 'illegal' based on immigration determinations categorising victimhood, forced migration and trafficking. The singular plural interactions that she was exposed to determine the journey and experiences with other refugees, human smugglers, and law enforcement officials. After she arrived in the UK with her children, Zainab claimed asylum and was sent to the Midlands. There, her experiences quickly become another statistic, as the technologies of immigration law identified her and her children as asylum seekers, and employment statistics as a non-UK worker looking for work and needing housing support and school for her children. Her experience, as ecotechnics, exceeds the categories of exclusion whereby very real legal boundaries and borders enforce difference and assess who is deserving or undeserving. At the same time, her experience is technologised, concretised by law, the nation-state, and capital.

Precarious, irregular, work is ecotechnical. An archetypal labour sector that relies on a workforce with precarious working conditions and often precarious employment status is care work. Care work, and the care industry, draws from a UK–citizen and non-UK–citizen labour force. Often, the more precarious the work, the more likely the workers will be drawn from a migrant labour force (Shutes 2014, 99). The act of caring, for persons who require support – most often elderly or disabled persons – has been commodified as a 'care sector' which can refer to privatised and public care provision, in residential care homes/institutions or private households (see Anderson and Shutes 2014). The Health and Social Care Act 2008 oversees care in residential and home care services, while the direct employment of care workers in private households by those who are privately funding care is not regulated. The less regulated, the higher the precarity in employment, and the more possible it is for someone with precarious immigration status to be employed due to recruitment deficits (Shutes 2014, 99). The privatisation of care provision, and cheaper forms of care, continue as public sector provisions are cut and underfunded. This has resulted in an increased reliance on underpaid labour often drawn from a 'global care chain' whereby migrant workers are employed to fill 'care deficits' where households are forced to work outside the home for income (see Hochschild 2002). Hayes (2017) describes three years of extensive interviews with care workers in the UK during which she documented the experiences of care workers working in the UK. Not only is care work, in particular privatised provision in private homes, under-regulated, precarious and 'irregular' in terms of the type of employment contracts offered (typically zero-hour contracts or self-employment contracts), the labour demand of care work embodies ecotechnics. Care work consists of the act of caring, and the relationship emerging from the care worker and care user. When this relationship does not exist, caring cannot take place (see Hayes 2017). Care work demands that the workers provide non-commodifiable emotion, give support, love and nurturing from one singular being to another. The act and emotion of care contradicts the demand that the worker and client participate in a marketised, contractual relationship assessed within the technologies of law and capital that calculate the working time, wages and skills required for the job, as if care was comparable to dropping off a package, or washing someone's floor. Capital technologies and infrastructures of law and market economy deny the sociality happening within caring to favour market economic productivity, not only by neglecting to regulate this sector (to ensure that adequate wages are provided and support is funded where needed) but also through the case law (see Chapter 3) where care has been constructed as 'help' rather than employment (Anderson 2014, 33). Critically, this distinction means that the worker can be seen as 'one of the family' rather than an employee deserving of employment law protection. This is in spite of the labour, in practice, being demanded of them (Salazar Parreñas 2014, 52). A worker engaged in care work, and a person receiving care, engage directly with the 'craft of dwelling', ecotechne. The relationship required in order to care exceeds technologisation and definition. Nevertheless, the overwhelming techne obscures the continuing *happening* (creative possibility) of care, subjugating care work as a less-valuable labour market sector requiring less skill, less regulation, and thus, precarious, irregular employment or family 'help'.

Ecotechnics – why?

An analysis through ecotechnics enables us to deconstruct the nexus of labour and migration. This is a pressing and important project because discourses and law in migration and labour/employment continue to shape political, legal and social dynamics, in the UK in particular. An ecotechnical analysis will contribute to the fields of labour migration, legal theory and subjectivity where existing studies already experience an impasse: programmes and categories (legal, political, economic) fail to address or remedy the situation of persons in the gaps, or grey areas, of the law – irregular migrants at work. This is because the terms of reference to diagnose the impasse and think through alternatives are themselves confined to the foundations of modern law, the nation-state, and ultimately ego-logical thinking. The circulation of sense and the circulation of techne, coexisting and distinct, shift the starting point from which to ask a fundamental question: what do we mean by *irregular migrant labour*? People moving across national borders for work is not inherently problematic. What is problematic, however, is the exploitation (taking advantage) of vulnerability, here meaning lack of access to protection against abuse as well as economic vulnerability where workers agree to work in substandard conditions due to limited labour market opportunities within a globalised labour force and market. The exploitation experienced by workers in irregular situations of work and citizenship status is exacerbated by the consolidation of territorial borders and differentiation based on national citizenship. While labour migration may seem to be a matter for transnational law, law, as it is conceptualised and practised, remains beholden to the nation-state. Whether law claims to be 'transnational' or 'international' the nation-state remains the primary site of legal recognition. Moreover, the legal response to labour migration is not transnational: workers experience simultaneous expansion and compression in opportunities, access, rights and protections from the nation-state where they are employed or gain work. In practice, 'the law' and 'the global' (including the 'global' market) derive from a limited conceptualisation of what it means to be in the world: being understood as participating in a plurality as citizenship, organised through a nation-state and recognised in economic production and modern law (see Butler and Athanasiou 2013; Quijano 2007). Through this, beings participate in the circulation of capital. Yet this participation is only possible because of the circulation of sense as singular plural beings happening beyond prescribed 'legal' and 'global' spaces.

The question that ecotechnics tackles is what are we *responseable* (what are we able to respond to) to do with the limit of our being singular plural – this limit being law, techne, but also possibly open and originary every time? This book does not aim to provide a definitive prescription or proposal. Rather my interrogation of this question offers a way to look at our present, and the particular challenge of 'irregular migration and labour' in discourse and law, as ecotechnics. In doing so, the particular emphasis departs from existing critiques of neoliberalism and the neoliberalisation of migration and labour by giving attention to the *eco* of ecotechnics: the circulation of sense in being singular plural (beings including nature, ecology). Such a perspective is valuable because it brings us back to the very foundation and constitution of law as emerging from the sociality present and happening, rather than a predetermined social (community, nation) that disenfranchises those deemed unworthy, or less valuable members. The sense of what is valuable, via ecotechnics, comes from the sense that is presence, being, living, relating. This is what is important to our world and ongoing, de/concretising world creation.

Generally, frames of analysis and critique assume that there is a form to which we strive to conform – as people, citizens, and broadly as human beings. Scholarly work often implicitly suggests that an extension of rights, legal recognition or judicial interpretation is the key to solving violence, exploitation or injustice. For example, adding rights for minorities in human rights law, extending rights to animals in animal law, or in adding care in labour law as if the addition of an 'ethic of care applied to concrete legal solutions' (Herring 2013, 5) would remedy exclusions in labour law. A similar common assumption in migration and employment analyses is that somewhere, somehow, order will be restored by the legal system within the nation-state (e.g. Collins et al. 2018; Costello and Freedland 2014; Guild and Mantu 2011; Alienkoff and Klusmeyer 2000). The ongoing chaos of political decisions regarding immigration laws and refugee policies throughout the world – what I refer to throughout this book as migration discourse – has been conceptualised as a temporary chaos to which normalcy will be restored, i.e. recognition of citizenship under a liberal nation-state system, and rights and privileges distributed from within this statist regime: regular migration and standard employment.

The rise of nationalist leaders advocating even more restrictive borders suggests one tactic of restoring such supposed 'normalcy': keeping migrants out and reinforcing nationhood by 'making America great again' as Donald Trump's campaign suggests for the United States of America, or Viktor Orban's Fidesz party in Hungary claiming to be the 'last defenders of Europe based on the nation, family, and Christianity' (Lendvai 2019). Immigration policies that have in the past accepted migration labourers often relied on an understanding that a migrant labour force is a temporary solution to a domestic, national economic problem. For example, the German gastarbeiter programme (Dinç 2015) or Braceros in the U.S. (Calavita 1992). An economic problem that, when remedied, will restore citizens and guest workers to their rightful homes. Similarly, labour law scholarship conventionally examines precarious labour/employment situations for their inability to fit the standard employment relationship with the goal of conforming these atypical employment contracts into a revised model of employment relationship (e.g. the personal employment contract, Freedland and Kountouris 2011). The remedy for precarious work has been to find greater legal protection for these workers so that they become less precarious (e.g. Langille 2011). What neither the traditional immigration lens nor conventional labour lens examine are the embedded normative processes of neoliberalisation as a redeployment of the nation-state that continue to create a demand for non-citizen and precarious, atypical workers precisely because they are included-as-excluded in the nation-state. Precarious, 'irregular', workers are of short-term financial benefit to the 'globalised' market economic system.

Policy proposals and critical analyses often assume that when conceived of, or applied correctly, the legal form can stretch to encompass everyone and perhapseverything. Critical scholars, moreover, recognise 'bad' law or 'bad' implementation of law, where law is used to wield power (colonial, patriarchal), institutionalise persons as commodities or statistics, facilitate greed and exacerbate vulnerability (see critical human rights debates in Baderin and McCorquodale 2007). We recognise law that facilitates, enables and enacts processes of neoliberalisation. Neoliberalism itself has been situated as a juridical project (see Brabazon 2018). We debate the potential for law to be used otherwise and celebrate these occasions, for example legal pluralism or human rights from the grassroots (Corradi et al. 2017; Isin and Neilsen 2008). These critical explications and interrogations provide a backdrop for my analysis through ecotechnics. However, digging deeply into 'the core logic of capitalism itself' (Oksala 2018, 226) as capitalising notions of economy and value link to the circulation of bodies and being in the world (ecology, our dwelling), ecotechnics opens onto a challenge beyond neoliberalism. Ecotechnics begins from an assertion that searching for a resolution to contemporary crises of migration and labour within existing structures is futile. Ecotechnics open up the analytical field beyond the constructed terrain of legal, political and economic systems to consider society as emerging through and from the relation of beings (human, animal, nature) in a plurality that is without ground. While this energy does undeniably coexist as techne, my point is that it is not defined by techne. The relationality of being singular plural gives society and law meaning, not the other way around. Society and law as a form, external to what is actively happening, do not create meaning. Ecotechnics shifts perspective to re-think the challenges presented through precarious labour, labour exploitation and irregular migration, leading to the final chapter which will discuss the relation of being singular plural as ecology.

Chapter outline

The methodological aim of drawing out labour migration as ecotechnics is not to impose new rational categories on the world as it is, or to idealise political and demographic change. Rather in identifying and examining the impasse in migration and labour law, the pursuit of this book is to open onto the alterity happening. The mundaneness or banality of 'irregular' migrants/foreigners/outsiders[5] at work provides a site to emphasise the ecotechnical spacings and sharings that compose the circulation of sense – creative singularities – from the ecotechnical spacings of the circulations of capital that express sovereignty through technical, market means. The political task is to conceptually fight to do away with grounding our being-in-relation (being singular plural, being as plurality) in self-justifying foundational norms that assign meaning before meaning takes place, e.g. legal categories and migration discourses. Thinking ecotechnics is a struggle against linear, deterministic assertions.[6] Yet this way of thinking of our being must resist being taken as forming a new ground, or one that serves a particular explicit 'political' (predefined, governance) purpose.

The ecotechnics of migration and labour, explored in depth in Chapters 2 and 3, leads to the suggestion in Chapters 4 and 5 that the potentiality within ecotechnics is unexplored because of the focus on the technologisation of movement, work, categories of recognition and hierarchies of belonging. Ecotechne is the possibility of the mobility of existence: migration/movement and labour/active life. Following from this, a uniform and predetermined signification of labour migration is not inevitable. As the chapters will explore, the potentiality within diagnosing our world as ecotechnics allows for possibilities to re-imagine work as a socio-ecological space, and our coming together as singular plural beings as a response to panic-inducing impasses in existing legal (theoretical, practical and epistemological) frameworks. Ecotechnics enables thinking of the simultaneity of techniques of capital, of labour markets and processes of neoliberalisation contingent on persons, beings, coming together as *originary sociality*. In originary sociality, the drive for determination, for categories and labels, is incommensurable with the material reality or experiences that are always exceeding the categories and frames. As incommensurable, techne does not supplant the eco. The techne forms, concretises, while the eco exceeds, simultaneously. The concretisation, a condition of modern reasoning to identify and define experience to signify meaning, swiftly cuts off experience itself. But experience is always in excess of the concretisation – it *is* simultaneously. Epistemological traditions of modernity, based on ideas of linear

5 In a critique of international law's response to irregular migration, Juan Amaya-Castro suggests that international law is able to respond to crisis and thus to the situation of temporary refugee status but does little to address what he refers to as the mundane realities of irregular migration. Amaya-Castro contends that international law fails to regulate irregular migration because it is not a 'crisis'. Whereas refugee status, for instance, is a temporary status whilst one either waits for permanent leave to remain, citizenship or is returned to their country of citizenship (Amaya Castro 2013).

6 For instance, Nancy has no determinate image of the human but still understands the immanence of the social being (see James 2015, 22). Understanding what Nancy is pushing at is only possible with a suspension of 'philosophy's legislative power' (James 2015, 28). I believe this is evident in the suspension of legislative and legal potential to address and remedy the situation of irregularity. Crucial to understanding Nancy's work is to see that he bases his thinking in the absence of the determined condition (ground). This, for Nancy, is freedom.

progress and dualisms, make it difficult to conceive of simultaneity. Traditions and knowledges that celebrate co-existence in conceptual, temporal and spatial understandings are therefore useful to support the onto-epistemological opening onto ecotechnics (Mignolo and Escobar 2010, more in Chapter 5).

Chapters 2 and 3 explore UK immigration and labour law, discourses, policy and debates. I begin with the assertion that 'irregular' migration and labour cannot be examined as distinct immigration or labour phenomenon. Both the regulation of movement across borders and a 'globalised' labour market are technologies that distil (i.e. make intelligible) experiences into predetermined categories. Laws that are expected, or intended, to regulate migration and work are at an impasse, often unable (due to legal provisions such as the doctrine of illegality or the Dublin agreement on port of entry and responsibility for asylum seekers, more in Chapter 2) to extend to the demographic most in need of legal protection as they cross territorial borders and/or engage in precarious work: persons and circumstances deemed 'irregular'. Legal restrictions limit the possibility of formal citizenship extending to those present in a given territory while social, economic and cultural practices mediate participation for those presumed to hold status as citizens. Laws create divisions and maintain them; for instance, the 'irregular' experience within migration and work is legally constructed where laws limit inclusion through exclusion. Political discourses of protectionism and national identity characterise labour migration as a threat to be feared. Meanwhile migration rhetoric obscures the benefit gained from 'irregular' migration and labour, a demographic that provides both cheap labour and a foil for national identity. Taking a step back from prescriptive solutions to irregular migration and labour, I ask first of all, what are we referring to when we speak of 'irregular migrant labour' (Chapter 2) and secondly, what is opening as a result of the circulation of sense and capital (ecotechne), as opposed to closing (Chapter 3). In ecotechnics 'something comes to an end, but something also comes to light for the first time' (Morin 2012, 121). Ecotechnics recognises an end and a beginning.

Chapter 4, Law as Ecotechnics, interrogates law more closely. Throughout the period of modernity or post-Enlightenment, classical thinking of law has evolved to construct law as if it were the pre-existing foundation or ground onto which sociality – community, state, nation – is built. However, law in and of itself provides no such ground; law is no*thing* but embodiment and materiality technologised in the world. This calls into question what we search for when we affirm legal categories in migration and labour, even when they do not match or reflect reality as lived experience. Theories of law suggest that law traces the limit of a sociality (Nancy 1993). In order for this definition of law to have meaning, the sociality needs to be alive and in movement (as originary sociality), as opposed to referring to a predetermined social or community. While law is not beholden to the nation-state system, law functions according to categories and frameworks understood within a statist structure: a predetermined social organisation that orders belonging along territorial and national borders, conjuring emotive belonging and notions of 'home'. Migration poses an existential crisis to this onto-epistemic frame. In contrast, the sociality *creating* in the being singular plural affirms law as ecotechnics, because law is a limit (order, structure) at the same time that it is responsive to the sociality, as originary and present. The living materiality of ecotechnics responds to the injustice of relegating an exploited labour force to legal grey areas, while capitalising on legal grey areas to further capital accumulation, within the state and beyond. Through ecotechnics we can recognise this incommensurability of law as order that cannot include-without-excluding, while uneasily recirculating what is included-as-excluded. Within ecotechnical circulation, moreover, nothing is external to the circulation of law, allowing law to be understood as an instrument that traces the limit of originary sociality: bodies and all singularities in the experience of ecology as the plurality that is world. Present, happening, now.

I do not claim to know the direct outcome of shifting analyses towards ecotechnics of the social. Consequently, rather than try to articulate without predetermination what a possible understanding of law emerging from the ecotechne of the plural world would be, Chapter 5 begins by considering what inhibits or blocks possibilities of openness to the plurality of sociality. In light of the evaluations and explorations in Chapters 2, 3 and 4, Chapter 5 interrogates the tenacity of the nation-state as an ideology and foundation. Focusing on the idea of hospitality, home and community, the fallacy of the nation as home and as a place of belonging – to be protected against the 'migration crisis' and labour pressures – is shattered through the deconstruction of migration and labour discourses. Beneath migration discourses and employment/work debates is a notion that the community, nationhood and citizenship need to be protected and maintained. The fear of losing a sense of nation underlies normative laws, bolsters the primacy of the individual as an appendage of the state and ultimately encourages social exclusion. Opening onto the ecotechnics of migration and labour, we see the simultaneous circulation of predetermined categories facilitating the circulation of capital accumulation and 'globalisation', the circulation of sense as the world creating itself. Furthermore, beneath the action of migration and labour we see the mythologies of nation-state and nationhood, propped by ego-logical ideologies and current ethnonationalist movements, unravel. Yes, capital circulation benefits from the suspended or limited subjectivity of labourers (cheap, deregulated labour) and persons deemed 'irregular' migrants. But the circulation of sense that is ecotechnical exposes sociality as happening in spite of formal citizenship and legal (state) recognition. The nation-state and its legal system do not form sociality. And if law traces the limit of sociality, then law-as-wedded to the nation-state is not a law that responds to sociality. This final fifth chapter brings together how migration and labour, movement and work, illuminate the craftsmanship, the technologies through which we dwell in common, in socialities. These technologies, however, are limited in their possibility and potentiality when we only see (analyse, critique) the cold, capital seizure of life – through market, nation-state and law. Revivifying eco-techne, eco-nomics and eco-logy opens onto pluriversal possibility for understanding, and experiencing, movement and work as and in the world.

Summary of main themes

Migration is a red herring, albeit one that holds massive political weight. The focus on immigration policy imbued with political ideas of what *should* be the world obstructs the circulation and experience that *is* the world. The frames, categories and strategies of the 'migration regime' do not match reality: the focus, discourse and actors are distorted. Therefore, the current frame – the status quo in migration analysis and debates – will not be rewritten to address labour migration from within the existing dominant paradigm of modernity and its legal, political, economic vocabulary. By opening and unravelling the legal categories and epistemological frames that have created migration, 'immigration', 'citizenship' and 'employment' such that we now seem to be in crisis, we find that there is no core. We have only historically, philosophically, ideologically constructed notions of being, of individuals, communities and political structures, without a singular material truth to differentiate being. The world is, in the issues and challenges of migration and work, revealed for what it is: a mess of bodies (human, non-human), material, circulating, singularities in relation that is plurality. Plurality in circulation that is techno-logical and eco-logical. In other words, ecotechnical.

Furthermore, migration, as a consequence of violence, foreign intervention, environmental emergencies sparked by ecological change, imperialism and colonial expansion, resource extraction and capital accumulation, is not an issue to be solved by immigration law. State-centred modern liberal legal regimes cannot, within their vocabulary and paradigm of recognition, remedy or stop the movement and mobility of persons around the globe. A vast and growing income divide around the world, as well as the lure of liberalism that promises lands (EU, North America) where freedom, democracy, equality and wealth await, only further incentivises the ruthless, reckless,[7] dangerous, at times selfless, acts of mobility that characterise much of the movement from the Global South to the North in the second decade of the twenty-first century. Rather than facilitate migrants' return to their countries of origin after a sojourn of labour or refuge, and rather than create larger spaces of employment protection within existing legal regimes to accommodate labour demands and mobility, we face a new normal where 'migrants' become permanent migrants either without a viable 'home' to return to, or their only home being the UK (for instance).

7 At the time of writing, it was reported that an Iraqi migrant attempted to cross the English channel wearing a lifejacket made from plastic bottles (Townsend 2019).

With regard to labour, precarious employment arrangements are validated within an entrepreneurial gig economy that takes pride in its fluidity, flexibility and ultimately, lack of consistency and security. In case law at the UK Supreme Court, 'irregular' labour migration is not linked to labour market deregulation and weak employment law protections. Employment discrimination as well as lack of recourse to employment protection in cases of abuse is relegated to exceptional modern slavery, the fault of the individual to not secure an employment contract, or to a lack of individual savviness to navigate self-employment (see *Hounga v Allen* [2014] UKSC 47 and *Taiwo v Olaigbe and another*; *Onu v Akwiwu and another* [2016] UKSC 31 in Chapter 2). Meanwhile, especially in times of fiscal austerity, national governments have preferred weak employment law protections to boost economic productivity with the understanding that strong employment law would be too costly (Hepple 2011). The practice and use of employment law and anti-discrimination law is disconnected from the reality of who is in need of protection from abuse at work (Hayes 2017). This disconnect is supported by the pre-eminence of capital accumulation and market growth. In other words, the techne, technological seizure of life distorts prerogatives of justice and fairness aiming to remedy inequalities. The scale of labour exploitation and irregularity in the systems, policies and practices of border crossing, immigration, labour and employment, sanctioned at the highest level of government, have become banal. In fact, they exist in spite of laws that ostensibly offer protection independent from government priorities and policies (according to principles of justice, equality and the rule of law, for instance).

In light of this observation, and the critique of law embedded in poststructuralism that leads to the diagnosis of the world as ecotechnics, it is untenable, irrational and irresponsible to assume that law in itself will produce a solution. When pushed to its limit, law is revealed as being empty but for being constituted by a sociality that imbues law with values, such as 'justice' 'equality' and 'rule of law'. As a concept in and of itself, law is no-*thing* but for the tradition of normative jurisprudential thought and statutes that assign rules to populations. Such 'law' finds its origin in a particular historically and socially constructed idea of law. Beyond discourses and interpretations, law in and of itself lacks any fixed, singular materiality. As an institution, law has become a spectacle, one that stages the world for us and 'by staging itself, alters not just the representation of the world but the world itself' (Philippopoulos-Mihalopoulos 2019, 213). Given the constructed-ness of legality itself, it is furthermore insufficient, as a method of critique, to circulate within debates of neoliberalism and law as a vehicle of neoliberalisation. This is not to deny capital's insatiable reach enabled by legal forms and practices, which exacerbate if not constitute violence in the form of poverty, racism, xenophobia, protectionism and rising inequalities. Yet, the techne of capital circulation that seems total and all-consuming is engineered and maintained through particular epistemological forms. Law, wielded as a tool of neoliberalisation, continues the violence of capital, yet neoliberalism does not solely define law's elemental constitution. Law as no-thing can, therefore, be the response – the enabling response – of the pluriverse of being singular plural. But, importantly, this is not a programmed enlightened idea of law. Law, in spite of being no-thing, inevitably is wielded as techne, technologising being at the limit of sociality. Thus, eco-techne crucially brings us back to the circulation of eco and techne, simultaneously.

The ecotechnics of labour migration, or seeing labour migration as ecotechnical, is a possibility of openness: diverse, plural, unknown. The sense that is happening and taking place in the world as world is creating (happening), is ecotechnical as much as the technological forces concluding, enclosing, signifying, interactions and relationality between singular beings. Techne is the proliferation of capital. The 'the conjunction of eco-technological enframing *and* of a vanishing of the possibilities of forms of life' (Nancy 2007, 95) threatens technologising an end to sense (Barrau and Nancy 2014, 54). Migration discourses and the neoliberalisation of work technologise communities (political and otherwise predetermined) to the extent that any spaces for the excess of sense to interrupt or disrupt are being eroded. Thus, the very foundation of sense is often obscured, and relationality is predetermined by profit maximisation, ideology (capital accumulation and individualism), and a fear of difference. Modern law has been shaped by these pursuits: the accumulation of wealth through epistemicide, championing a totalising global narrative of progress and European superiority over other cultures, peoples and nature. Colonial expansion was premised on the ability for European colonial powers to build their nations and institutions of knowledge off the exploitation and territorial seizure of previously inhabited lands. Immigration and employment law, as will be discussed in Chapters 1 and 2, are configured by this tradition of exclusive rights, which exacerbate difference and create conditions for exploitation. Migration discourses – us versus them, deserving versus undeserving – and the labour market of the twenty-first century – 'globalised' 'free market' and 'competitive' – are chapters in the same narrative.

On the one hand this narrative has been successful in onto-epistemologically destroyed the sense of world by technologically supplanting life as diverse, plural. On the other hand, this destruction – or, framed differently, this hegemony over knowledge through the 'colonial matrix of power' (Quijano 2010) – gives no choice but to create world from the eco/*oikos*/dwelling that *is forming as* life continues: as 'world' continues. At the heart of sense and the circulation of being is the sharing out of singularities in our singular plural existence that *is happening*. What is equally ecotechnic to the seizure of life into capital circulation are the processes of being that are not solely ego-logical. Ego-logical thought comes from the Western, modern/modernity, obsession with the Cartesian centrality of the individual and rational thinking self-subject (see Mignolo 2010, 314). Yet there are other ways of seeing being, starting here from the ontological being singular plural but extending to various lived understandings of communion, interdependence, sociality, pluriversality and sharing (i.e. sharing economies, solidarity economies and so on, discussed in Chapter 5). A technological circulation of sense dominates what we know of as our world. But sense has not, and cannot, become technological. Sense is phenomenological being, bodies, materiality, in motion, not contained in categories and definable being. To have techne – capital and capitalism and circulation – sense is necessary; and as such, sense is the world and the world is sense.

The global reality, in other words the world, is ecotechnical. Within this same world, globalisation – connected to the notion of a 'global' reality' – is destroying 'the world' (Barrau and Nancy 2014, 34; Nancy 2007, 1997, 160). What we refer to as 'the world' has been reduced to accumulation, or 'proliferation through value' (Barrau and Nancy 2014, 46). Rather than unite us, globalisation and 'the global' exacerbate difference, poverty, and the exploitation of those marginalised by modern liberalism. The claim to globality, to the existence of a 'global' or 'globalised' world, is nevertheless ecotechnical. It is from within technologically charged economic growth that capital has claimed, captured and acquired a totalising presence, seizing not only human production but also life – our dwelling, eco and ecology. Ecological circulation has been subsumed to the advancements of technology and globalisation, both in terms of natural resource extraction and exploitation and the *eco-logos* of plant, animal and human exchange and interdependence. Technologically fuelled expansion and growth is not a new, twenty-first–century phenomenon. 'Development', 'progress' and colonial expansion since the sixteenth and seventeenth centuries were similarly based on conquering nature (Quijano 2010, 23) and seizing control of circulation – physical, epistemological and ontological. Globalisation has been pursued by 'blind technological and economic exploitation' (Nancy 2007, 34), since the expansion of European empire through the 'colonial power matrix of the world system' (Quijano 2010, 27; Grosfoguel 2010, 71). The world system creation of colonial expansion, which paved the way for 'globalisation' and 'the global', was economic (for instance, the transatlantic slave trade and resource extraction) and paradigmatic. Ecotechnics allow us to revisit these historically conditioned onto-epistemological origins by reminding us in our critique that the techne is not total. There is sense that exceeds and happens in excess of the techne.

As theorists Quijano (2010) and Dussel (2003) explain, the international division of core and periphery territories and cultures ordered an epistemic (spiritual, linguistic, sexual) hierarchy that privileged European knowledge (Grosfoguel 2010, 70–71). The Euro-centric production of knowledge 'made it possible to omit every reference to any other 'subject' outside the European context' (Quijano 2010, 27). Through this production of knowledge, political philosophy centred the individual (man) as a participant in the city, a presupposed community, and the individual in the city – the political – as the origin of society. This is traceable from Aristotle's *logos politikos* through Rousseau and the social contract, and is evident in Marx and theories of communism (see Nancy 2000, 23–24). The triumph of such world-system creation, or globalisation, lay in creating a blocked sociality where true communication and the interchange of diverse knowledge has been prevented for the past five hundred years (Quijano 2010, 28). Thus, the 'global' that lays claim to the 'world' is built on the historically constructed omission of difference; an atomistic image of social existence that denies the very idea of a social totality (Quijano 2010, 27) and of social creation (Nancy 2000, 24). This has, in the twenty-first century, become physically evident in financial economic globalisation which is no longer geographically confined to a Western or explicitly European sphere: the largest supranational hubs of financial power are in London, New York, yes, but also Singapore, Shanghai, Abu Dhabi, Dubai. The 'global' further lies in the expansion of technological communications and artificial intelligence (AI), which is powered by what Gray and Suri refer to as 'ghost workers' (2019). The totalisation of 'blind technological and economic exploitation', acting *as if* it were the entirety of our world system, continues through the primacy of capital accumulation via financial growth. Capital accumulation, under the auspices of free market economics, proliferates to the extent that not even the promise of the West (liberalism, 'political civilisation' through individualism and human rights) maintains a dominant narrative. Universal human rights and democratic freedoms are publicly denied even in Western democracies, while financial and therefore 'global' power is growing specifically through a rejection of Western liberal values in China and Russia, for example (Pabst 2019). Notwithstanding, life continues. Sense exceeds this dominant narrative – the being singular plural relationality of the aforementioned coffee, Zainab travelling with her children, care work existing as a labour sector that constantly defies commodification – the life happening in our world is as much a part of it as the techne.

Globalisation's destruction of the world means that it is not only possible, but it is imperative to rethink the world, or worlds, as creative, creation. The alternative is that intellectual critique remains within the same cold circulation of stale hegemonic modernist tropes that are not experienced in actual sociality. These tropes deny the being singular plural in favour of predetermined existence, reaffirming the same onto-epistemology that persists in exclusion, exploitation and prioritising capital. Nancy draws attention to the French word for globalisation: *mondalisation* (*monde* – world, from Latin *mundus*, cosmos). Translated back to English, rather than 'global' creation we have 'world' creation, or worldisation. For Nancy, world is 'a totality of meaning, where things genuinely take place' (Nancy 2007, 42). World is a totality of sense, sense being what happens in the singular plural. Sense is the excess, the exposure that makes being exist. Therefore 'world' can never be something separate from us, from me. Rather, 'as a world appears to me, I already share something of it' (Nancy 2007, 42). World is only world insofar as it is a totality, a resonance of shared existence. But it is not 'the' unitary, universal, totality. Rather, the world is the mutual interpellation of singularities, the coming together of singular beings in/as plural to form sociality, or shared existence. World is 'not deciding in advance what an existence is worth, what a meaningful life is, yet at the same time providing the material condition for such an existence to expose itself "meaningfully"' (Morin 2012, 7) – meaning coming from *sense*: 'to be engaged in, to be responsive to and responsible for existence as sense' (Morin 2012, 6). Existence is creation, *our* creation (Nancy 2000, 17).

The limits of existing legal, political vocabularies and the sensationalised outsider-characters that solidify operating categories through inclusion and exclusion have been explored by scholars, most notably Anderson (2017, 2013). Given these critical studies, this book aims to explore what *is* happening: if migration discourse obscures, what does it obscure? On an meta level, it obscures how the world now is ecotechnical. Ecotechnics is a way of seeing what is happening in the global circulation of capital and of sense: the global circulation of sense. Sense, rather than garnering attention for its difference and transformative potential, has been subsumed and *made technological* (technologised) in the systems, structures and categories that order and organise our Western, contemporary, economically driven world. Politics, evident through migration discourse, is now in many ways synonymous with economic concerns recognised through the market economic system. There is no economic system that is separate from the globalised economic system; no alternative to bring us back to what eco-nomos, law of dwelling, might look like now. Meanwhile, value or what holds value cannot be represented 'in simple equivalences of money and commodities' (Conely and Goh 2014, 89). There is much more happening in the world, taking place and experienced, than the cold categories that are used to define globalisation, or globalised labour.

The next chapter will explore the happening of migration, migration law and migration discourses, particularly in the UK, as ecotechnical. Migration discourses and migration law at the nexus of migration and labour reveal a disconnect between the constructed categories and technologies of migration, and the circulation of movement and creative happening as the world.

References

Alienkoff, T. Alexander and Douglas Klusmeyer. 2000, *From Migrants to Citizens*. Washington, DC: Carnegie Endowment for International Peace.

Amaya Castro, Juan. 2013, 'International refugees and irregular migrants: Caught in the mundane shadow of crisis' in *Netherlands Yearbook of International Law*. The Hague: Springer.

Anderson, Bridget. 2017, 'Towards a new politics of migration' *Ethnic and Racial Studies* vol. 40, no. 9, pp. 1527–1537.

Anderson, Bridget. 2015, '"Heads I win. Tails you lose": Migration and the worker citizen' *Current Legal Problems* vol 68, no. 1, pp. 179–196.

Anderson, Bridget. 2013, *Us & Them: The Dangerous Politics of Immigration Control*. Cambridge: Cambridge University Press.

Anderson, Bridget and Isabel Shutes. 2014, *Migration and Care Labour: Theory, Policy and Politics*. London: Palgrave Macmillan.

Baderin, Mashood and Robert McCorquodale (eds). 2007, *Economic, Social, and Cultural Rights in Action*. Oxford: Oxford University Press.

Barrau, Aurélien and Jean-Luc Nancy. 2014, *What's These Worlds Coming to?* New York: Fordham University Press.

Brabazon, Honor (ed). 2018, *Neoliberal Legality*. Abington: Routledge.

Butler, Judith and Athena Athanasiou. 2013, *Dispossession: The Performative in the Political*. Cambridge: Polity Press.

Butler, Patrick. 2018, 'Welfare spending for UK's poorest shrinks by £37bn' *The Guardian* 23 September 2018, viewed 28 September 2019 www.theguardian.com

Calavita, Kitty. 1992, *Inside the State: The Bracero Program, Immigration and the INS*. New York: Routledge.

Collins, Hugh, Gillian Lester and Virginia Mantouvalou (eds). 2018, *Philosophical Foundations of Labour Law*. Oxford: Oxford University Press.

Columb, Seán. 2020, *Trading Life: Organ Trafficking, Illicit Networks and Exploitation*. Stanford: Stanford University Press.

Conely, Verena and Irving Goh (eds). 2014, *Nancy Now*. Cambridge: Polity Press.

Corradi, Giselle, Eva Brems and Mark Goodale (eds). 2017, *Human Rights Encounter Legal Pluralism: Normative and Empirical Approaches*. Oxford: Hart Publishing.

Costello, Catherine and Mark Freedland (eds). 2014, *Migrants at Work*. Oxford: Oxford University Press.

De Genova, Nicholas. 2018, 'The "migrant crisis" as racial crisis: Do Black lives matter in Europe?' *Ethnic and Racial Studies* vol. 41, no. 10, pp. 1765–1782.

Derrida, Jacques. 2006, *Politics of Friendship*. London, New York: Verso.

Dinç, Cüneyt. 2015, 'Gastarbeiter in Germany' in *The Wiley Blackwell Encyclopaedia of Race, Ethnicity, and Nationalism*. A. D. Smith, X. Hou, J. Stone, R. Dennis and P. Rizova (eds). Hoboken, NJ: Wiley Blackwell.

Dussel, Enrique. 2003, *Beyond Philosophy: Ethics, History, Marxism, and Theology of Liberation*. Lanham, MD: Rowman and Littlefield Publishers.

Dustmann, Christian and Tommaso Frattini. 2014, 'The fiscal effects of immigration to the UK' *Economic Journal* vol. 124, no. 580, F593–F643.

Dustmann, Christian and Ian Preston. 2019, 'Free movement, open borders and the global gains from labor mobility' *Annual Review of Economics* vol. 11, pp. 783–808.

Fitzpatrick, Peter. 2012, 'Reading slowly: The law of literature and the literature of law' in *Reading Modern Law: Critical Methodologies and Sovereign Formations*. Ruth Buchanan, Stewart Motha and Sundhya Pahuja (eds), pp. 193–210. Abington: Routledge.

Fitzpatrick, Peter. 2009, 'Finding normativity: Immigration policy and normative formation' in *A Right to Inclusion and Exclusion? Normative Thought Lines of the EU's Area of Freedom, Security and Justice*. Hans Lindahl (ed), pp. 118–135. Oxford: Hart Publishers.

Fitzpatrick, Peter. 2008, *Law as Resistance: Modernism, Imperialism, Legalism*. Aldershot: Ashgate.

Forrester, Katrina. 2019, *In the Shadow of Justice*. Princeton: Princeton University Press.

Freedland, Mark and Nicola Kountouris. 2011, *The Legal Construction of Personal Work Relations*. Oxford: Oxford University Press.

Gray, Mary and Siddharth Suri. 2019, *Ghost Work: How to Stop Silicon Valley from Building a New Global Underclass*. Boston: Houghton Mifflin Harcourt.

Grice, Andrew. 2013, 'Voters "Brainwashed by Tory welfare myths", shows new poll' *The Independent* 7 January 2013, viewed 28 September 2019 www.independent.co.uk

Grosfoguel, Ramón. 2010, 'The epistemic decolonial turn: Beyond political-economy paradigms' in *Globalisation and the Decolonial Option*. Walter Mignolo and Arturo Escobar (eds), pp. 65–77. New York: Routledge.

Guild, Elspeth and Leonie Ansems de Vries. 2019, 'Seeing refuge in Europe: Spaces of transit and the violence of migration management' *Journal of Ethnic and Migration Studies* vol. 45, no. 12, pp. 2156–2166.

Guild, Elspeth and Sandra Mantu (eds). 2011, *Constructing and Imagining Labour Migration*. Aldershot: Ashgate.

Hayes, Lydia. 2017, *Stories of Care: A Labour of Law*. London: Palgrave Macmillan.

Hepple, Bob. 2011, 'Enforcing equality law: Two steps forward and two steps backwards for reflexive regulation' *Industrial Law Journal* vol. 40, no. 4, pp. 315–335.

Herring, Jonathan. 2013, *Caring and the Law*. London: Bloomsbury.

Hochschild, Arlie Russel and Barbara Ehrenreich. 2002, 'Introduction' in *Global Woman: Nannies, Maids, and Sex Workers in the New Economy*. A. R. Hochschild and B. Ehrenreich (eds), pp. 1–13. New York: Henry Holt and Company.

Hutchens, Benjamin. 2005, *Jean-Luc Nancy and the Future of Philosophy*. Montreal: McGill-Queens University Press.

Isin, Engin and Greg Neilsen. 2008, *Acts of Citizenship*. Chicago: University of Chicago Press, Zed Books.

James, Ian. 2015, 'The ground of being social' in *Being Social: Ontology, Law, Politics*. Daniel Matthews and Tara Mulqueen (eds). Oxford: Counterpress.

Kothari, Ashish et al. 2019, *Pluriverse: A Post-Development Dictionary*. New Delhi: Tulika Books.

Langille, Brian. 2011, 'Labour law's theory of justice' in *The Idea of Labour Law*. Guy Davidov and Brian Langille (eds). Oxford: Oxford University Press.

Lendvai, Paul. 2019, 'The transformer: Orban's evolution and Hungary's demise' *Foreign Affairs* September–October 2019, viewed 28 September 2019 https://link.gale.com/apps/doc

Lloyd, Moya. 2007, *Judith Butler*. Cambridge: Polity Press.

Marks, Susan. 2011, 'Human rights and root causes' *The Modern Law Review* vol. 74, pp. 57–78.

Medland, Linda et al. 2019, 'The "future" of work? A call for the recognition of continuities in the challenges for conceptualising work and its regulation' in *Perspectives on Work Faculty Research Group*, Law Research Paper Series #001. Bristol: School of Law, University of Bristol.

Mignolo, Walter. 2010, 'Globalisation and the decolonial option' in *Globalisation and the Decolonial Option*. Walter Mignolo and Arturo Escobar (eds), pp. 303–368. New York: Routledge.

Mignolo, Walter and Arturo Escobar (eds). 2010, *Globalisation and the Decolonial Option*. New York: Routledge.

Miller, J. Hillis. 2012, 'Ecotechnics ecotechnological odradek' in *Telemorphosis: Theory in the Era of Climate Change*. Tom Cohen (ed). Ann Arbor: Open Humanities Press, University of Michigan Library.

Morin, Marie-Eve. 2012, *Jean-Luc Nancy*. New York: State University of New York Press.

Nancy, Jean-Luc. 2012, 'The political and/or politics' Unpublished lecture for Derrida Konferenz, Goethe-Universitat Frankfurt am Main, Frankfurt, Germany, 14 March 2012.

Nancy, Jean-Luc. 2007, *The Creation of the World, or Globalisation*. trans., François Raffoul and David Pettigrew. New York: State University of New York Press.

Nancy, Jean-Luc. 2000, *Being Singular Plural*. trans., Robert Richardson and Anne O'Byrne. Stanford: Stanford University Press.

Nancy, Jean-Luc. 1997, *Sense of the World*. trans., Jeffrey S. Librett (1st edition 1993). Minnesota: University of Minnesota Press.

Nancy, Jean-Luc. 1993, *Experience of Freedom*. trans., Bridget McDonald. Stanford: Stanford University Press.

Nancy, Jean-Luc. 1991, *The Inoperative Community*. trans., Peter Connor. Minnesota: University of Minnesota Press.

Oksala, Johanna. 2018, 'Feminism, capitalism, and ecology' *Hypatia* vol. 33, pp. 216–234.

Pabst, Adrian. 2019, 'The fall of freedom's armed missionaries' *New Statesman* 10–16 May 2019. London.

Peck, Jamie. 2013, 'Explaining (with) neoliberalism' *Territory, Politics, Governance* vol. 1, no. 2, pp. 132–157.

Peck, Jaime and Nik Theodore. 2019, 'Still neoliberalism?' *The South Atlantic Quarterly* vol. 118, no. 2, pp. 245–265.

Philippopoulos-Mihalopoulos, Andreas. 2019, 'Law and the aesthetic turn' in *Research Handbook on Critical Legal Theory*. Emilios Christodoulidis, Ruth Dukes and Marco Goldoni (eds), pp. 201–222. Cheltenham: Edward Elgar.

Philippopoulos-Mihalopoulos, Andreas. 2015, *Spatial Justice: Body, Lawscape, Atmosphere*. Abington: Routledge.

Quijano, Aníbal. 2010, 'Coloniality and modernity/rationality' in *Globalisation and the Decolonial Option*. Walter Mignolo and Arturo Escobar (eds), pp. 22–32. New York: Routledge.

Quijano, Aníbal. 2007, 'Coloniality and modernity/rationality' *Cultural Studies* vol. 21, no. 2–3, pp. 168–178.

Salazar Perreñas, Rhacel. 2014, 'Migrant domestic workers as "One of the family"' in *Migration and Care Labour*. Bridget Anderson and Isabel Shutes (eds), pp. 49–64. London: Palgrave Macmillan.

Slater, Tom. 2014, 'The myth of "Broken Britain": Welfare reform and the production of ignorance' *Antipode* vol. 46, pp. 948–969.

Shutes, Isabel. 2014, 'A right to care? Immigration controls and the care labour of noncitizens' in *Migration and Care Labour: Theory, Policy and Politics*. Bridget Anderson and Isabel Shutes (eds), pp. 87–109. Basingstoke: Palgrave Macmillan.

Thomas-Pellicer, Ruth and Vito De Lucia. 2016, 'Introduction: Exploring reimbodiments' in *Contributions to Law, Philosophy and Ecology*. Ruth Thomas-Pellicer, Sian Sullivan and Vito De Lucia (eds), pp. 1–24. Abington: Routledge.

Trilling, Daniel. 2019, 'How the media contributed to the migrant crisis' *The Guardian* 1 August 2019, viewed 28 September 2019 www.theguardian.com/

Trilling, Daniel. 2018, *Lights in the Distance: Exile and Refuge at the Borders of Europe*. London: Palgrave Macmillan.

Townsend, Mark. 2019, 'Channel smugglers cram 30 migrants into boats made for six' *The Guardian* 1 September 2019, viewed 28 September 2019 www.theguardian.com/

Viveiros De Castro, Eduardo. 2004, 'Exchanging perspectives: The transformation of objects into subjects in Amerindian ontologies' *Common Knowledge* vol. 10, no. 3, pp. 463–484.

Wacquant, Loïc. 2012, 'Three steps to a historical anthropology of actually existing neoliberalism' *Social Anthropology* vol. 20, pp. 66–79.

Wild, Antony. 2005, *Coffee: A Dark History*. New York: W. W. Norton & Company.

Case Law

Hounga v. Allen [2014] UKSC 47

Taiwo v. Olaigbe and another; Onu v. Akwiwu and another [2016] UKSC 31

2 Migrants at work as ecotechnics

UK employment laws, migration policies and immigration laws condition the ongoing irregularisation of working conditions for low-waged workers, the most vulnerable of whom are migrants without secure immigration status. Immigration policies are designed to keep out the 'global poor' while opportunities for work with the promise of making more money than accessible in their country of origin are attractive and often irresistible, in spite of restrictive law and policy. Citizenship, loaded with a promise of belonging and privilege, is an instrument of exclusion, which creates 'legal non-personhood' (DeGenova 2018, 192) for persons who manage to enter the territory but who are excluded by being denied legal status. The processes of state power exercised through citizenship also shape the legal personhood of the labouring subject, or 'worker-citizen' (Anderson 2013). The worker-citizen's labour is valued against the cheaper, more precarious standards accepted by a worker who is denied legal status, be it as a consequence of lacking citizenship or being reduced to 'low-skilled' labour (socially constructed) that is under regulated and denigrated.

In the UK, weak employment and labour regulations together with restrictive immigration policies contribute to the functioning of a particular 'global' market economic system, one that relies on the technologies of the nation-state to bolster capital accumulation (e.g. processes of neoliberalisation discussed in the previous chapter, Peck et al. 2012). While labour and employment laws largely fail to extend protection to precarious workers in contemporary work, migration discourses target blame towards 'migrants'. In the UK, discourses, laws and policies of labour and migration (for example, Immigration Acts 2016 and 2014; Immigration, Nationality and Asylum Regulations 2019; the Employment Rights Act 1996; National Minimum Wage Regulations 2015) enforce difference through the exclusion of non-citizens and those not considered 'employees' engaged in a contract of employment. Moreover, by strengthening borders, deregulating employment and commodifying work/ers, neoliberalisation processes facilitate capital accumulation at the expense of social welfare support. The breakdown in social welfare, and increasingly precarious working conditions correspond with steep increases in in-work poverty (Barnard 2018).

Racial, cultural and economic difference is mobilised to focus disparity and discontent in labour markets onto immigration control as if migration was the locus of current 'crises' (Shabi 2019).

Where is the alternative? Where can the processes be disrupted in order to extend protection or recognition to persons most vulnerable to exploitation and precarious work? The ecotechnics of labour migration draws attention to the grounded, material experiences of social circulation in spite of, and because of, technologies of capital embedded in processes of neoliberalisation (nation-state, economy and law). Within the circulation of capital there is the possibility of coming together, as 'we' do in the singular plural, in not-yet-determined modalities. Ecotechnics reveals that all that we have is what is being produced and reproduced by being singular plural. This chapter explores what this ecotechnical lens can offer to both a deconstruction of migration in the UK and the conditions of *irregular* migrant labour in employment law. The aim is to open our thinking of irregular migrant labour to see what is included-as-excluded within the legal and discursive categories. Discourses of migration and weak employment protections exacerbate the vulnerability of precarious workers, identified as 'foreign' or 'migrant', within a broader context of labour precaritisation.

'Migrant', used as a broadly encompassing label, technologises difference along constructed divisions of territorial borders and nation-state (including race, ethnicity and culture), disciplined according to notions of Good Citizenship, belonging and home. The category of 'migrant' worker, juxtaposed to the 'citizen' worker, ultimately denies the *sense* of people coming together in a given territory. The eco, happening, of how people get by, work, get along, and are response-able for each other is obscured by categories that define who is deserving or undeserving of recognition, state protection and status: irregular migrant, migrant worker, citizen worker, precarious worker. Nevertheless, the people that we are, and choose to be, responsible for (see Flusser 2003, 11) are the people that form our plurality, our sociality – this *happens* and is *happening*. When the singular plural *happens*, and a sociality is 'formed' or constituted, this is a technologisation of eco. But, vitally, this techne does not necessarily or inevitably have to be as capital circulation (discussed in more detail in Chapter 5 and Nancy 2008, 91). Migration, as the act of crossing national borders, facilitates sociality; it does not stifle or prevent it. Migration discourses, however, seize movement as capital and fit experiences into predetermined frames of economy, nation, belonging and home. These discourses deny the movement that is the world and world-creating (as being singular plural) in place of a 'global' order, which capitalises economy (eco-nomos) and being into a historically specific, onto-epistemology (modern, neoliberal, colonial, patriarchal).

In order to address the political-legal configuration of migration and labour, this chapter illustrates the nexus of labour migration and precarious work as ecotechnical. Ecotechnics explores both the technological-global circulation of capital fuelling international migration that induces, and is induced by, shifts in labour markets, and the circulation of beings, or socialities, that continue above, beyond and in excess of, nation-states, formal legal categories and frames of modern subjectivities. Such a deep interrogation, uprooting the very onto-epistemological foundations underpinning migration law and its connection to labour and employment, is crucial if we are to think through the impasse of existing categories and the normative violence these categories enable. In this chapter, I will firstly situation the discourses of migration and irregular migration within processes of neoliberalisation and the nation-state. From there, I will dig deeper into what is meant by the term irregular migration. Then, I will explore the connections between precarious employment and migration discourses, leading to a discussion of the imagination, or fantasy, of citizenship. This is followed by an examination of UK employment law as it affects irregular migration and illegality. Finally, this chapter will conclude with an interrogation of migration discourses and labour markets, in particular how this nexus of migration and labour has been shaped in the European Union.

Migrant discourses and neoliberalisation

As discussed in the previous chapter, through processes of neoliberalisation and the securitisation of nation-state regimes, *irregular* migration and *irregular* labour have become 'new normals' to discuss the movement of persons across territorial borders and globalised labour markets. Deemed irregular, in that these workers do not fit into the standard employment model or conform to shifting immigration policies, these persons are often in vulnerable situations where their income, health and safety, and legal status is insecure. Such an experience of movement and work is not unique to people with precarious immigration status or migrants at work, in spite of this being a demographic with the most experience of 'irregular' and precarious statuses. Labour protections and regulations, even when tested in tribunal and court proceedings, capture only a segment of the labour force. Precarity broadly affects the labour market experiences of workers across immigration statuses. The experience of irregularity is heightened according to race, gender and class. That irregular status at work and precarious forms of work are not limited to or reserved for those considered 'migrant' ultimately exposes the lack of substance and materiality in the imagined condition, or privilege, of citizenship. The circulation of these categories as opposed to, or in spite of, the experiences that both underpin and undermine them is ecotechnical.

Migration is a function of labour market demand, while labour market demand exceeds territorial (national) boundaries because of migration. As one and the same phenomenon, labour migration can be analysed as a product or process of neoliberalism. As outlined in Chapter 1, neoliberalism relies on the centrality and redeployment (Peck and Theodore 2019) of the state to 'foster and bolster the market' while deflecting responsibility and enforcing punitive social control (Wacquant 2010). Undeniably, migration is created by the state and a bordered international space. Yet people do not migrate solely because of the nation-state. Neither are decisions to migrate for work based on market-based decisions alone. Labour, conversely, is a fundamental condition of life (*vita activa*, Arendt 1958) regardless of territory, nation and borders. The globalised market economy has transcended the nation but still works through nation-state entities and benefits from punitive controls that may restrict 'free market' movement. The 'free' market exists for some, but not for those whose labour is necessary to enable freedom for others. Loïc Wacquant refers to this as centaur state capitalism where those on top are enabled to be successful while those on the bottom are subjected to punitive controls (Flint 2018; Wacquant 2016, 2010). The reinforcement of borders and punitive migration controls do not contradict or ignore labour market needs. Rather, migration controls enable the performance of borders which at once consolidate the nation and citizenship against particular (undesirable) bodies and permit these undesirables to carry out essential (cheap and hidden) labour to bolster the market and allow businesses to remain competitive. Migration discourses, fixated on the border and the nation-state, promote and foster processes of neoliberalisation.

The construct of the mutually beneficial national (internal, domestic) market and the global, international (common) market continue processes that are identified as neoliberalisation. Neoliberalisation, as different from neoliberalism, is an ongoing process that is 'a crisis induced and crisis inducing form of market-disciplinary regulatory restructuring' (Peck et al. 2012, 268). The movement of neoliberalisation is characterised by a chronic instability and patterned tendency of the contemporary, neoliberal market (Peck et al. 2012, 269). Neoliberalisation within the globalised labour market intersects with the nation-state, where seemingly fixed borders and citizenship categories are purportedly protected and upheld by immigration laws and policies (and government priorities, such as the 2017 Conservative party manifesto to decrease net migration to 'tens of thousands'). Meanwhile, more flexible, capital-driven priorities steer practices of labour market demand and supply, facilitating migration flows. For example, the frequent adjustments made to National Health Service (NHS) work and shortage occupation lists (Launder 2019). Neoliberalisation as a process allows the demand and supply of labour, as *migrant* and at other times throughout history as domestic or indentured, to continue to be sanctioned by a legal regime that espouses labour rights, social equity and a bounded nation-state. Meanwhile, neoliberalism is itself based on economic efficiency and claims to ethical self-responsibility where 'structural causes of social problems are erased by a discourse of moral culpability that manifests at the individual level' (McNevin 2011, 61). In the UK, this is evident in the deferral of responsibility to 'migrants stealing British jobs', 'foreigners draining the social system' and to widespread blame placed on the EU entitling Britain to 'take back control' of its borders. The 'migrant' is resoundingly blamed for the chronic instability and patterned tendency of the contemporary, neoliberal market.

Ironically, the mobility inherent in market fluctuation contradicts the belief that formal citizenship, guaranteeing status and protection, is the ideal. In other words, neoliberalisation opposes a concretisation of (the fantasy of) citizenship: citizenship as a ticket to protection, stability and security would stifle neoliberal marketisation. Neoliberalisation moves within a fluid nation-state system that is redeployed to bolster financial markets in the ostensibly global circulation of capital. Ultimately the success of neoliberalisation lies in its ability to encompass and conform to human action, mobility, our dreams and aspirations, while concretely, materially, undermining, disabling, their fruition. People on the ground live and work with the hope that their labour will help them achieve stability and security. Yet the promise of citizenship, of 'making it', is directly contradicted by the pursuit of capital accumulation in a neoliberalising system. Thus, while 'world' is being created through lives lived/living in excess of technologisation, in particular in the reality of precarious work and the insecurity of irregular immigration status, neoliberalisation (as techne) seizes life, thereby stifling world creation. But life cannot be totally concretised as techne. The pursuit or aspiration driving people to cross territorial borders to secure work for a 'better life' and the aspiration fuelling engagement, energy and determination to persist even in the worst conditions cannot be written off as purely a pursuit of capital accumulation and neoliberalisation. Undoubtedly, this is the most common critical lens to shed light on the most hegemonic, pervasive form of economic, political, legal and social organisation. But techne, and capital, does not precede eco. Eco, as that which simultaneously with techne exceeds signification, exists. Both eco and techne are world. The pursuit of citizenship, while a technologising movement, is also a movement of sense, sense happening in the being singular plural. This is important to the deconstruction of migration discourses and labour because ecotechnics enables us to see what techne obscure not only in terms of legal gaps and impasses, but what socialities, pluralities exceed capitalisation.

'Irregular' migration: categories of movement, work and status

The fervour of anti-migration discourse, now quasi-normalised in the UK (and U.S., Europe), precipitates from a massive deferral of responsibility (Medland et al. 2019). Government and political leaders are neglecting to take responsibility for economic and social sustainability after austerity and cuts to social services were used to mitigate the aftermath of the financial crisis of 2008 (Partington 2019; Castells et al. 2012). Instead of addressing the impact of austerity measures on communities, leaders in the UK have stoked resentment and anger towards 'migrants' (BBC 2019; Mehta 2019; ITV 2016). In the wake of the financial crisis outsourced production, automation and technological advancement in manufacturing have further caused dramatic shifts in socio-economic (including employment) conditions. On the one hand, the deferral of production to other countries and distant geographies makes it seem as if workers are no longer physically involved in industry, as if industrialisation was over and 'work' now purely consisted of service-oriented jobs. On the other hand, production has been offset to distribution warehouses where workers on night-time shifts stay invisible to daytime workers and commuters (Pickard 2018; Agerholm 2017). In spite of technological advancements, including artificial intelligence (AI) and robotics, labour has not disappeared, but continues to be offloaded to the other countries and other workers. These workers are, furthermore, often marginalised based on race, gender and mobility (Gray and Suri 2019). With the globalisation of production and the breakdown of the social welfare state, the UK is experiencing a state of profound and shocking change. But it is misguided and misleading to consider this to be caused by migration. The political and policy focus on immigration is a red herring.

The evolution of migration debates, discussions and policies in the UK points to much more profound movement and change in the relationship of people to the nation-state and the global circulation of bodies, goods and finances – in other words, to capital. Immigration, discussed and debated in UK politics with significant impact on the Brexit referendum in 2016, is not solely an issue of persons crossing territorial borders. Neither is 'migration' simply about people moving (and working) in countries where they do not hold citizenship. Migration has become a widely used and pejorative term to encapsulate social, cultural and economic experiences that have unsettled imagined, largely fantastical, notions of belonging and security within a nation-state. Focusing specifically on migration as crossing borders by non-nationals masks more fundamental questions about foundational assumptions and ways of knowing, or understanding, how we come together. Essentially, understanding through being singular plural (see Chapters 1 and 5).

Migration discussions and policies often compartmentalise 'migration' as if it were a distinct experience that could be captured in isolation. 'Migration' as a phenomenon is separated from employment, family, war and violence, environmental catastrophe; subcategories that are addressed and treated by new categories, with distinct criteria and policies. Migration, as a discourse and an experience, cannot be disentangled from work, employment and labour. The global movement, and circulation, of bodies as capital intertwines migration for work with financial interests mediating the movement of persons around the world. Having people willing to work is economically necessary. However, containing people and maintaining them in positions of precarity has developed as a necessary practice in the current neoliberal global economic market. While it is true that people often move to secure better opportunities for employment and a future, policy formulas that feed into legal categories and practices do not easily adapt to complex reasons or motivations. For instance, if a person is migrating to find better work and income (economic migration) they are presumed not to be primarily fleeing war and violence (forced migration). Or if one agrees to migrate for work in a given job with a given employer (labour migration) it is difficult for the migration regime to imagine this conscious, consenting person could also be exploited and placed in a vulnerable situation (forced labour, trafficking). Additionally, under the UK point-based system, a worker cannot change from one employer to another without exiting the country and reapplying from their country of origin. The imagined freedom of a liberal, autonomous individual is assumed and juxtaposed to the extreme alternate case of an exploited, non-consensual, hapless victim. Such compartmentalisation, founded in modern liberal thought (and law, legal subjectivity), works in tandem with a free-market globalised economy that offers anyone and everyone 'willing to work for less' a job. This 'free' market maintains opportunities for people's labour to be exploited, ostensibly for the good of the economy and health of the market, both national and international.

Therefore, what we have is an experience of migration, an infrastructure of migration discourses, debates and policies that distort and compartmentalise these experiences within a reality of market competitiveness whereby everyone, no matter their experience or citizenship, is made part of the global circulation of capital and market. In so far as they are willing to be exploited. Indeed, while work is conceptualised and regulated by law, 'global mobility, trade, migration and global finance' are changing the way that work is experienced and deregulated (Medland et al. 2019, 11). This has created conditions whereby irregular migration and atypical work are increasingly recognised as a norm in labour practices.

Migration discourses, debates and analyses, both in academic and policy circles, struggle to encompass the complexities under the category of 'migration' (Ruhs and McAuliffe 2017). According to the International Labour Organisation (ILO), there are an estimated 150.3 million migrant workers around the world, 11.5 million of these working as domestic workers (ILO 2015). Migrant workers account for more than 70% of international migrants of working age, with the highest percentage of these workers engaged in 'service' work in high-income countries (Ruhs and McAuliffe 2017, 28). The 2018 International Organisation of Migration (IOM) report affirms that irregular migration is difficult to quantify (Ruhs and McAuliffe 2017, 306). Therefore, little is known about irregular migrant flows. However, it is widely acknowledged that migrants in irregular situations are particularly vulnerable to abuse due to their lack of legal recognition and security (i.e. their lack of recourse to state protection). In particular, migrant domestic and care workers working in private homes are relegated to 'private' situations beyond the ambit of public oversight and employment law (OHCHR 2015). In the UK, the live-in domestic worker visa binds the person migrating for work to their employer, such that without that particular employer the worker has no permission/right to be in the UK. A special category of visa, moreover, exists for non-British citizens who employ their own 'staff' through the domestic worker visa. These visa arrangements have resulted in situations of 'extreme exploitation' (Fudge and Strauss 2014) where, as will be discussed ahead, migrant workers are afraid to leave situations of abuse and exploitation (or do not even know how to leave), for fear of being arrested, criminalised and deported (see below *Hounga v Allen* [2014] UKSC 47; *Reyes v Al-Malki* [2017] UKSC 61; and in Chapter 3: *Taiwo v Oliagbe* and *Onu v Akwiwa* [2016] UKSC 31).

Migrant categories

According to the International Organisation of Migration (IOM), irregular migration is defined as 'movement that takes place outside the regulatory norms of the sending, transit and receiving countries' (IOM 2019). The OHCHR report in 2015 described migrant workers in irregular situations as migrants who:

> are 'invisible'. For the authorities of their country of employment, they do not exist; they are unrecorded in population statistics and other administrative data. This invisibility often makes it difficult for them to claim and enjoy their rights. The misperceptions and myths that surround irregular migration can also contribute to stigmatization and abuse. For example, it is often assumed that irregular migrants are a burden on the national economy. In fact, they contribute to the economy and often pay taxes.
>
> (OHCHR 2015)

This 'invisibility' is not based on a lack of economic participation, but a lack of determined legal status. The individuals considered to be 'irregular' can exceed recognised categories of migration because their entrance and stay (act of migration) is regular while their employment constitutes the irregular element. Conversely, an immigration status can be considered irregular as a result of changing immigration legislation, lack of access to security in their immigration and employment status, and subsequently – or as a consequence of their immigration/residency/work restrictions – an inability to be employed by other employers or in other sectors (Dauvergne 2008, 14–15). In particular the UK foreign worker visa system requires a single employer to sponsor foreign workers (and often contribute towards the costly visa process), both for specific temporary work (Tier 5) and long-term work (Tier 2). If the employer changes, the work permit or visa is void and needs to be renewed by the new employer at an increased cost, in some circumstances with the worker reapplying from their country of origin outside the UK (see Gov.UK 2019).

It is difficult to identify irregular migrant labourers who may not have any direct immigration irregularities due to family sponsorship, study permits or EU and EEA mobility (pre-Brexit), but are working in contracts where they are not recognised as employees under s 203 ERA 1996, often in temporary or casual work. Through family sponsorship these migrants would not necessarily be entirely 'invisible', but their work status and economic participation may be undeclared or 'informal'. Also, because the term 'migrant' in political and social (including media) discourses may not match a specific legal category, persons who hold UK nationality and have acquired citizenship may be popularly considered 'migrants'. A contributing factor to the widespread use of the term migrant is the racialisation of certain labour sectors which are associated with, or employers demonstrate a strong preference towards, particular racial and ethnic backgrounds (Wills et al. 2010). After multiple generations of migration networks, Eastern European or Turkish small business and shop owners for example, or food processing workers in the Midlands, have come to provide an ethnically specific supply of labourers (Ruhs and Anderson 2010, 25). These businesses and the labour they demand can be popularly identified as 'migrant' due to the particular labour sector being racially identified as foreign and non-national, not because of the workers' actual legal status (immigration and/or employment status and right to reside and work). The racialisation of labour sectors therefore contributes to the wide reach of (anti)migration discourses. Bridget Anderson and Scott Blinder agree that the term 'migrant' in public debate 'often conflates issues of immigration, race/ethnicity and asylum' (Anderson and Blinder 2019).

The exclusion of migrant labourers considered 'irregular' from what is considered normal citizenship, and from the legal protections of the nation-state due to insecure employment or immigration status, is not definite: 'irregular' is not 'illegal'. In fact, the term irregular came into popular usage as an alternative to the widely acknowledged derogatory term of 'illegal migrant'. Migration activists, for example the international movement No One Is Illegal, brought public attention to the derogatory label 'illegal' (No One Is Illegal 2012). Scholars such as Dauvergne, in *Making People Illegal*, have used the term illegal because of its pointed, specific implication of the law. Dauvergne discusses the process whereby labels make people illegal and create divisions of 'us versus them'. The term 'illegal' is the clearest example of this separation (Dauvergne 2008, 16–19). 'Il-legal' has a direct association with criminality. Meanwhile, the legal ambiguity of the term 'irregular' allows it to be applied to a demographic of labourers beyond a specific legal category (Dauvergne 2008, 4). Policy makers and researchers may use the term 'irregular' to refer to a subset of labourers who are not plainly contravening immigration or labour laws but nevertheless are marginalized in the shadow of regulations. Media, international organisations, and advocacy channels also adopted the term 'irregular' to replace the use of 'illegal' (National Union of Journalists 2014).

'Irregular' is a legal grey area, but grey to the extent that it may not directly implicate the law. The adjective 'irregular' is not innocent: it presupposes a 'regular' form of what it modifies. Irregular signifies that the presumed regular is negated – not regular. Because the term 'irregular labour' refers to a broad assortment of employment circumstances, it blurs the distinction between the legal and illegal. Moreover, the term 'migrant' increasingly has become used as a comprehensive phrase that serves not to define a particular experience or complex legal status, but to further confound meaning while reinforcing the notion of citizenship as non-migrant. The construction of legal boundaries and definitions directly create the space that is, then, irregular. Irregular situations exacerbate labour exploitation and vulnerability. According to the Office of the United Nations High Commissioner for Human Rights (OHCHR),

> migrants are more likely than nationals to work in the informal economy, which may increase their economic insecurity and isolate them from mainstream human rights protection and services. Migrants in an irregular situation are less likely to be aware of services, including health care, social protection and legal aid, that are available to them.
>
> (OHCHR 2015)

The definition of migrant in reference to migrant labourer or worker is also unclear. According to the UN International Convention on the Rights of Migrant Workers and Members of their Family (UNCRMW), article 2 (1) defines a migrant worker as 'a person who is to be engaged, is engaged or has been engaged in a remunerated activity in a State of which he or she is not a national' (United Nations 1990). The International Organisation of Migration (IOM) defines labour migration as 'the movement of people from one country to another for the purpose of employment' but does not define what would constitute employment. The International Labour Organisation (ILO) has defined 'migrant for employment' in Convention No. 97 article 11 (1), as 'a person who migrates from one country to another with a view to being employed otherwise than on his own account and includes any person regularly admitted as a migrant for employment' (ILO 1949/1952). The preceding definitions specifically refer to individuals crossing international borders.

In the UK it is difficult to distil how the popular definition of 'migrant' is applied in data collection and research. The Labour Force Survey (LFS) and Annual Population Survey (APS) are typically used to measure the impacts of migrants on the UK economy and define migrant as 'foreign born'. Based on this definition, calculations of a migrant population would include those who have citizenship and who would not be counted as migrants if 'migrant' were defined as those who are subjected to immigration control or distinguished by an identified nationality distinct from the UK. For data according to the LFS, 'migrant' is defined as a foreign national. In the Office of National Statistics (ONS), 'migrant' is defined according to the UN definition, where a migrant is someone who is residing in a country other than his or her usual residence for at least a year. ONS data is used in the UK for measuring net migration, with significant impact on immigration policy and political promises concerning immigration reduction (see Conservative and Unionist party 2017, 54). The ONS data does not include statistics on actual departures from the UK. Length of stay is based on terms stipulated in migrant visas and self-reporting (Anderson and Blinder 2019).

The differences in definitions used in UK government surveys are not insignificant. In practice, foreign nationals and foreign-born workers have different relationships with the labour market based on whether the intention to stay is permanent or temporary. Temporal restrictions and status concerns for foreign nationals impact the intensity of working hours and length of contract these individuals will agree to. These differences cannot be fairly summarised in most political debates, policy and legal concerns about a migrant labour force that form part of the UK's 'migration discourse'. Furthermore, asylum seekers require different treatment under international law and refugee policies. They too are included in data as 'migrant'. The use of the term 'migrant' can exploit the inconsistent statistical definitions of migrant to further political agendas. Political discourses significantly impact who is popularly considered to be a migrant labourer, and consequently treated as a foreigner and non-citizen. Political support for tighter immigration controls, such as Theresa May's infamous 'hostile environment', obscures the structural labour market (economic) reasons for precarious work as well as the reality of who is carrying out that labour. It is difficult to determine who is a migrant if the term is broadly used to discuss 'foreigners' but refers to persons working in temporary, insecure or precarious low-waged ('low-skilled') labour. Moreover, within the EU, EU citizen workers are not migrants subject to border or immigration controls (articles 18, 21 TFEU, non-discrimination, free movement of labour). Nevertheless, non-British citizens may be considered migrant against a citizen-national, UK passport holder.

Recent political events in the UK demonstrated that citizenship even with a UK passport may be disputed, based on ethnicity and race (Bridle 2019). In February 2019, Shamima Begum stated her desire to return to her home: the country of her birth and country of citizenship, England. As the wife of a former ISIS fighter, her request was met with fear and hostility. In spite of her British citizenship, then Home Secretary S. Javid stated publicly that she would have her citizenship revoked. This sparked controversy, and questions concerning a potential contravention of international law: her lack of dual citizenship elsewhere (her parents are from Bangladesh) meant that a revocation of her British citizenship would essentially make her stateless. Fears of terrorism and Brexit have compounded differentiation of citizenship and ethnicity (racism and xenophobia) with significantly harmful effects (Rzepnikowska 2019; Virdee and McGeever 2018).

Implications of 'irregularity' for the labour market

Notwithstanding the question of who, actually, is a migrant, the demand for migrant workers is structurally embedded in neoliberalising processes of market growth. This returns our focus to the labour market. Migrant labour is desired, in fact demanded, in the UK because migrants, especially temporary migrant workers, are often considered a guaranteed hard-working labour force. Migrants are perceived as a 'self-regulating' and 'self-sustaining labour supply' due to their economic and legal vulnerability (Anderson and Ruhs 2010, 25). When demand for their labour is high, many non-British citizens will come to the UK and supply their labour. When demand is low, migrants – EU citizens included – may choose to stay in their country of nationality or (more permanent) residency. According to Piore, writing in 1979, migrants are disproportionately available for work regardless of over-qualification because they may choose temporary work or due to the 'wage differential with their country of origin' (Anderson and Ruhs 2010, 17). This remains a factor where workers may be relegated to a temporary work status in spite of holding EU citizenship (seasonal work, for example) and thus forego entitlement to existing labour rights and protection contingent on a continuity of employment (see Barnard, in Costello and Freedland 2014, 193–215). Temporary status implies that migrants may be subjected to substandard working conditions and demands to which citizen workers usually would not consent.

Labour markets structured by the preference for a flexible labour force have created path dependencies in the form of labour traditionally provided by migrant workers. Indicatively, agriculture and food processing sectors have restructured job requirements and classification to allow employers to rely primarily on a migrant labour force, where hiring British workers is not seen as an option (Anderson 2012). Moreover, where attention has been given to combat forced labour and human trafficking in these sectors, the more banal exploitation experienced due to the lack of oversight to ensure decent working conditions has continued to devalue work in these sectors. The 2018 White Paper on Immigration post-Brexit proposed a temporary worker scheme to allow workers from 'low-risk' countries to come work in the UK for up to 12 months. Although not explicitly stated by the authors of this White Paper, this is a clear example of where immigration laws are adapted and used to serve market needs or preferences. Consequently, immigration controls have focused on both keeping out potential migrants and sanctioning opportunistic employers, but nevertheless enabling lower cost temporary workers to define labour sectors such as agriculture. Since 'migrant' can be defined in a way that includes EU citizens with access to the labour market as equal to British citizens, the reliance in these labour sectors on a *migrant* labour force is not a consequence of lax immigration controls. Regulatory attention to immigration rather than oversight and regulation within business and employment practices has exacerbated the pervasiveness of precarious work.

Concerns about immigration for the purposes of work have significantly informed political agendas for over two decades (ILO 2010, 6). Immigration policies have focused on reducing the influx of immigrants identified as irregular, illegal, unauthorised or otherwise undesirable (Blinder 2012, 2, 6). Equal attention has not been given to what is *happening* in labour/business practices that seek out workers who are willing to work in precarious, insecure conditions and who are denied access, due to their work arrangement or contractual agreement, to employment law. In particular since the 2008 financial crisis, the UK government has preferred a flexible labour market with weaker employment law protections. A flexible market is believed to keep the economy 'happy'. Meanwhile governments turn a blind eye to businesses that seek out the cheapest forms of employment and support a labour market built on insecurity for employees and workers. The labourer is expected to be thankful that they are able to serve the 'happy economy' – especially where workers are seen to be easily replaceable, by citizen or non-citizen workers – which translates to wealthy employers and business owners.

Precarious employment, work and migration

Rodgers and Rodgers, in 1989, defined precarious employment as work that involves a combination of 'instability, lack of protection, insecurity and social or economic vulnerability' (3). The condition of precariousness does, however, cut across all forms of remuneration. According to the European Parliament resolution in 2017, precarious work is defined not only by 'non-standard' or atypical employment because 'not all atypical or casual work is precarious' (European Parliament 2017). Notwithstanding, precarious work is most often associated with casual work, agency work, subcontracted labour or contractual arrangements that specifically are not 'employment' arrangements, as per ERA 1996 s. 230. Yet neither are precarious contracts clearly self-employment contracts. The European Parliament, as of July 2017, defined precarious employment according to non-adherence to existing employment regulations, and employment that

> does not provide sufficient resources for a decent life or adequate social protection'. Notwithstanding the implicit belief that EU, international and national standards are known and applicable to all workers, this definition supports Rodgers and Rodgers in suggesting that precarious employment is linked to a lack of social protection, and vulnerability. The International Labour Organization (ILO) defined precarious employment as a 'work relation where employment security which is considered one of the principal elements of the labour contract, is lacking. This term encompasses temporary and fixed-term labour contracts, work at home and sub-contracting.
>
> (ILO, Industrial Relations Dictionary)

That being said, there is no single 'robust legal definition of precarious work' (McKay 2013, 194). Precarious work and precarious employment therefore can be used to identify divergent experiences, including Guy Standing's suggestion that the 'precariat' form a new class of worker worldwide. Standing argues that trends of restructuring labour markets, employment and purportedly globalised markets have formed the Precariat. He contends that due to fragmentation, deregulation and privatisation, these workers are prevented from seeing the social and economic situation that is creating and producing a common set of vulnerabilities. This destroys solidarity and a shared identity as a collective 'working class' (Standing 2011, 25). A concern for migrant labour in the UK indicates a strong connection between precarious employment in low-waged low-skilled sectors and a racialised labour force considered to be outside the boundaries of community (national) belonging (see De Genova 2018, 1768, 1777). Albeit, not as a cohesive 'immigrant' demographic but a fragmentation of non-citizen or sub-citizen disenfranchised Others. By maintaining a focus on migration, policy attention is deflected away from increasing employment precarity as a contemporary labour norm for citizens and non-citizens alike.

Low-waged, low-skilled labourers are distinguished into two equally contrived categories: 'irregular migrants' contrasted to 'work shy' 'benefits scroungers' (Anderson 2012). Precarious citizens and workers are pitted against each other and blame each other for their subjugated and disadvantaged position (Barnard 2014, 194; Anderson 2013). The broader economic and political system is not blamed for systemically enforcing precarious situations and disadvantaging, marginalising and 'excluding' certain members of the population. Rather, these Failed Citizens provide a vehicle for social regulation, to dissuade people from transgressing the law, but also to juxtapose the Good Citizen against the Failed Citizen. These forms of control are focused in the 'community of value' as the reference point of worthy membership/belonging (Anderson 2013, 4, 178). The community of value lies beyond legal categories where social membership and belonging are arbitrated. According to Bridget Anderson,

> the Illegal Immigrant and Benefit Scrounger serve as powerful warnings to benefit claimants and legal migrants of what they might become, and what they must dissociate themselves from. In the same way that the immigrant is faced with actual and rhetorical slippages into illegality, the claimant must constantly beware the slippage into the scrounger.
>
> (Anderson 2012, 14)

Neither the irregular migrant nor the benefit scrounger is able to achieve the rank of 'model citizen', 'public' or 'taxpayer', in spite of their actual social and economic participation and formal legal status. Research in migration can often inadvertently place persons considered to be irregular migrant labourers into two camps – either as victims or villains – without drawing attention to how this dichotomy simplifies otherwise complex social and economic relationships.[1] Unless the concept of citizenship is analysed, citizenship norms can continue to be reconstituted on neoliberal lines, according to market priorities.

1 Good versus Bad Citizen, like victim migrant versus villain migrant, can be seen to justify measures of control, such as limits on immigration and work permits, to maintain the regular status quo. The dichotomy established between the regular and the irregular serves to organise the nation-state. This apparently necessary, or natural, separation obscures the way economic business priorities are met because of a fragmented responsibility to labourers, and de-centred accountability away from the nation-state to individual employers and industries.

Proposals for legalisation and citizenship can reaffirm flexibility and insecurity as a form of civic virtue if these proposals do not problematise the labour demand for precarious labour (McNevin 2011, 151).

Precarious migrant workers

Judy Fudge, drawing from Bridget Anderson, maps a taxonomy of the 'nexus between precarious migrant status and precarious employment' (Fudge 2012, 109). The taxonomy demonstrates that the causes of precarious migrant status overlap with factors of precarious work. Categories in immigration create precarious statuses for migrants while legal categories of employment similarly produce a spectrum of precarious legal recognition for workers.

The relationship between precarious labour and immigration involves a process whereby uncertainty is institutionalized. Employers favour workers who are in a state of temporariness and insecurity, for instance on zero-hour contracts (Rigby 2013). The availability of workers from within the EU, and with Brexit

Box 2.1 Fashioning precarious workers

Conditions of entry

- Migrant worker: skill level, age, gender, country of origin, marital status
- Family accompaniment
- Employer: occupation, sector
- Temporal: duration of visa
- Spatial: mobility to leave and re-enter receiving country and to move around it

Employment relations

- Labour market mobility: dependence on an employer
- Duration of employment relationship
- Terms and conditions of employment: wages, hours, health and safety
- Legislative protection: employment standards, occupational health and safety, collective bargaining, workers compensation
- Unionization

Institutional insecurity

- Social citizenship entitlements: health, unemployment insurance, social assistance
- Pathways to more secure migrant status
- Family reunification

Source: J. Fudge 2012, 14–15 from Anderson, 'Fashioning Precarious Workers', 307–312.

the possibility of workers external to EU borders whose labour is not regulated by EU labour standards, supports a deregulated labour market that encourages and promotes a labour supply to meet a demand for precarious workers. This is demonstrated in the post-Brexit proposed temporary workers permit (2018 White Paper), which would grant 12-month working visas for nationals of 'no risk' countries to work in the UK without any access to national services, support or protections. However, importantly, the ideal flexible worker does not include workers whose immigration status depends on their employment. For precarious work, 'employers must avoid being tied into sponsorship and other obligations' (Anderson 2013, 81). While discursively it seems the opportunistic labour market choice would be to hire foreign workers, realistically the cheapest workers are those already present in the country. Temporary work programmes and the legal employment of third-country nationals are highly regulated and costly. For work to truly be flexible and malleable it is not the 'foreign worker who would be the most desirable worker. Immigration controls '*construct* certain types of workers through selection of legal entrants, and the requiring and enforcing of certain types of employment relations' (Anderson 2013, 91). Citizen workers are left with little choice but to adapt and conform. Workers who, for various reasons, are desperately in need of income – a need exacerbated by cuts to welfare services, housing benefits and job seekers allowance – are the 'ideal' flexible (precarious) workers. Hired and fired at the employers will, without access to ERA employee status, training opportunities, or continuity of employment to develop skills and status, these workers are told that they should be thankful that they have a job (Van Arsdale 2016).

Although migrant labourers are integral to maintain a supply of a particular type of temporary, flexible and precarious worker, the labour demand for this worker (flexible, temporary, precarious) extends to citizen-workers. Increasingly, this labour demand will be met by citizen workers as, for example, entering the UK becomes more difficult and expensive. Employers consistently demand what they 'think they can get from the various pools of available labour, while at the same time, labour supply often adapts to the requirements of demand' (Anderson 2010, 6). Thus, employers can demand the same cheap, expendable, flexible labour from all workers (low-waged, considered low-skilled) whether they are 'migrants' or not. Workers in these labour sectors have little choice but to follow suit and supply this type of labour, which is characterised by a lack of security and precarious circumstances. The perception that these are 'migrant' jobs heightens animosity against anyone suspected of being a foreigner, even if such suspicions are evidently racial, discriminatory and ultimately unfounded.

The perceived availability of a migrant labour force has facilitated a reduction in training programmes and incentives to invest in local workers (Gov.uk 2015). The lack of training and investment weakens the connection between the state, industry and people, which builds a system of social welfare. Workers without opportunities for further training can become trapped in in-work poverty, where individuals may be employed but living without enough income and without access to skills development, wage increases and/or progression. According to the Joseph Rowantree Foundation, 4 million workers in Britain live in poverty with rates of in-work poverty rising faster than employment rates (Barnard 2018). Popular methods practiced by employers to maintain workers in this employment stalemate is to offer non-permanent contracts to 'self-employed' workers rather than hiring them as 'employees' or relying on zero-hour contracts (without mutuality of obligation,[2] see *Autoclenz* [2011] discussed in Chapter 3; Hayes 2017).

If workers are either technically self-employed or not legally defined as 'employees', employers are able to evade the legal responsibilities that they would owe to 'employees'.[3] Employment law enables this: the basis of the employment contract is a traditional distinction between contract of services (commonly the employer-employee relationship) and contract for services (temporary contract for specific period of time and specific service, commonly self-employment contracts). Whether one is contracted *for* services or in a contract *of* services allows certain rights claims for employment malpractice to be made or refused. When one's employment relationship is not recognised as a contractual employment relationship but a contractual agreement, the possibility of being considered 'irregular' and in legal grey areas is much greater. Less regulation of employment practices is encouraged through political priorities focused on economic growth, where governments prize economic competitiveness in a local and global labour market. This has allowed employers to hire and fire at will, enforce nonrenewable fixed term or temporary contracts, and remain malleable (competitive) to market fluxes.

Techniques of precarity

The UK has infamously weak labour regulations (Medland et al. 2019; Hepple 2013). Employers avoid contractual employment obligations by relying on subcontracted labour, or outsourcing. Subcontracting has become the paradigmatic form of labour in the twenty-first century (Wills 2009). Subcontracting

2 The lack of recognised mutually of obligation waves workers' entitlement to an employment contract, the reasoning being that they are not obligated to continue providing services (working) with that contracting party. If the relationship is not concretised according to predetermined definitions of obligation and mutuality, then the law does not intervene. Without an employment contract, workers do not have established grounds for grievance procedures, termination of contract, sick pay, pension or benefits. The contract law model operates on an individual contractual basis, without any consideration overarching the contractual agreements to provide individuals with assistance towards their well-being or social welfare. These benefits are believed to be the mandate of *public* services, not the *private* realm of contractual agreements. Due to the decentralisation and de-regularisation of industries and labour, for the sake of encouraging a free market economy, the public social welfare system is increasingly unable to provide for individuals outside of their private employment relationships. After *Carmichael,* but before clarification in *James* [2008] casual, or agency workers, engaged in a discontinuous contractual relationship were, by law, not considered employees. The obligation to provide support and protection to workers is interpreted as mutually reflected in the obligation of a worker to continue working.

3 According to the UK Employment Rights Act 1996 (ERA), 'workers' are entitled to national minimum wage, health and safety protections, whereas rights and responsibilities are granted only to 'employees'.

in labour most often means that workers are placed in precarious situations where they are not considered employees in a standard contractual employment relationship because they are hired by a third party or agency. Avoiding the 'employee' definition (s 230 ERA 1996) absolves the employer from extending statutory protection to these workers. The worker is left to depend on the market for her/his well-being.

Subcontracting functions in tandem with deregulation. After a primary contract is negotiated between those demanding labour and those supplying (contractors), those responsible for supplying the labour in turn enter into another contract with workers to provide a portion of the labour. In other words, outsource. These workers are not the primary contractors and are responsible for only a specific aspect of the total job. Subcontracted workers can be more precarious because they are vulnerable to the demands of the first contract and second contract, the second or subsequent contracts often holding fewer guarantees of protection and obligations.[4]

The International Labour Organization (ILO) has raised international concern with subcontracting, particularly in construction industries (ILO 2011). Subcontracting is common in construction industries where a construction company will subcontract pieces of the work: a kitchen refurbishment company may subcontract an electrician, or a flooring company; or a building construction company will subcontract installation of windows, plumbing or cleaning. Similarly, in the hospitality industry, catering companies may rely on subcontracting and/or outsourcing to provide food for hotel events, or cleaners in large hotel chains. Commonly, workers in hospitality services are hired through an employment agency or outsourcing firm and then subcontracted to third party employers who are not the direct employers of that worker. This is in contrast to hospitality staff being hired directly through the human resources (HR) department of a large hotel chain, for example, and thereby entering into an employment contract with that business. Outsourcing and labour contracted through employment agencies are sold on the promise of reducing business overhead costs involved in HR departments and payroll (Van Arsdale 2016). While many outsourcing firms do have human rights statements and anti-modern slavery policies to ensure compliance with corporate social responsibility, outsourcing agencies may not provide their employees and workers with the means to report disputes or mismanagement (see Van Arsdale 2016).

Practices of outsourcing labour involves businesses (including governments, public institutions) subcontracting from firms – 'outsourcing companies' – which are now operating worldwide. Serco, Sodexo, G4S and Mitie are among the largest. The operation of these multinational firms has been facilitated by 'global trade agreements [that] have opened labour and manufacturing markets in developing regions allowing companies to outsource, offshore, and relocate

4 The law regulating third parties to contracts could be relevant in an expanded discussion of this point. For example, in the Privy Council case of *New Zealand Shipping Co. Ltd. v. A. M. Satterthwaite & Co. Ltd.* [1974] UKPC, [1975] AC 154.

production operations efficiently and expeditiously' (Van Arsdale 2016, 10). The British Hospitality Association (BHA) lobby the UK government in favour of increasing the outsourcing of hospitality services in schools and public sector businesses including the National Health Services (NHS), prison services and National Defense. This outsourcing enlists services through private multinational firms. Most of the BHA Board of Directors are representatives of such private multinational firms. Serco refers to itself as 'reimagining public services' working in five core sectors: defense, justice and immigration (detention centres), transport, health and citizen services (Serco 2017). Their stated 'purpose and ambition' is to 'be a trusted partner of governments'. With clear independent statements of their corporate human rights, social responsibility and anti-slavery and human trafficking policies, Serco is not bound by one particular national legislation, in the sense of being accountable to public oversight or regulation. In a shocking example of Serco's private corporate management of public, social affairs, in April 2019 the high court of Scotland ruled that the company's Move On protocol was not illegal (Scottish Legal News 2019; Serco 2019). While it is impossible to find details of Serco's 'Move On' protocol online, the protocol rolled out in Glasgow (2018, 2019) involves changing locks on residences of asylum seekers who have had their claims rejected by the Home Office, thus rendering them without the right to remain in the UK. Serco had been contracted to provide housing for asylum seekers. However the Move On protocol rendered these people homeless (Serco 2019). Serco's instance on the legality of their actions was supported by the April 2019 High Court of Sessions decision, whereby Serco was deemed to be in fulfilment of its contractual obligation to the property owners by vacating the properties where persons are 'illegally' residing. Moreover, Serco have promised £150,000 to support homeless charities in Glasgow, as if recirculating capital (money) would remedy the physical problem of homelessness that they created. With more details on this explored in Chapters 3 and 4, this example nevertheless demonstrates how outsourcing to for-profit companies detaches from engagement with the social reality of people and their work, or livelihoods. The transactions are legally sanctioned business processes, led by capital.[5]

5 Like Serco, Sodexo call themselves a 'quality of life services' company with 420,000 employees in over 29,000 sites. Sodexo similarly offer everything from catering services to private prison security to hospital staff and waste removal services. Sodexo have their own human rights policy where they 'promote respect for human rights' and 'ask suppliers to abide by a code of conduct' which is based on the ILO Group Supplier Code of Conduct. However, Sodexo is not governed by national or international law in the way that the government and public sector of a nation-state (in a liberal democratic nation) ostensibly is. The lack of enforcement or accountability guiding Sodexo and their code of conduct (or its adherence to the ILO standards) means that they are able to operate in a legal grey area of their own. These companies exist within, and provide services to, the public sector. Meanwhile, they hold no accountability to any 'public' at all: they are for-profit, multinational companies (similarly, G4S specializes in logistics and security services. Mitie, an 'outsourced facilities management firm' manage (and compete for contracts within) hospitals, prisons and detention centres).

Currently, economic growth under a flexible, 'global' labour market and restricted immigration are assumed to be necessary for the good of the economic system and the nation-state. The intensive production expectations of workers are contingent on a labour force that is willing to work for less. Workers from economically weaker EU member states and British nationals in disadvantaged positions can consent to work for less, for indeterminate periods of time, within a labour market that looks to international flows of workers as if this would supply a steady, self-regulating stream of labourers when needed. Yet, due to restrictive immigration policies and the pursuit of a 'hostile environment' towards migrants, these factors not only result in downward pressure on wages but also in conditions where individuals, citizens and non-citizens, are not employable or hireable unless they conform to lower standards of employment and pay. In other words, unless workers are willing to become 'migrant' and 'irregular', the jobs are not available (see Anderson and Ruhs 2012, 3).

Employers and industries concerned with cutting costs and maintaining market competitiveness prefer irregular, precarious workers. However, an overt demand for the type of worker embodied by the migrant would belie the purported values of the twenty-first-century liberal democratic nation-state. If liberal democratic nations explicitly demanded an easily exploitable irregular labour force, this would contradict foundational elements of their constitution. The difficulties of engaging in coherent discussions about migrant labour outlined previously and heightened by the experience of movement within the EU suggest that modern-day labour market practices and the nature of citizenship, its purpose and rhetorical power, are a more pertinent focus than immigration controls.

Imagined citizenship

Nationality laws traditionally recognise citizenship as a legal status following either of two definitions: *jus soli* which is citizenship based on birthplace and *jus sanguinis*, based on nationality of parents. The collective, or community, of people who are within that territory form the nation-state, and thus engage in a reciprocal relationship with the governing authorities who, presumably, have been democratically elected to govern the population of citizens. It is difficult to determine what point in history best illustrates the fallacy of this citizenship myth. Whether it be the selective citizenship represented in early twentieth-century suffrage, or the globalised movement of persons moving on trade routes, uprooted during the trans-Atlantic slave trade or colonisation that saw European settlers colonise territory in the Americas claiming it as theirs and their new identity as 'Americans.' It could seem that citizenship as we know it now, as a legal concept, only came to fruition in the twentieth century. The upheaval and disruption of the first and second World Wars, the creation of refugee status and condition of 'statelessness' illustrates the volatile nature of citizenship: it can be lost, gained, denied, even purchased. Even when possessed, even when one is a citizen with a passport documenting this citizenship, participation in the collective or community in a reciprocal relationship with the governing authorities can be withheld or denied. Citizenship under the law, formal citizenship, suggests a universalised belonging, because it promises that there is an attainable legal status for all persons within a territory. In practice citizenship is 'characterised by inclusion and exclusion' (Kraamwinkel 2012, 323).

Citizenship has been associated with political-economic participation that is based on a liberal, individual, male, property (land)-holding subject being recognised as a citizen of a political community, namely the nation-state. Since the emergence of the modern nation-state and subsequently the modern welfare state, the distinction made between citizen and non-citizen has become further intertwined with socio-economic entitlement. The liberal democratic nation has been identified as 'the dominant form of the modern state' (Held 1995, 51). Citizenship is a key feature of membership in the political community of the nation-state (Carens 2000). Citizenship, under a liberal democratic nation, is believed to enable autonomous individuals to participate in democratic systems and establishes 'rights and duties, liberties and constraints, powers and responsibilities' (Held 1995, 66). In its legal form, citizenship is meant to offer civil, social and political rights, together with the right to the law and its protection (to everyone, as Carens argues in favour of open borders 2000, 2013). Citizens, in turn, grant legitimacy to governments and legal systems through representative democracy and participation in the modern capitalist economy (Held 1995, 70). The state is 'supposed to service the matrix for the obligations and prerogatives of citizenship. It is that which forms the conditions under which we are juridically bound' (Butler and Spivak 2010, 3).

Citizenship as social entitlement differs from citizenship as a legal status. Moreover, citizenship as social participation is different from citizenship as political/governance participation. Citizenship, as a term and legal form, can therefore be used to close off membership even when one supposedly possesses it. For example, as mentioned earlier, in the spring of 2019 then British Secretary of State Sajid Javid revoked Shamima Begum's British citizenship as a consequence of her involvement with the Islamic State in Syria (Clarke 2019). That the Secretary of State felt emboldened to take such an action without proper assurance that he would not render Begum stateless, and the subsequent fervour of debate and research into her case, demonstrates the fragility and insecurity of citizenship as a legal concept. While surely Begum would have been prosecuted, as any citizen would, if she was to return to the UK, her skin colour and heritage moreover reinforced that she is not a 'British problem'. The UK responded to Begum by attempting to wash its hands of any responsibility, denying her citizenship based on her alleged crime. Migration then becomes the problem rather than, as in her case, juvenile disenfranchisement, poor education, community breakdown and radicalisation.

The myth of citizenship

The right of a nation-state to mediate its population and citizenry has been debated within theories of justice (see Carens 2000; Rawls 1999; Walzer 1983). The right of a nation-state to enforce boundaries has clear implications for the constitution of the political as a bounded population. Hannah Arendt explored the concept of the bounded political (Arendt 1958) and contemporarily Seyla Benhabib has explored this through a concept of rights de-territorialised from the nation-state (Benhabib 2004). Walzer (1983) questioned an obligation to citizenship beyond the nation-state as 'aid' (Walzer 1983, 47) and others have explored an uprooted, cosmopolitan citizenship (Kok-Chor 2017). Yet the nation-state, as a political governing structure and bureaucracy does not alone determine the limits of acceptable behaviour. Neither do the legal system, legislation and their application (more in Chapters 4 and 5). As Anderson (2013) explores through the categories of the 'migrant worker' and 'worker-citizen', social, cultural and economic controls shape belonging along lines of acceptable citizenship and value.

Movement across territorial boundaries – the movement of persons who are economically active in a place where they are not a citizen – affects the myth of citizenship by allowing non-citizens to live and work in the 'community' that conceivably would be the commonality from which not only citizenship is granted, but law is formed. If the community forms the limit that is then concretised in law, the imagined modern nation-state is a community made up of citizens who form the limit concretised into national law. In reality, the community (*persons coming together*) is made up of citizens and non-citizens; 'migrants' and 'British'. Significantly, the work carried out by migrants in the settlement country is economically welcomed and integral to the host country's economy. Yet the law, juridical law, acts as if it regulated and existed for citizens alone. Indeed, determining privileges offered to citizens through a recognised legal status can be seen as the sovereign prerogative of a nation-state's legal system. Labour migration raises questions about the role and constitution of community as it informs, and is ordered by, law. The same law that, now constituted by the nation-state, controls who is and who is not granted citizenship along notions of deserving and undeserving. The law technologised in this way as 'nothing but a technique' (Nancy 2003, 25) recognises beings that fit into predetermined categories rather than physical presence and participation in sociality. The presence, happening, that exceeds techne and capitalisation is written out of the law, as are the bodies living and working in the shadows of legal status and the labour market economy.

The social function of a community of value is an implicit acceptance of liberal values including autonomy, individual rights and economic market participation. These values are grounded in a particular and specific European idea of the Enlightenment individual (male), which was built against the communal, embodied, 'savage' other (see Quijano 2010). 'Migrants', particularly those stuck in low-waged, low-skilled labour, engaged in different cultural and linguistic communities within the nation-state of their work/residence, provide a convenient foil for the ideal community 'member'. But other others include anyone who does not conform to, or rejects aspiring towards, the ideal of the liberal, autonomous male: persons carrying out traditionally female work (care work, work in the home); persons with disabilities whose work and labour may not be within the dominant economic market; people living in ways that reject capitalism and/or formal employment, such as artists, nomads, subsistence farmers or local community activists. Rather than reify migration as the site of 'crisis', migration scholars such as Bridget Anderson as well as decolonial theorists (see Mignolo and Escobar 2010) trouble the imagined ideal of the liberal nation-state as a territorially bounded community of citizens who equally participate and share in the nation-state while those excluded from this participation do so by virtue of their own individual failings. The myth of inclusion through citizenship is sustained by the implicit exclusion of those who are seen as 'less worthy': marginalised due to race, class, gender, ability, age and so on.

Cultural, historically specific values, enshrined within liberal philosophical notions of the individual being, as well as economic market measures and ideas of progress, bolster a regulatory community of value (colonial matrix of power, Quijano 2010). While the community of value elusively regulates membership, the ideal conditions of desirability have become entrenched and embodied as social norms. For example, the biopolitics that regulate ideas of 'acceptability' in the social sphere are especially evident in physical, bodily conformity (dress, fashion, 'appropriate attire' as well as discrimination against obesity, expectations around conformity with gender norms) that, while to a certain extent are being challenged and stretched, nevertheless continue to be prominent in communities, workplace norms and social media.

UK employment law and immigration illegality

Many labourers in low-waged and low-skilled sectors live with insecurity. This parallels the lack of certainty involved with precarious immigration status which Nicholas DeGenova calls 'the deportability of everyday life' (DeGenova 2002, 149). Taken together, the insecurity of precarious employment and uncertainty of living without secure immigration status forms a shared space of irregularity even if individuals do not experience both at the same time (see Wills et al. 2010, 59–93). Persons in precarious employment situations who live and work in legal grey areas are maintained in this position due to multiple political, social and economic factors, not only immigration status. The market economic benefit provided to the state and industry by persons working in legal grey areas, as precarious workers, encourages the complicity of labour/employment and immigration law tacitly supporting the current marginalisation of irregular workers.

A supply of precarious labour keeps labour costs down. A migrant workforce can be 'cheapest' until the employer can face sanctions for employing workers in contravention of immigration law, at which point their cheap labour is dispensable. A 2018 review of employment in the UK concluded that there are 'serious gaps in labour market enforcement' (Metcalf 2018). Lax employment regulations may encourage employers to find workers who will accelerate their firms' competitiveness in the market economy. Employers in sectors that disproportionately favour precarious workers may continue employment practices that regularly undermine existing laws with relative impunity, as long as they contribute to economic growth.

Criminal sanctions against employers in the UK were introduced in the 2016 Immigration Act. However employers are not liable for employing persons without the 'right to work' if they have ensured proper identification checks have been carried out. While employers do not have a legal obligation to provide information to the Home Office, cooperation reduces the penalty fine against employers. A particularly callous example of employer collusion with immigration enforcement, conceivably in order to reduce their financial liability for employing irregular workers, is the episode of Byron Burger in 2016 (see Bales 2017). The burger chain – ironically one that prides itself in high quality products ('properly sourced British beef') and participating in a 'one feeds two' campaign funding school meals for children around the world – responded to the 2016 Immigration Act imposing penalties against employers. Multiple Byron Burger locations in London called a meeting of their kitchen staff, many of whom would have been paid £10/hour and worked up to 70 hours per week. This was part of a 'carefully planned "intelligence-led" raid by the Home Office' that 'brought together workers who were known by the management to not hold valid work permits' (O'Carroll and Jones 2016). In total, 35 workers were arrested, 'around 20 were deported by the Home Office' (O'Carroll and Jones 2016), some of whom had worked for Byron Burgers for over 11 years. The doctrine of illegality (see *Patel v Mirza* [2016] UKSC 42 and *Hounga v Allen* [2014], discussed in more detail ahead) legally overrode any duty of care employers had to their employees.

Economic and immigration concerns oscillate between government efforts to ensure that the UK is attractive to 'skilled workers' (those earning above the debated £30,000/yr threshold, Sabbagh and Syal 2018) and vigilance to preclude lax post-Brexit policies that might encourage opportunistic and presumably low-skilled migrants to remain in situations where they are irregular or 'illegal' (Gov.uk 2018). The Conservative government into the time of writing in early 2020 did not relinquish its 2017 manifesto to decrease net immigration by the 'tens of thousands', while still maintaining a policy that 'will attract the brightest and best to a United Kingdom that is open for business' (May 2018). According to the 2018 White Paper on (post-Brexit) Immigration, the government committed itself to a short-term workers permit that would bring migrant workers (from 'low risk countries'– in Europe and some of the Commonwealth) into the UK, without any promise of resettlement, or access to rights and entitlements, including no access to public funds (Javid 2018, 5). This move does not reform labour practices but exacerbates migrant-foreign workers' vulnerability. Working without access to public support creates an indentured labour force. Yet the link between government migration policies and the perpetuation of conditions of servitude evaded the authors of this newest rendition of UK immigration policy.

The most vivid illustration of the lack of consideration given to the link between immigration policies and labour market demands and conditions has been the government focus on modern day slavery. In the 2012 ECHR case of *CN v UK*, it was found that the UK provided insufficient protection against trafficking and article 4 of the ECHR's prohibition against slavery and forced labour. Following from this, the 2015 Modern Slavery Act and judicial considerations of modern-day slavery (see *Reyes* 2017; *Taiwo* and *Onu* 2016; *Hounga* 2014) recognised a need to protect against the exploitation of vulnerable workers. Theresa May's 2017 election manifesto promised to combat trafficking for the purposes of labour exploitation by 'cracking down' on criminal employers. Nevertheless, neither the 2015 Act nor the Supreme Court judgements connect unscrupulous employment practices with labour market deregulation and legally embedded, *common*, exploitative practices (see Mantouvalou 2018). In Miss Hounga's employment situation discussed next (and Ms Taiwo and Ms Onu discussed in Chapter 3), the existence of employment contracts seemed to sanction an autonomous employment relationship, albeit in Miss Hounga's case one that was founded on immigration illegality and thus the doctrine of illegality was considered. These employment contracts assume the parties to be consenting adults, freely entering into a contract, in spite of the power imbalance and exploitation that characterises the entire contractual arrangement and relationship as a whole. For Ms Reyes, not only was she party to an employment contract, her entry in the UK was further deregulated by being tied to her employer through the Tier 5 domestic worker visa (and questions in the SC case referred to issues of diplomatic immunity).

Hounga v Allen

In the 2012 Court of Appeal case of *Hounga v. Allen and Another* [2012] EWCA Civ 609, the contract of employment was 'tainted with illegality'. This illegality overwhelmed the discrimination case pursued by Mary Hounga (under the Race Relations Act). According to the doctrine of illegality, Mary Hounga's dismissal discrimination claim was not allowed as a result of her illegal immigration status and employment as a live-in *au pair* without a work permit. In Hounga, the Court of Appeal followed *Vakante v. Governing Body of Addey and Stanhope School* (No 2) [2005] ICR 231. Both cases concerned foreign nationals whose illegality was based on their lack of permission to work in the UK. The UK Supreme Court overruled Miss Hounga's 2012 Court of Appeal decision in 2014, based on conditions akin to modern day slavery, not based on the doctrine of illegality. Thus, the contract law principle of illegality remains intact to be applied to cases of immigration status 'illegality'.

While the Supreme Court in 2014 refused to condone illegality, it remained silent about the illegal (criminal assault: offenses against the persons) behaviour of the Allens. The labourer was blamed for her own illegal situation, in spite of the ongoing labour demand for an illegal, 'captured' labour force. Hounga's employment as a live-in *au pair* in the Allens' house challenged the scope of responsibility and assumed consent to one's illegal situation. The majority (Lord Wilson, Lord Kerr and Lady Hale) found that 'Hounga was the victim of forced labour' (*Hounga v Allen* [2014] at para 39). Consequently, the majority ruled that 'it would be a breach of the UK's international obligations under the Convention for its law to cause Miss Hounga's complaint to be defeated by the defence of illegality' (*Hounga v Allen* [2014] at para 50. Dissenting opinion, however, stated that in spite of Hounga being abused by the Allens, her participation in immigration illegality meant that she would not be protected by trafficking provisions. Meanwhile the Supreme Court referred to parliamentary attention to modern slavery but not to the extent that they overruled the application of the doctrine of illegality. The SC clarified the factors that need to be considered when applying the doctrine, but the basis remains that if the illegality is known and intentional, on a balance of competing public policy considerations, the doctrine will likely render employment rights void (see Byron Burger, Bales 2017).

The legal debates in *Hounga, Taiwo, Onu*, or *Reyes* have not taken into account what economic and labour market forces may benefit from decisions to limit non-nationals from accessing labour rights. Labour that takes place outside of the private home holds labour market value and subsequently creates a demand for domestic home workers. While encouraging labour market participation, the nation-state (law, politics, economy) re-enforces a concurrent disinterest in the well-being and labour market presence of those working inside the home. So-called private employment situations exemplified by the work carried out by the migrant women in all four of the cases (Hounga, Taiwo, Onu and Reyes) are private in contrast to labour law's public subjects: workers outside the home. Private forms of work, including care giving and care work inside the home, are excluded from conventionally recognised formal employment (more detail in Chapter 3). Albin argues that the culture of particular labour sectors has a significant impact on the type of labour and treatment of workers regardless of citizenship status or indeed access to the law (Albin 2010, 975). This is especially true where there is no organising collective that formalises this labour and the labourers, a point also raised by Standing and the Precariat: fragmentation, through casual work, zero-hour contracts, gig economy labour and self-employment exacerbates precaritisation.

A compounding factor adding to the experiences of precarity, Albin explores how workers in the service or hospitality industry are expected to embody the labour and company for which they work. Like care work and work in the home, this type of labour is much more demanding of physical and emotional presence and can constantly necessitate workers to exceed their contracted hours, as well as blur lines between contractual obligations and emotional, even familial or friendly, relationships. This expectation applies both in cases of high-waged business services, such as consulting firms, and low-waged catering, hospitality services and care work. Although divided by income, these sectors exemplify employment practices that go beyond what can be recognised within a fixed idea of labour regulation and can be considered forms of precarious work. Hounga's situation, made exceptional in the Supreme Court ruling [2014] through the emphasis placed on the horror of forced labour and not the structural shortcomings of existing labour law remedies, illustrates how contemporary labour practices are external of labour law and labour legislation. The exploitation of workers in precarious situations has only been addressed by the law as a singular criminal act committed by individuals. The modern framework of law and legal analysis struggles to address its own complicity in structural labour exploitation (see Mantouvalou 2018).

Migration discourses and labour markets

Migration scholarship that is concerned with labour migration and precarious labour outside the scope of employment legislation, when charged with suggesting alternatives or resolutions, tends to focus on expanding existing statutory provisions or including migrants into existing legal categories (e.g. Costello and Freedland 2014; Cholewinski 2006). Rarely does this attention extend to an investigation of the conditions of sub-citizenship demanded by labour markets or a consideration that rights may be ineffective protection for those who fall outside of the scope of legal recognition; Bridget Anderson's work being a rare, yet significant exception. As long as state-centric legal structures remain the common reference point of scholarly analyses, the barriers to secure work and employment cannot be addressed. 'Migration' needs to be disentangled from political discourses and sensationalised fears of foreigners affecting a fantasised stable economy full of opportunities for (loyal) citizens. The figure of the migrant, in border control, immigration policy and labour practices, exposes disempowering mechanisms of control and dependence (Anderson 2017). These mechanisms function as bio-political governance beyond the subjects of immigration and labour. Not only do discourses of migration and 'the migrant' cause unrest and discord within localities and communities (Gerlich 2018), individuals regulate and check their behaviour against notions of deserving and belonging. For example, in a study looking at employment agencies and job centres, Van Arsdale explores how people remain in a system that exploits their underpaid work. Workers are often sold a promise, an ongoing hope, that *maybe their contract will become permanent* or that the rigidity of standard work would be worse for them then the daily uncertainty of agency deployment and zero-hour contracts (Van Arsdale 2016).

The technologisation of governance and differentiation of subjects happen within the sphere of immigration's purported control. A passport, for instance, distinguishes a British citizen from a citizen of a different nation-state; a valid work permit versus an asylum claim or someone who does not have any legal permit to work (entry on a tourist visa, for example). Yet control over labour migration can give way to 'control which is no longer about labour nor even about migration as the citizen and foreigner are equally subject to control' (Guild 2011, 225). The regulatory and legal mechanisms that perpetuate the discursive distinction between migrant and citizen maintain situations of precarious labour and migration that harm both citizens and non-citizens alike – all the while benefiting the neoliberalisation of the market economic system and the circulation of capital beyond the individual nation-state, seizing ecotechnics into seemingly all-consuming capital. The UK government has effectively decentralised its border control to employers, landlords, banks, educators and health professionals. Due to fear of their own liability, employers in the UK require all workers and employees to provide evidence of passports and proof of the right to work for all employment. Employers can also require employees to declare of all foreign travel. Universities monitor student attendance to protect themselves against accusations of facilitating student visa overstayers, and landlords ask tenants for their passports as proof of citizenship required for renting properties. Similarly, banks ask potential bank account holders and borrowers for similar evidence. Depending on the area and clinic, NHS services can ask for certain forms of ID to be shown to demonstrate one's 'right' to access essential health services. Universal credit, which replaced previous welfare schemes such as housing or childcare support, furthermore requires that individuals have a permanent postal address, something that is difficult, if not impossible, for persons who are most vulnerable: homeless or in-transit without any social/community support. With varying degrees of legality and/or obligation, public services have adopted regulatory practices that internalise, and put into practice, restrictive border policing of 'deserving' versus 'non-deserving' members of society.

The idea that there exists such a reality as a truly global, or universal, market or global economy allows individual countries to avoid responsibility for the persons living and working within their borders who are not considered national citizens. Persons recognised as 'migrants' may not be directly excluded; rather the 'logic of boundaries' is such that 'boundaries do not simply include and exclude; they *include by excluding*' (Lindahl 2009, 425) and exclude by including. These boundaries are not only of citizenship where the identified citizenship signifies belonging in the nation-state, but opportunities for employment and legal protections in cases of employment malpractice, abuse, and discrimination. Labour migration and migrants at work expose the logic of boundaries where 'the twofold process of inclusion and exclusion' assumes 'certain interests [determined] as worthy of legal protection' (Lindahl 2009, 424). Such practices exclude the fact that the national labour market is dependent on sub-citizens, willing to work for less and in substandard, deregulated work. Emerging from this, the ostensibly global economy is believed to capture those who participate as 'global' labour suppliers and therefore external of recognition from within the particular nation-state, yet vital to the circulation of capital. Nation-states thereby maintain an exclusive hold on their supposedly 'domestic' economic market, while accessing labour more broadly in the EU and beyond. Furthermore, the global market economic model remains situated within, and supported by, the modern liberal nation-state. Thus the 'domestic' economy is intricately linked, even intertwined, with the so-called international or global (this is not a new phenomenon, Harvey 2005). Domestic, yet economically available, while the protections of the law are unavailable to the 'migrant' labourer.

Government priorities within the globalised market economy and processes of neoliberalisation (Peck et al. 2012, 268) crave cheap labour, no matter the implications that this opportunism has on the mythologised nation with its dream of a contained and equal citizen population. But it is not only neoliberalisation that chisels at this myth; people move and seek new opportunities whether because of war, violence, forced displacement, a need for adventure, family, education, climate or a desire for a different future, no matter what the reason. The European Union offered elements of this myth: that EU citizen workers may be protected by legal frameworks that are beyond the particular nation-state where EU migrant labourers are living and working (*Zambrano* [2011]; *CN v UK* [2012]; *Siliadin v France* [2005]). EU Directives have instructed national legislation to secure protections and freedoms, in particular in employment law (Agency Workers Directive, Part Time and Fixed Term Regulations). Nevertheless, reciprocity within the EU and allegiance is enlisted by enforcing differences based on who is 'inside' versus 'outside', both in terms of EU citizens (see *Viking* and *Laval*[6]) and non-EU nationals (*R(HC) v Secretary of State for Work and Pensions* [2017] UKSC 73).

In the clarification of *Zambrano,* the case of *R(HC) v Secretary of State for Work and Pensions* [2017] distinguished between EU citizens and third-country nationals to reinforce an external border against non-EU nationals. 'Inside' the EU reaffirms a mythology that these nations reflect shared values, namely European values inscribed in the Treaty of Lisbon.[7] The ECJ *Zambrano* decision in

6 Case C-438/05 *International Transport Workers' Federation and Finnish Seamen's Union v Viking Line ABP and OÜ Viking Line Eesti* [2008] IRLR 143; Case C-341/05 *Laval un Partneri Ltd v Svenska Byggnadsarbetareförbundet* [2008] IRLR 160. The cases of *Viking* and *Laval* juxtaposed the right to work in an EU host state against the EU host state's own domestic labour law protections (in particular, collective bargaining and the right to strike). There is no express entitlement within EU law to allow freedom-of-movement workers to engage in collective bargaining. Therefore, UK collective labour law and EU free movement laws 'exacerbate inequalities' differentiating EU migrant workers from domestic UK workers.

7 Treaty Of Lisbon, Amending The Treaty On European Union And The Treaty Establishing The European Community 2007/C 306/01 Preamble 1 (a): Drawing inspiration from the cultural, religious and humanist inheritance of Europe, from which have developed the universal values of the inviolable and inalienable rights of the human person, freedom, democracy, equality and the rule of law.

2011 created a non-legal category known as 'Zambrano carers': where a non-EU citizen is a primary carer of an EU citizen, they cannot be deprived of their rights insofar as deprival would force the EU citizen to leave the EU. This has ostensibly granted some carers the right to live and work in the UK. *R (HC) v Secretary of State for Work and Pensions* [2017] tested this right of residence to include a right to quality of life. It was held in the Supreme Court that EU law only obligated nation-states to offer to Zambrano carers the 'practical support sufficient to avoid their being obliged to leave the EU.' In spite of *R (HC)* contesting that without financial support she was unable to care for her British children, this interpretation excluded non-citizens to claim entitlement to financial assistance beyond 'limited support'. As discrimination based on immigration status is insufficient grounds for protection under the Equality Act 2010 (see *Taiwo and Onu* [2016], discussed in greater detail in Chapter 3), differentiation between EU citizens and third country nationals was reaffirmed in spite of *Zambrano*. This is in spite of the implied family discrimination experienced by the children whose mother was denied support.

The reciprocity envisioned within the European Community is therefore not a reciprocity that extends beyond an imagined European sphere in its own right. The reciprocity that is meant to protect non-nationals within the European Community (EU citizens) rests on the belief in a more fundamental and all-encompassing political sphere where European values are seen as 'universal'. These values are furthermore permitted to remain 'universal' while enforcing exclusion of difference in the form of non-nationals. In the recent (2015–2019) political chaos and panic around migrants arriving by sea to European shores, this universality visually stops at the white, Judeo-Christian European border and difference is highlighted in black, Muslim bodies (see De Genova 2018). The boundary is both figuratively inside and literally being reinforced outside through third-country agreements, externalising the 'dirty work' of an exclusive Europe. Migration within the European member states is limited based on the rules of the Dublin regulation, which deems that asylum seekers are tied to the country where they entered the EU (they must register in the country that is their first port of entry, and can be returned to this member state if they try and move[8]). However, differentiation is reinforced by extra-legal exclusion from, and within, labour sectors that limit employment opportunities along racial, gendered and socio-economic (class) bias. The EU external borders have, moreover, been reinforced by agreements that aim to mitigate Europe's responsibility for migrant flows (see Ryan 2019, 203). The most detailed of these agreements is the Joint Action Plan between

8 Regulation (EU) No 604/2013 of the European Parliament and of the Council of 26 June 2013 establishing the criteria and mechanisms for determining the Member State responsible for examining an application for international protection lodged in one of the Member States by a third-country national or a stateless person. http://data.europa.eu/eli/reg/2013/604/oj

the EU and Turkey agreed in 2016, otherwise known as the EU Turkey Deal. This 'joint action plan' oversees the transfer of 6 billion Euro for the Turkish government in exchange for the resettlement of migrants arriving to Turkey who intend, it is believed, to travel to Europe (see Columb 2020). Similar agreements have been made since 2012 between the EU and Libya (Naceur and Rollins 2017).

Conclusion: ecotechnics of mobility and work

Migration discourse, dominant in current political, economic and social debate, suspends the diversity and heterogeneity of all bodies living and working within a particular space. The precarious, non-regular working bodies categorised as 'migrant' suggest that (a) there is a common experience of all persons who are not remaining in their country of birth and/or nationality and (b) the non-migrant, or citizen, is protected by their citizenship from the precariousness and lack of recognition embodied in the 'migrant'. The 'migrant' and 'migration' provide an empty container for the excess of existing categories and ways of diagnosing the upheaval and challenges experienced within the UK, and the European Union, today. 'Migration' as a blanket term persists and is maintained through the agenda and priorities of immigration and employment law, arguably because it is easy; this term identifies a threat and sees that threat as foreign. Furthermore, there is an implication that the threat *should* be stopped at the territorial border. Rather than examine what has happened with the global financial system, privatisation, globalisation, austerity, multicultural communities and so on, migration identifies the problem physically at the border and politically at immigration policy. When 'migration' continues, in other words the challenges and changes brought about by the global financial system, privatisation, globalisation, austerity, climate change, multicultural communities and so on, the emphasis and attention is turned towards making the laws and policies *better* – more law, harsher law, stricter controls and more widespread policies. The frenzy over 'migration' does not consider whether migration is even the real issue of concern. Instead, migration rekindles a fervour around citizenship and the nation-state, one that is all too keenly taken up by nationalist groups who believe protection against change and threats to an imagined identity must be first and foremost in a government's policies and priorities.

The idea of the nation-state is potent when membership is mediated through belonging in the aforementioned community of value. The community of value recognises and rewards membership of the Good Citizen, who is deemed to share values of the national community. In the UK and Europe, these values are liberal, and tied to market economic values and success. The Good Citizen is rewarded in contrast to the Failed, or sub-citizen, who is exemplified by the 'migrant' who does not conform to the parameters of national community membership and is therefore a threat (Anderson 2017). The community of value supports exclusionary participation and reinforces situations of sub-citizenship from within a liberal democratic nation-state. Indeed, the idea of the liberal state, with its fantasy (Anderson 2017) of citizenship, democracy and a modern legal system where all subjects are equal and free, has crashed into the experience of the twenty-first-century neoliberal state. The discord, or the truth of mere fantastical ideals, mourned by those most fiercely obsessed with 'migration', cultivates sentiment against difference. Yet this performance against migration is in spite of the fact that membership in the community of value can be strictly guarded and prohibited to those that slip into precarity, dependence and difference from the ostensible 'inside'.

While citizenship may seem to be a matter of legal techniques and requirements (techne), it is based on conditions of desirability according to the community of value: a technologised *eco*. The sense of beings coming together always happens, but here, within citizenship and migration categories, the sense of what exceeds conditions of desirability is silenced and ignored. The conditions of desirability embodied in a (neo)liberal ideal make practical membership for some impossible (Honig 2003, 54). As a popular category, the ideal of the 'Good Citizen' excludes those who, through circumstances such as gender, ability or occupation, fall through the cracks and become the Failed or sub-citizens. There are many examples of citizenship being contested and/or experienced in ways that complicate formal, legal, state-centric, interpretations of the term. The UK labour force has always included the marginalised, devalued labour of those historically, and currently, not considered full citizens: women (Conaghan 2006, 8), colonial subjects, slaves or indentured servants (Blackett 2011, 420–421), disabled persons (Addas 2012, 53; Rigg 2005, 2), prison inmates (Zatz 2008) and children (van Beuren 1998, 263). The experiences of persons designated within these categories further demonstrate that legally possessing citizenship status does not ensure equal recognition of rights in the nation-state (Anderson 2013, 4). Social and economic inequalities isolate certain sectors of the citizenry, who subsequently are relegated, through the labour market, into irregular labour situations that are neither fully inclusive nor exclusive (Wills et al. 2010, 1). The idea that there is a global economy supports a myth of global belonging, which works within a framework of national citizenship but suggests a belonging that supersedes the nation. The layers of myth and fantasy remain grounded in an ideology of modernity (colonial and patriarchal).

Existing legal mechanisms, if un-interrogated, buttress the imagined universality of a global community and market economy. Interrogating the techne of migrant discourses reveals processes of neoliberalisation that maintain a demand for precarious work, supplied by persons in the ambiguous spaces of irregular migrant work. With a focus on migration as the problem, the symbolic structure of the nation-state is upheld by a fiction of formal legal citizenship as signifying membership in a benevolent social welfare state. This fiction relies on the marginalised presence of superfluous populations, those persons whose presence contests categories of 'regular' 'citizen' 'worker'. In other words, the structure of the nation-state relies on the idea of formal legal citizenship to facilitate belonging and recognition. Meanwhile the practices of citizenship and the economic system that uphold the nation-state include a demographic of labourers who are considered irregular and treated as sub-citizens. Yet due to the embeddedness of the nation-state and market economic system, the *eco* (dwelling, home) is recognised only from within the paradigm of the liberal modern nation-state (with global economic capital, citizenship and its consequences). Thus, the tenacity and universality of citizenship, the nation-state and the globalised market are unassailable. The law and legal instruments regulating migration and work are complicit in obscuring the reality of persons living and working within a certain territory. The jurisdiction of immigration and labour law is established based on the limited conditions of possibility embedded in the system of the nation-state, the market economy and the global circulation of capital.

The very real situations of abuse and exploitation that are experienced by persons in irregular labour market situations make it difficult to take a step back and consider the underlying paradigm of thought that conditions categories and frameworks surrounding the institutions involved. Indeed, there are immediate ethical, justice claims that demand attention, such as forced labour, modern slavery and in-work poverty (Barnard 2018). However, responses to these exigencies reaffirm nation-state borders as a necessary evil that enable governments to organise populations into liberal nation-states, and thereby to support liberal democratic values. The state and its institutions are always our addressees in labour and immigration law. In Bonnie Honig's words, 'when they self-privilege as our most important addressees, we are called into and by their perspective and we lose hold of our capacity to imagine politics otherwise' (Honig 2009, 135). Thus, existing frameworks are reaffirmed. The values believed to be contained within the nation-state and its institutions seem incontrovertible because of the universal benefit they offer. Values include the primacy of the individual and the idea of the autonomous citizen-producer as an economic unit as well as social welfare as determined by political priorities and state governance.

Thinking of solutions away from the political frame of the nation-state demonstrates how ecotechnics traces both the techne of capital and the interactions and relations of sociality – of our being together in pluralities. This plurality exceeds the categories of belonging in the nation-state or what is recognised as participation in the globalised market economic system. It also exceeds the way law is instrumentalised, illuminating that law does not just happen, but its activation and practice is part of the circulation of capital and of sense: ecotechne. The aporia between the claims of the nation state as bordered and the state's economic welcome of foreign workers is highlighted as is the limited extension of rights to persons labelled irregular or illegal, although economically essential. Law's limits belie the claims embedded into modern law, to be not only universal (or global), but just.

The next chapter looks more closely at the part that labour and labour law plays in the constitution of 'irregular' migrant labour and crises in both migration and employment. The diagnosis of labour as ecotechnics brings us deeper into the deconstruction of normative categories, which will then lead us to think to the possibility of openness in ecotechnics explored in Chapters 4 and 5.

References

Addas, Jihan. 2012, 'A Legacy of Exploitation: Intellectual disability, unpaid labour and disability services' *New Politics* vol. 14, no. 1.

Agerholm, Harriet. 2017, 'Amazon workers working 55-hour weeks and so exhausted by targets they "fall asleep standing up"' *The Independent* 27 November, viewed 8 September 2019 www.independent.co.uk/

Albin, Einat. 2010, 'Labour law in a service world' *The Modern Law Review* vol. 73, no. 6, pp. 959–984.

Anderson, Bridget. 2017, 'Towards a new politics of migration' *Ethnic and Racial Studies* vol. 40, no. 9, pp. 1527–1537.

Anderson, Bridget. 2013, *Us & Them: The Dangerous Politics of Immigration Control*. Cambridge: Cambridge University Press.

Anderson, Bridget. 2012, 'What does "The migrant" tell us about the (Good) Citizen?' in *Centre on Migration*, Policy and Society Working Paper 94. Oxford: University of Oxford.

Anderson, Bridget. 2010, 'Migration, immigration controls and the fashioning of precarious workers' *Work, Employment and Society* vol. 24, no. 2, pp. 300–317.

Anderson, Bridget and Scott Blinder. 2019, 'Who counts as a migrant? Definitions and their consequences' (6th revision) 10 July 2019, viewed 15 December 2019 https://migrationobservatory.ox.ac.uk/wp-content/uploads/2017/01/Briefing-Who-Counts-as-a-Migrant-Definitions-and-their-Consequences.pdf

Anderson, Bridget and Martin Ruhs. 2012, 'Reliance on migrant labour: Inevitability or policy choice?' *Journal of Poverty and Social Justice* vol. 20, no. 1, pp. 23–30.

Anderson, Bridget and Martin Ruhs (eds). 2010, *Who Needs Migrant Workers? Labour Shortages, Immigration and Public Policy*. Oxford: Oxford University Press.

Arendt, Hannah. 1958, *The Human Condition*. Chicago: University of Chicago.

Bales, Katie. 2017, 'Immigration raids, employer collusion and the 2016 immigration act' *Industrial Law Journal* vol. 46, no. 2, pp. 279–288.

Barnard, Catherine. 2014, 'Enforcement of employment rights by migrant workers in the UK: The case of EU-8 nationals' in *Migrants at Work*. Cathryn Costello and Mark Freedland (eds), pp. 193–215. Oxford: Oxford University Press.

Barnard, Helen. 2018, 'UK poverty 2018' *Joseph Rowantree Foundation*, viewed 28 September 2019 www.jrf.org.uk/report/uk-poverty-2018

BBC News. 2019, 'Nigel Farage: Breaking point poster transformed politics' *BBC News* 12 May 2019, viewed 28 September 2019 www.bbc.co.uk/

Benhabib, Seyla. 2004, *The Rights of Others: Aliens, Residents and Citizens*. Cambridge: Cambridge University Press.

Blackett, Adelle. 2011, 'Emancipation in the idea of labour law' in *The Idea of Labour Law*. Guy Davidov and Brian Langille (eds), pp. 420–436. Oxford: Oxford University Press.

Blinder, Scott. 2012, *Briefing: UK Public Opinion Towards Immigration: Overall Attitudes and Public Concern*. Oxford: Migration Observatory University of Oxford.

Bridle, James. 2019, 'Shamima Begum's case shows us citizenship can never protect our rights' *The Guardian* 5 March 2019, viewed 28 September 2019 www.theguardian.com/

Butler, Judith and Gayatri Chakravorty Spivak. 2010, *Who Sings the Nation-State?* New York, London, Calcutta: Seagull Books.

Carens, Joseph. 2013, *The Ethics of Immigration*. Oxford: Oxford University Press.

Carens, Joseph. 2000, *Culture, Citizenship, and Community: Contextual Political Theory and Justice*. Oxford: Oxford University Press.

Castells, Manuel, João Caraça and Gustavo Cardoso (eds). 2012, *Aftermath: The Cultures of the Economic Crisis*. Oxford: Oxford University Press.

Cholewinski, Ryszard. 2006, *Irregular Migrants: Access to Minimum Social Rights*. Strasbourg: Council of Europe.

Clarke, Steve. 2019, 'Shamima Begum and the public good' in *Practice Ethics*. Oxford: University of Oxford http://blog.practicalethics.ox.ac.uk/2019/05/shamima-begum-and-the-public-good/

Columb, Seán. 2020, *Trading Life: Organ Trafficking, Illicit Networks and Exploitation*. Stanford: Stanford University Press.

Conaghan, Joanne and Kerry Rittich. 2006, *Labour Law, Work, and Family: Critical and Comparative Perspectives*. Oxford: Oxford University Press.

Conservative and Unionist Party. 2017, 'Forward together: The conservative manifesto' viewed 28 September 2019 www.conservatives.com/manifesto

Costello, Cathryn and Mark Freedland. 2014, *Migrants at Work*. Oxford: Oxford University Press.

Dauvergne, Catherine. 2008, *Making People Illegal*. Cambridge: Cambridge University Press.

DeGenova, Nicholas. 2018, 'The "migrant crisis" as racial crisis: Do Black lives matter in Europe?' *Ethnic and Racial Studies* vol. 41, no. 10, pp. 1765–1782.

DeGenova, Nicholas. 2002, 'Migrant "Illegality" and deportability in everyday life' *Annual Review of Anthropology* vol. 31, no. 1, pp. 419–447.

European Parliament Resolution of 4 July 2017 on Working Conditions and Precarious Employment 2016/2221(INI) s.1.2.

Flint, John. 2018, 'Encounters with the centaur state: Advanced urban marginality and the practices and ethics of welfare sanctions regimes' *Urban Studies Journal* vol. 56, no. 1, pp. 249–265. Doi:10.1177/0042098017750070

Flusser, Vilém. 2003, *The Freedom of the Migrant*. Trans., Kenneth Kronenberg, Anke K. Finger (ed). Chicago: University of Illinois Press.

Fudge, Judy. 2012, 'Precarious migrant status and precarious employment: The paradox of international rights for migrant workers' *Comparative Labor Law and Policy Journal* vol. 34, no. 1, pp. 95–132.

Fudge, Judy and Kendra Strauss. 2014, 'Migrants, unfree labour, and the legal construction of domestic servitude: Migrant domestic workers in the UK' in *Migrants at Work*. Cathryn Costello and Mark Freedland (eds), pp. 160–179. Oxford: Oxford University Press.

Gerlich, Karolina. 2018, 'I'm a care worker. The £30k immigration rule would decimate the sector' *The Guardian* 19 December 2018, viewed 28 September 2019 www.theguardian.com/

Government UK. 2019, 'Domestic workers in a private household visa' viewed 28 September 2019 www.gov.uk/domestic-workers-in-a-private-household-visa

Government UK. 2018, 'The UK future skills-based immigration system' Cm 9722 viewed 28 September 2019 www.gov.uk/government/publications/the-uks-future-skills-based-immigration-system

Government UK. 2015, 'The impact of migrant workers on UK businesses' *BIS Research Paper No. 217*. Department for Business Innovation and Skills, viewed 28 September 2019 https://assets.publishing.service.gov.uk/government/uploads/system/uploads/attachment_data/file/406760/bis-15-153-impacts-of-migrant-workers-on-uk-business.pdf

Gray, Mary and Siddharth Suri. 2019, *Ghost Work: How to Stop Silicon Valley from Building a New Global Underclass*. Boston: Houghton Mifflin Harcourt.

Guild, Elspeth. 2011, 'Equivocal claims? Ambivalent controls? Labour migration regimes in the European union' in *Constructing and Imagining Labour Migration*. Elspeth Guild and Sandra Mantu (eds), pp. 207–228. Abington: Routledge.

Harvey, David. 2005, *A Brief History of Neoliberalism*. Oxford: Oxford University Press.

Hayes, Lydia. 2017, *Stories of Care: A Labour of Law*. London: Palgrave Macmillan.

Held, David. 1995, *Democracy and the Global Order: From the Modern State to Cosmopolitan Governance*. Stanford: Stanford University Press.

Hepple, Bob. 2013, 'Back to the future: Employment law under the coalition government' *Industrial Law Journal* vol. 42, pp. 203–223.

Honig, Bonnie. 2009, *Emergency Politics: Paradox, Law, Democracy*. Princeton: Princeton University Press.

Honig, Bonnie. 2003, *Democracy and the Foreigner*. Princeton: Princeton University Press.

Industrial Relations Dictionary. No date, 'Precarious work' *Eurofound*, viewed 28 September 2019 www.eurofound.europa.eu/observatories/eurwork/industrial-relations-dictionary/precarious-work

International Labour Organisation. 2015, 'ILO global estimates on migrant workers' December 2015 viewed 28 September 2019 www.ilo.org/global/topics/labour-migration/publications/WCMS_436343/lang--en/index.htm

International Labour Organisation (ILO). 2011, *Search – Subcontracting ILO*. Geneva: International Labour Organisation. Viewed 28 September 2019 www.ilo.org/

International Labour Organisation. 2010, *International Labour Migration: A Rights-Based Approach ILO*. Geneva: International Labour Organisation.

International Labour Organisation (ILO). 1949/1952, 'Migration for employment convention (Revised) No. 97' *ILO*. Geneva: International Labour Organisation.

The International Labour Organisation (ILO), *Convention concerning Migration for Employment* (Revised 1949). Entry into force: 22 January 1952.

International Organisation for Migration (IOM). No date, 'Key migration terms' viewed 28 September 2019 www.iom.int/key-migration-terms

ITV Report. 2016, 'Is britain full?' *ITV News* 31 March 2016, viewed 28 September 2019 www.itv.com/news/2016-03-31/is-britain-full-tonight/

Javid, Sajid. 2018, 'White paper on (post-Brexit) immigration' in *The UK's Future Skills-Based Immigration System*. Cm 9722. Government UK, viewed 28 September 2019 https://assets.publishing.service.gov.uk/government/uploads/system/uploads/attachment_data/file/766465/The-UKs-future-skills-based-immigration-system-print-ready.pdf

Kok-Chor, Tan. 2017, 'Cosmopolitan citizenship' in *The Oxford Handbook of Citizenship*. Ayelet Shachar, Rainer Bauböck, Irene Bloemraad and Maarten Vink (eds), pp. 695–710. Oxford: Oxford University Press.

Kraamwinkel, Margriet. 2012, 'The imagined European community: Are housewives European citizens?' in *Labour Law in an Era of Globalisation: Transformative Practices and Possibilities*. Joanne Conaghan, Richard M. Fischl and Karl Klare (eds), pp. 321–338. Oxford: Oxford University Press.

Launder, Mimi. 2019, 'Lack of nurses 'most concerning' shortage in NHS, report finds' *Nursing in Practice* 8 October 2019, viewed 15 November 2019 www.nursinginpractice.com/professional/nurse-shortages-most-concerning-nhs

Lindahl, Hans. 2009, 'In between: Immigration, distributive justice, and political dialogue' *Contemporary Political Theory* vol. 8, no. 4, pp. 415–434. https://doi.org/10.1057/cpt.2008.50

Mantouvalou, Virgina. 2018, 'Legal construction of structures of exploitation' in *Philosophical Foundations of Labour Law*. Hugh Collins, Gillian Lester and Virginia Mantouvalou (eds). Oxford: Oxford University Press.

May, Theresa. 2018, 'Foreword' *The UK Future Skills-Based Immigration System* Cm 9722.

Medland, Linda et al. 2019, 'The "future" of work? A call for the recognition of continuities in the challenges for conceptualising work and its regulation' in *Perspectives on Work Faculty Research Group*, Law Research Paper Series #001. Bristol: School of Law, University of Bristol.

Metcalf, David. 2018, *Labour Market Enforcement Strategy*. Government UK www.gov.uk/government/publications/labour-market-enforcement-strategy-2018-to-2019

McKay, Sonia. 2013, 'Disturbing equilibrium and transferring risk – Confronting precarious work' in *Resocialising Europe in a Time of Crisis*. Nicola Kountouris and Mark Freedland (eds). Cambridge: Cambridge University Press.

McNevin, Anne. 2011, *Contesting Citizenship*. New York: Columbia University Press.

Mehta, Suketu. 2019, 'Immigration panic: How the west fell for manufactured rage' *The Guardian* 27 August 2019, viewed 28 September 2019 www.theguardian.com/uk-news

Mignolo, Walter and Arturo Escobar (eds). 2010, *Globalisation and the Decolonial Option*. New York: Routledge.

Naceur, Sofian Philip and Tom Rollins. 2017, 'Europe's migration trade with Egypt' 1 February 2017, viewed 15 November 2019 https://madamasr.com/en/2017/02/01/feature/politics/europes-migration-trade-with-egypt/

Nancy, Jean-Luc. 2008, *Corpus*. Trans., Richard A. Rand. New York: Fordham University Press.

Nancy, Jean-Luc. 2003, *A Finite Thinking*. Simon Sparks (ed). Stanford, CA: Stanford University Press.

National Union of Journalists. 2014, 'Updated NUJ race reporting guidelines and EFJ manifesto' *NUJ* 16 May 2014, viewed 15 November 2019 www.nursinginpractice.com/professional/nurse-shortages-most-concerning-nhs

No One Is Illegal (NOII). *Website*, viewed 13 February 2012 www.noii.org.uk/.

O'Carroll, Lisa and Sam Jones. 2016, 'It was a fake meeting': Byron hamburgers staff on immigration raid' *The Guardian* 28 July 2016, viewed 28 September 2019 www.theguardian.com/uk-news

Office of the High Commissioner on Human Rights (OHCHR). 2015, *Behind Closed Doors: Protecting and Promoting the Human Rights of Migrant Domestic Workers in an Irregular Situation*. New York, Geneva: OHCHR, viewed 28 September 2019 www.ohchr.org/

Partington, Richard. 2019, 'Britain risks heading to US levels of inequality, warns top economist' 14 May 2019, viewed 28 September 2019 www.theguardian.com/

Peck, Jaime and Nik Theodore. 2019, 'Still neoliberalism?' *The South Atlantic Quarterly* vol. 118, no. 2, pp. 245–265.

Peck, Jaime, Nik Theodore and Neil Brennar. 2012, 'Neoliberalism resurgent? Market rule after the great recession' *The South Atlantic Quarterly* vol. 111, no. 2, pp. 265–288.

Pickard, Jim and Ram, Aliya. 2018, 'Union voices safety fears at Amazon UK warehouses' *The Financial Times* 1 June 2018, viewed 28 September 2019 www.ft.com/

Quijano, Aníbal. 2010, 'Coloniality and modernity/rationality' in *Globalization and the Decolonial Option*. Walter D. Mignolo and Arturo Escobar (eds), pp. 22–32. New York: Routledge.

Rawls, John. 1999, *A Theory of Justice*. Cambridge, MA: Harvard University Press.

Rigby, Elizabeth, Duncan Robinson and Andrea Felsted. 2013, 'Zero-hour work kept down dole queues, says CBI' *Financial Times* 6 August 2013, viewed 28 September 2019.

Rigg, John. 2005, 'Labour market disadvantage amongst disabled people: A longitudinal perspective' in *CASEpaper (103) Centre for Analysis of Social Exclusion*. London: London School of Economics and Political Science.

Rodgers, Gerry and Janine Rodgers (eds). 1989, *Precarious Jobs in Labour Market Regulation: The Growth of Atypical Employment in Western Europe*. Geneva: ILO.

Ruhs, Martin and Marie McAuliffe (eds). 2017, *IOM World Migration Report 2018*. Geneva: International Organisation for Migration.

Ruhs, Martin and Bridget Anderson (eds). 2010, *Who Needs Migrant Workers? Labour Shortages, Immigration and Public Policy*. Oxford: Oxford University Press.

Ryan, Bernard. 2019, 'The migration crisis and the European union border regime' in *EU Law Beyond EU Borders: The Extraterritorial Reach of EU Law*. Marise Cremona and Joanne Scott (eds). Oxford: Oxford University Press.

Rzepnikowska, Alina. 2019, 'Racism and xenophobia experienced by Polish migrants in the UK before and after Brexit vote' *Journal of Ethnic and Migration Studies* vol. 45, no. 1, pp. 61–77.

Sabbagh, Dan and Rajeev Syal. 2018, 'May's cabinet split over £30,000 immigrant salary threshold' *The Guardian* 19 December 2018, viewed 28 September 2019 www.theguardian.com/

Scottish Legal News. 2019, 'Serco lock change challenge dismissed by court of sessions' *Scottish Legal News* 15 April 2019, viewed 28 September 2019 www.scottishlegal.com/

SERCO. 2019, 'Update on the status of accommodation being provided by Serco to former asylum seekers in Glasgow' 12 July 2019, viewed 28 September 2019 www.serco.com/

SERCO. 2018, 'Statement by Serco on Asylum Seeker Accomodation in Glasgow' SERCO, viewed 28 September 2019 www.serco.com/

SERCO. 2017, 'Slavery and human trafficking statement' SERCO, viewed 28 September 2019 www.serco.com/media/2385/slavery-and-human-trafficking-statement-2017.pdf

Shabi, Rachel. 2019, 'Racism in political parties reflects pervasive prejudice in Brexit Britain' *The Guardian* 7 May 2019, viewed 28 September 2019 www.theguardian.com/

Standing, Guy. 2011, *The Precariat: The New Dangerous Class*. London, New York: Bloomsbury Academic.

United Nations. 1990, *International Convention on the Rights of Migrant Workers and Members of their Family*, article 2, no. 1. New York: United Nations.

Van Arsdale, David. 2016, *Poverty at Work*. Leiden: Brill Publishing.

Van Beuren, Geraldine. 1998, *The International Law on the Rights of the Child*. The Hague: Martinus Nijhoff Publishers.

Virdee, Satnam and Brendan McGeever. 2018, 'Racism, crisis and Brexit' *Ethnic and Race Studies* vol. 41, no. 10, pp. 1802–1819.

Wacquant, Loïc. 2016, 'Revisiting territories of relegation: Class, ethnicity and state in the making of advanced marginality' *Urban Studies* vol. 53, no. 6, pp. 1077–1088.

Wacquant, Loïc. 2010, 'Crafting the neoliberal state: Workfare, prisonfare, and social insecurity' *Sociological Forum* vol. 25, no. 2, pp. 197–220.

Walzer, Michael. 1983, *Spheres of Justice: A Defense of Pluralism and Equality* (New edition). New York: Basic Books.

Wills, Jane. 2009, 'Subcontracted employment and its challenge to labour' *Labor Studies Journal*, special issue on community unionism vol. 34, no. 4, pp. 441–460.

Wills, Jane, Kavita Datta, Yara Evans, Joanna Herbert, Jon May and Cath McIlwaine. 2010, *Global cities at work: New migrant divisions of labour*. London, New York: Pluto Press.

Zatz, Noah. 2008, 'Working at the boundaries of markets: Prison labor and the economic dimension of employment relationships' *Vanderbuilt Law Review* vol. 61, no. 3.

Case Law

Autoclenz Limited v. Belcher and others [2011]

Carmichael v. National Power plc [2000] IRLR 43

Consistent Group v. Kalwak [2008] EWCA Civ 430

CN v. The United Kingdom [2012] Application no. 4239/08

Halawi v. WDFG UK Ltd T/A World Duty Free [2014] EWCA Civ 1387

Hall v. Woolston Hall Leisure Ltd [2001] ICR 99

Hoffman Plastic Compounds v. NLRB, 535 U.S. 137 [2002]

Hounga v. Allen [2014] UKSC 47

International Transport Workers' Federation and Finnish Seamen's Union v. Viking Line ABP and OÜ Viking Line Eesti [2008] IRLR 143 Case C-438/05

James v. Greenwich London Borough Council [2008] EWCA Civ 35

Laval un Partneri Ltd v. Svenska Byggnadsarbetareförbundet [2008] IRLR 160 Case C-341/05

New Zealand Shipping Co. Ltd. V. A. M. Satterhwaite & Co. Ltd. [1974] UKPC, [1975] AC 154

Patel v Mirza [2016] UKSC 42

R (HC) v. Secretary of State for Work and Pensions [2017] UKSC 73

Reyes v. Al-Malki [2017] UKSC 61

Sharma v. Hindu Temple and Others [1990] EAT/253/90

Siliadin v. France, App No. 73316/91, Judgment of 26 July 2005

Taiwo v. Olaigbe and another; Onu v. Akwiwu and another [2016] UKSC 31

Uber BV & ors v. Aslam & ors [2018] EWCA Civ 2748

Vakante v. Addey & Stanhope School 4 AII ER 1956

Zambrano [2011] C-34/09, of 8 March 2011

3 Labour as ecotechnics

As the previous chapter identified, modern law's categories limit recognition in employment law to citizen-employees, usually in high-valued, high-income jobs in identified employment relationships. Low-income, precariously defined working arrangements and transactions are less regulated, with work increasingly administered by intermediary agencies, contractors or private individuals. For instance, the care or domestic work arrangements of Miss Hounga and Ms Reyes discussed in Chapter 2, and Ms Taiwo, Ms Onu and Ms Mruke discussed ahead. Persons working in private households are often the most vulnerable to being exploited and abused, especially where their status in the country is dependent on their employer (see *Reyes* [2017]). However, as noted in the previous chapter, while citizenship can refer to a formal legal status that entitles one to rights in the nation-state, in practice the benefits of citizenship are allocated according to accepted membership in a 'community of value' (Anderson 2013). Labour practices of subcontracting and outsourcing work can deprive workers of an identifiable employer-employee relationship through zero-hour or self-employment contracts. Moreover, membership in the community of value is often dependent on participation in the economic market, where value is assessed according to socio- cultural norms as well as financial productivity and economic status. In other words, income value. Consequently, participation in the market economy has become an indication of one's 'good' or valid participation in society. Persons recognised as less economically productive exist external to employment law, for example people whose working arrangements are temporary, transient, or where workers' labour involves caring for persons who themselves are not, and will not become, economically productive such as the elderly, disabled (see Hayes 2017; Fudge 2014). Therefore, these persons at work are less protected by existing labour standards (including National Minimum Wage) and more vulnerable to exploitation in the labour market.

Migration discourses portray an irregular, non-citizen labour force as problematic. Irregular protection through a denial of labour rights is attributed to an absence of the benefits of recognition granted by citizenship. 'Irregular' migrant workers are assumed to be undocumented and working illegally in the shadow economy. However, factors that condition labour market participation and membership in a so-called national community, and in its absence irregular status, are not solely based on citizenship. The modern legal system recognises the ideal legal subject-citizen as an autonomous, liberal individual who participates in the external ('public'), formal market economic system. Those who, through their work, fail to conform to this frame experience marginalisation, sub-citizenship often manifest through low wages and a lack of regulation simply because their work is not seen to be of value. Nevertheless, they are participating in the market economic system and the circulation of capital. Their labour is technologised *as* invisible and 'irregular'.

This chapter addresses the state of UK employment/labour law in order to understand labour and the precarity experienced at work particularly by persons considered to be 'irregular' 'migrants' as ecotechnical. As the previous chapters have described, ecotechnics refers to the circulation of techne – technologies of capital, of law, of intelligibility – that circulate at the same time as we are existing in eco, the sense that sustains and maintains being in the world. To diagnose the world as ecotechnical is to say that everything, everyone, every being, moves as techne (overwhelmingly experienced as capital) and eco – this is how we live, create and give meaning to our reality. Labour/employment law is a technique that concretises at the limit of a sociality. However, beyond or before law, ecotechnics reminds us that the singular plural is happening in the originary – open and potentially new every time – sociality. Within this sociality, that is embodied by bodies labouring, or bodies-at-work, ecotechnics also recognises that there is an ethical imperative to be response-able to what is happening; what is happening as embodied through bodies at work. This chapter explores precisely these spaces where work as eco (dwelling, home, environment) intersects with techne and technologies of law and capital, namely the market economic system. At this intersection, if we are to imagine extended recognition through the valuing of bodies at work, work and labour need to be understood beyond the marketised, concretised techne of law and the nation-state. In this chapter, I examine the 'feminisation of labour' and work that fails to conform to standard market, and legal, frames by examining the state of labour/employment law at three levels of analysis: meta, meso and micro. In particular, in-house domestic and care work, as an extreme of atypical work, illustrates bodies-at-work that do not conform to the technologies of capital and marketisation.

Technologies of labour

Work, and working, mediates if not determines relationality through our participation in exchange and production. Labour – what we *do*, not limited to waged work – is integral to the co-appearance of being together in our world as sociality. While immigration laws and policies administer the movement of persons across constructed borders and territorial boundaries, labour is integral to our basic sociality. Often, work (finding work, needing work) is what motivates migration and determines one's arrival and incorporation, or not, into a new territory and sociality. One's employment status based on work carried out external of the home or family for a wage, however, is the form of work that is embedded in modern law and gains a person legal recognition. Employment selectively frames membership in an exclusive sociality through citizenship. Currently, the dominant model of employment law persists as the standard employment contract, a form which has inherited much of the language and construction of work from the industrial model. The contractual model of employment continues within a specific political-juridical system that ultimately focuses on labour through material production and labour market participation as 'public', waged work. Normative categories of 'work' and 'labour' expose ecotechne: we experience the seizure of work as capital production and accumulation simultaneous with the excessive energy that is also work but that cannot be concretised or capitalised. In other words, the labour that exceeds work. The practice of law and the modern legal system, however, recognises work only through categories of employment, based on a contractual relationship whereby employment is the privileged (i.e. protected) participation in a political-economic-legal community, and ultimately the nation-state.

Labour, juridically and practically understood through labour market participation and capital accumulation (production and exchange), has become a technique. Labour has become *technologised* where tangible, physical, manual work is increasingly distinct from experiences where labour takes place behind a computer screen or a smart phone and may not even seem 'laborious' at all. Labour, 'eclipsed as production by technology' (Nancy 1997, 101), distorts and shifts the ways in which we understand bodies at work, our participation in production and exchange, and its regulation. Where does labour happen? By whom? For what? While physical labour has not disappeared, manual work has largely been displaced to invisible spaces, distant lands and onto distant bodies, only to be filtered (experienced) through technology as if technology was replacing the very labour itself. For example, work in call centres where someone calling for assistance with an item or product or service in the UK may end up speaking with someone hired through an 'offshore' call centre typically based in English-speaking countries such as the Philippines, India or South Africa (Jongkil et al. 2012). This displacement contributes to regulatory gaps and the continuing invisibility of work carried out by persons in subjugated, 'irregular' situations.

Digitalisation, artificial intelligence and technological advancements seem to present a threat that the need for the physical labour of human bodies, and physical interaction between bodies, will disappear. Such a displacement is lamented by those whose livelihood is dependent on their physical labour and presence – how else will industrial workers, for instance, earn a wage and participate in economic sociality if the factories close? Such concerns for shifts in labour are not new. However, it is the techne of globality (based on the idea of a globalised world) whereby production is technologised, minimising time and space, and its maintenance and function displaced unto poorer, more invisible ('irregular', see definition in Chapter 2) bodies and locations, that is emerging as a unique experience in the twenty-first century. The invisibility or irregularity has multi-pronged effects. Not only are human bodies still part of exploitative processes of resource extraction, such as mining, processing, but 'when AI advances, it creates new temporary labour markets for human fixers', in other words, humans often working in substandard, hidden conditions, are needed to oversee, remedy, correct and manage the technology that is assumed to have progressed beyond factory, manual labour (see Gray and Suri 2019; referenced in O'Brien 2019, 17). Furthermore, 'irregularity' is created by the displacement and demands of labourers outside of the home, where time and space are again condensed while requiring an online, quasi-emotional presence that chisels away at personal time and privacy. This can be experienced both in precarious zero hour contract work, where one is required to be 'on call' without pay, and in higher paid work, such as consultancy or Google-model industries where one's life is seized by the company through family-home–like working conditions and office spaces that blur the line between life and work. Yet another prong of irregularity is the creation of temporary labour markets in private (home) settings that attempt to fill the gaps created by a formal, 'public' labour market, increasingly demanding of time and emotion. Irregular, invisible, labour is in demand to provide care, emotional and physical support, for the young, the elderly, the disabled and ill. Thus, the technologisation of work is fundamentally linked to the demand for 'irregular' labour, a demand that has become transnational and 'global'. The displacement of labour demand from family, traditionally the women in the family, to privatised services, for example 'domestic workers in private households' facilitated through the unique visa programme offered by the UK government (Gov.uk 2019a), has awkwardly and ineffectively commodified the 'job' of nurturing and caring in a home environment.

Work is a normative category rather than descriptive (Medland et al. 2019, 2). The techne of labour law increasingly struggles not only with the falsity of boundaries between public and private realms of labour, but with the falsity of 'employment'. Employment, as a legal category, is not able to capture work taking place in, and out, of the formal labour market. The concerns raised by work and labour market participation are awkwardly addressed under labels of industrial law, labour law, employment law, work law, equality law, social law or social security law (Collins et al. 2018, 9). The multifaceted nature of labour, law and economy has caused much debate amongst scholars as how best to address the challenges of law and work in the twenty-first century. In an attempt to organise the ecotechnics of labour, this chapter will explore labour/employment law as ecotechnics on three levels: meta, meso and micro. The three levels of analysis suggest that, as ecotechnics, labour law reveals the incommensurability of labour as sociality with labour as market. As a field, labour law has been characterised by reflexive internal debate as to its purpose, aim and scope. Labour law's relationship with the economic market, followed by proposed theories and alternatives will be considered towards the end of this chapter, according to the possibility opening onto what sense can be found through ecotechnics.

On a meta level, this chapter recognises how historically the 'private', social reproductive work traditionally carried out by women has been discounted (Fudge 2014, 17; Fudge and Strauss 2013, 14; Busby 2011; Picchio 1992). The dominant patriarchal conception of work (linked, traditionally to citizenship) is labour that is 'public' and paid work juxtaposed to 'private' and unpaid work in the home, whether it be one's own home, or someone else's. The 'feminisation' and informalisation of work since the 1980s has resulted in precarious working situations becoming increasingly visible in the labour market for women and men, citizens and non-citizens (Zahn 2019; Fudge and Strauss 2013; Standing 2011). Similarly, 'nature' and ecology has been absent from labour law debates and discussions, in spite of a growing acknowledgement of the interrelatedness of work and ecology (Routh 2018; Zbyszewska 2018). It is with new urgency that emerging scholarship calls for a socio-ecological concept of labour to respond not only to the limited paradigm of labour law, but the climate crisis (see Zbyszewska 2018). This section explores ecotechnical labour in particular with reference to care and 'domestic' work and the awkward, or impossible, commodification of caring that necessarily challenges the scope of labour law to be widened and expanded to socio-ecological awareness.

On a meso level, the relationship between labour law and labour markets – the two are not synonymous – and resulting labour practices reveal discrepancies between the injustices that labour law purports to address and market economic goals that privilege differential citizenship and favour limited regulatory power. Before the nineteenth century, the market was but one facet of a broader socio-economic system (Polanyi 2001, 52). Once labour power became disciplined into an economic market, the market became the primary recognised mode of economic organisation. A belief in the primacy of the market, and with this, processes of neoliberalisation (Peck et al. 2012), have shaped the development of labour law in the twentieth century, particularly in the latter decades. Increases in precarity, casualisation, fragmentation and in-work poverty challenge labour law to respond not only to issues in the workplace, but social security and welfare. The ecotechnics of labour law features the seizure of labour as a marketised and market-based activity (including treating labour as a commodity), at the expense of attention given to the circulation exceeding marketisation.

On a micro-level, UK judicial decisions at the tribunal and court level are carving space for some atypical work arrangements to receive some legal protection. However, these decisions are slow-moving. Prominent Supreme Court cases (*Autoclenz* [2011] and *Aslam v Uber* [2018]) have successfully gained employee and worker status for atypical workers. Yet these trades privilege citizen-based arrangements in defined work arrangements that continue to be male dominated. The ambiguously commodified work of care and domestic (in-house) labour continues to be marginalised by, or absent from, judicial decision making, as will be discussed looking at *Taiwo and Onu* [2016] and *Mruke* [2018] and in Chapter 2 exemplified by *Hounga* [2014]. The lack of consistency in these decisions indicates a failure to extend thorough protection to the most vulnerable workers in the UK labour market. This will be discussed in the context of the particular structure of the dominant political-economic-legal order that seizes the happening of work into recognisable categories of law and legal subjectivity.

Metalevel: labour and care

The economic market, capital accumulation and global finance determine political priorities in the majority of the world. Economic labour market participation, however, is not the only way to live in the world. Not only is it not the only way to live, but the capital system continues its circulation because of the sense that exceeds it. This sense includes the labour and work that circulates above and beyond market capitalisation – for example, what I will call ecological labour, including but not limited to caring, sustaining and consciously respecting human and non-human life. Ecological labour is absent from what is recognised as 'work' and employment in the standard, modern liberal (individualist, ego-logical) frame.

On a metalevel, women's labour, ecological labour, i.e. care, caring, sustaining and reproducing, has been left out of the scope of employment (Conaghan 2018; Hayes 2017; Fudge 2014; Busby 2011). The limited frame of mainstream UK employment/labour law has been broadly recognised and critiqued by labour law scholars. Calls to rethink labour law in the twenty-first century identify labour law's original mandate to be a legal field that not only arbitrates work relations, but in doing so addresses the 'subordination, injustice and indignity endemic in our society' according to a 'broad and deep critique of our society and political economy' (Arthurs, vii in Collins et al. 2018). In spite of a proliferation of monographs and edited collections discussing labour law's future, past and present (see Collins et al. 2018; Busby et al. 2016; Bogg et al. 2015; Mantouvalou 2015; Bogg and Novitz 2014; Davidov and Langille 2011), the question remains unanswered of how labour law can exist (methodologically, practically) as a distinct legal field or framework while encompassing the breadth and scope of subordination based on labour, work, wages and social welfare (see Blackham et al. 2019). Ruth Dukes (2014) addresses this challenge from within the frame of constitutional law by suggesting that the law of labour is constitutional and needs a social approach that is consolidated in the very make-up of the nation-state and its legal structure. Yet considering ecological labour, or labour as ecological, we are urged to think deeper at an ontological level to consider the relationship between the techne of law, work, value and ecological being within a social and natural environment.

As noted in the previous chapter, labour law in the UK is most commonly practiced as employment law, regulating the contract of employment and rights administered under the Employment Rights Act 1996. Employment status, under the ERA 1996, represents a contractual employer-employee relationship. The contract plays a role in the (market) economic system by regulating labour markets. Work, in employment law, is waged labour (a work-wage bargain) that originates from participation in commodity production and exchange. This is distinct from what can be referred to as direct life-sustaining actions, whereby labour migration, for instance, offers a conceptual locus of two vital aspects of life: work and movement. The first, labour is 'the first need of life', according to Marx as opposed to what labour has become in capital production, which is a 'means of life' (Marx 1844). Elemental to birth, basic survival, reproduction, art, creativity and evolution, labour arguably can be synonymous with life itself. For Hannah Arendt (1958), labour and work (although the two words are not always synonymous), is the basis of action, necessary not only for material gain, but also political freedom. The second, as a freedom, especially in the Marxist sense of labour facilitating the passage to freedom, labour would have to be considered not only on the level of the proletarian revolutionary, but as an esoteric action. Labour is what exceeds the limit and, in the Nancean sense, touches the being singular plural. Ecotechnics shows how labour circulates as capital, within a market, and as that which exceeds capital circulation excessive of concretisation and commodification. The excess of capital labour is the labour of sustenance, ecological and social, exceeding the capital concretisation whereby labour equals work equals income (i.e. productivity and participation in the labour market). Employment law, conversely, as a technique of modern law, refers to a specific legal, statutory, definition. Not only are other forms of employment arrangements – casual, subcontracted, agency work – written out of 'employee' status and full recognition under the ERA 1996, forms of labour happen beyond the contractual exchange model and work-wage bargain that are economically necessary but denied recognition and protection.

Historically, unpaid work in the home was seen as 'women's work' and formally not as 'work' at all. The idea that women were predominantly working in private, domestic environments versus the predominance of male workers on standard employment contracts and/or in industries with union organisation reinforced an imagined division between the public (male) and private (female) spheres (see Conaghan 2018, 208).[1] Relegating women to the

1 The gendered division of labour is a construction reinforced by Victorian middle-class ideals, working class women throughout the industrialised era worked outside the home in factory-type labour or as domestic servants to middle and upper-class women. Conaghan suggests the opportunities for women's economic independence began to diminish as early as the late seventeenth century (Conaghan 2018, 280).

so-called private, domestic, sphere stems from a historically embedded notion that the reproductive (private, home) is a 'feminine responsibility' (see Hayes 2017, 37, 80 – women's social inferiority reinforced in the development of science and law). While it has been broadly recognised that women since the late twentieth and early twenty-first century are more actively and widely participating in the labour market economy (so-called public sphere), there is still a gap between the overall experiences of women versus men in the labour market. For instance, concerns over equal pay and the 'gender pay gap' (Parliament.uk 2015), as well as the so-called feminisation of labour. The feminisation of labour recognises a trend in labour towards more precarious, flexible employment for men and women, such as part-time, agency/intermediary work, and with this an increase in in-work poverty (Zahn 2019). Moreover, in spite of domestic (home) work being recognised as a labour sector and in many cases now is 'waged-work', this work is often significantly underpaid and women are particularly at risk of abuse when they work in private, domestic settings (OHCHR report 2015, 15–17).

The feminisation of labour

The rise of flexible labour considered as the feminisation of labour coincided with changes to industrial labour, through privatisation, and a shift towards a globalised 'free' market economy. The shifts both in industrial sectors and more women participating as wage earners in the formal labour market impacted employment norms: the jobs that women took on were often more precarious, casual, part-time and lesser paid, just as the shifts in industrial labour fractured the power of British trade unions and collective labour law. Both shifts signified the beginning of the end of the short-lived, post–World War II social welfare state, and triggered growing attention to labour migration (immigration) as a threat to a domestic, citizenship labour force. Increasingly in the 1980s and 1990s, labour was organised around individual employment contracts, rather than sector-led collective bargaining units. The feminisation of labour across socio-economic classes transformed the middle-class home (arguably, poorer, peasant and working-class women always worked inside and outside the home). The work that women had previously predominantly carried out in the home was now vacated due to their wage-earning responsibilities. This created a new demand for domestic workers in middle-income, dual-waged earner households. This influenced a new marketisation of work in the home. Work in middle-income homes, which was previously non-marketised, un-waged and relegated to a 'private' sphere, was integrated into labour market demand. However, this new labour demand remained external to the standard contractual employment relationship and organised labour even when employees had to be hired outside of the home and/or the family. That the standard contractual employment relationship is the point of reference for identifying labour market participation means that formerly non-waged labour, most notably but not exclusively home and care work, continues to not be readily recognised as labour within the market. This is in spite of the labour itself (housework, care work) becoming, not exclusively but predominately, marketised and waged.[2]

Care is perhaps the archetypal historically and culturally feminised form of labour: care for bodies, care for the home, care for communities and care for environment. Since being recognised within the labour market, care work remains stigmatised as a burden on the economic system, rather than accruing value (Hayes 2017; Fudge 2014; Picchio 1992). The pervasive notion that the home is a private, enclosed space outside the ambit of 'public' law and regulation condemns domestic workers, in particular those considered 'irregular' and 'migrant', to unregulated labour arrangements where exploitation is common. This rendering of care to the private home means that the home is simultaneously private and public: it is outside the scope of standard employment categories but also elemental to the functioning and order of the public. Cultural norms around domesticity and femininity reinforce an assumption that workers in 'home' spaces should assume more responsibility than if they were in a workplace, or that their time is exploitable because they are treated 'like family' (see *Ajayi v (1) Abu (2) Abu* [2017] EWHC 1946; *Nambalat v Taher & Anor: Udin v Pasha & Ors* [2012] EWCA Civ 1249 and family exemption from minimum wage requirements, reg. 57(3) National Minimum Wage Regulations 2015). Salazar Perreñas refers to this as a 'culture of maternalism' where domestic workers are expected to assume the role of a 'shadow mother' as an extension of their being women in a home environment (Salazar Perreñas 2014, 52). Even in waged care work as distinct from domestic live-in work, weak regulation and a lack of political attention and will ultimately allow care agencies and companies to avoid legal entitlements such as a minimum wage. For example, care workers working with multiple clients cannot count their time spent between clients (i.e. travel time) towards minimum wage. The working time is considered only when they are physically in contact with clients (Hayes 2017).

The commodification of care provides a normative dilemma (Lutz 2017). Although traditionally 'private' labour, such as work in the home or care work, has been commodified insofar as there is a price paid for services rendered through agencies (domestic cleaning, child/elderly care or support for persons with disabilities etc) or 'care-providers', the act of caring cannot be isolated through a checklist or formula. Indeed, if persons want to perform the job or work well, care workers constantly need to go beyond what the sector or 'profession' (i.e. job specification) not only requires but permits (see Hayes 2017, Chapter 3). The failure of legal recognition, as well as the continuing abuse in care situations in particular where care is demanded under conditions of low

2 Where does family life end and exploitation that begs attention from labour law and protections begin? This question was broached in a case in the European Court of Human Rights: *Siliadin v France*, App No. 73316/91, Judgment of 26 July 2005. See Mantouvalou 2006.

pay and low value denigrating both the carer and person needing care, demonstrates that recognising care or domestic work as 'work' has not facilitated greater social value or capital for those in these labour sectors (Briskman et al. 2012; Curry et al. 2001). But this is precisely because care happens in excess of techne, in excess of capital circulation.

An often irregular labour force, supplying care work also raises racial, class and gender issues: care as a marketised labour sector and an industry may be liberating for women who are 'freed' to participate in the labour force as breadwinners; someone else can be hired to take care of the(ir) care responsibilities. But their liberated situation simultaneously marginalises care responsibilities away from everyday experiences and offloads 'care' onto para-professional workers whose economic disadvantage relegates them to the private sphere of foreign houses, often in foreign countries (Anderson and Shutes 2014; Mantouvalou 2006). Care responsibilities are seen as an individual burden that is emancipated through the market, a 'burden' that is placed onto global supply chains of foreign workers that supply care work in ostensibly 'economically productive' or 'economically active' (meaning, neoliberal) countries. Meanwhile, the foreign workers who migrate to supply care work in highly marketised countries leave behind a care gap in their own families and countries of origin that is then filled by aging parents, siblings, or other carers. This is also part of the circulation of an apparently globalised market economic system, and the eco-technical circulation of capital and sense in the world.

Care's normative dilemma illustrates the limits of legal, market recognition. Capitalist development and with it legal recognition within a modern legal system that is intertwined with capital circulation (e.g. neoliberalism) is not progressive (Federici 2008, 92). Increased legal recognition together with being incorporated into the market economic system will not necessarily improve a person's experience of work and labour. The commodification of care work has not led to care and its predominantly female and migrant workers to be valued as equal to other labour sectors. This lack of recognition has been complicated by the changes within the structure of the nation-state. As Federici explains in the context of workers with care responsibilities,

> In England the government has given caregivers the right to demand flexible work schedules from employers, so they can "reconcile" waged work and care work. But the dismantling of the "welfare state" and the neoliberal insistence that reproduction is the workers' personal responsibility, have triggered a countertendency.
>
> (Federici 2008, 117)

Existing legal strategies are often insufficient to address gaps in labour market participation for women, and men, in marginalised, precarious work. Legal remedies of redistribution (see Kotiswaran 2011, labour law's redistributive potential) may technically put more people to work, and recognise their action as 'labour', yet these work arrangements may offer 'unfavourable welfare' where people are 'at work' but in jobs that are not sufficiently paid to facilitate workers out of poverty (Albin in Collins et al. 2018, 299). Employment figures in the UK indicate a decrease in unemployment rates at the same time that rates of in-work poverty are increasing (Joseph Rowantree Foundation 2019). For example, people may have to work multiple jobs, including shift-work or work in the gig-economy, in order to meet basic housing payments or provide for dependents. And, their dependents may miss out on the care they require, whilst their caregivers are providing care services elsewhere for a minimal wage – not just in the global care gap explained in the previous paragraph, but in the UK, for UK-based workers and their families.

The commodification of care work and a care-work industry in the UK privatises social responsibility and the responsibility of the welfare state to provide for its citizens through social support. The shift to a professionalised care-work sector radically shifts models of employment from classic workplace domains, with set hours of 'work' (public) in contrast to hours 'at home' (private). The persons employed for this work are often employed through temporary work agencies, as self-employed and/or casual labourers with zero-hour contracts and are therefore engaged in 'contracts *of* services' without the protection of statutory employment protections (see Chapter 2). Especially in the case of live-in caregivers, labour and employment take on a very different quality, with new sets of concerns and regulatory needs. This labour sector, under trade in services where women migrate to work as caregivers in homes, is further characterised by 'constructed precariousness under temporary migrant schemes, limited community market access rules, and channels of perpetual irregularity' (Blackett 2011, 430).

When care work persists in being underpaid and socially denigrated as work for 'irregular' employment, particularly for migrant labourers, those working as carers are often unable to provide the care actually needed in order for the person needing support to thrive. A notion such as Judy Fudge's 'care activation' (Fudge in Davidov and Langille 2011, 135) could mean that the work of care becomes a recognised aspect of economic life as it affects everybody's labour market participation and possibilities. Such a shift in the economic value of care and care work would only be possible if we dismantle the foundational contingencies of what is value(d), which underlie the very idea of market economics. Thinking of care, and care as vital to the circulation of sense, reminds us of what it is that *is* valuable to individual beings and the being singular plural (the being together) in the sense of the world, prior to economic markets and financial measures. The act of 'care' and 'caring' are non-productive but a vital part of the circulation of bodies and sense. Care, in the very material bodily practices, happens in the *sense* of the being singular plural. A bodily understanding of care exceeds capital circulation and poses a fundamental, ontological and *ecotechnical* challenge to neoliberalisation and the dominant economic market model, including the *sense* of the market. We encounter sense through bodily materiality, and caring is the sense of being that exceeds capitalisation. Thus care work is the excess, or the sense, of labour.

Through care work and care as a responsibility that *is* an aspect of the originary sociability and not an imposed burden of individuals, labour law is forced to contend with the responsibility of being as singular plural, what Marie-Eve Morin calls 'being more than one' (Morin 2012). This recognition is similar to the 'ethical subjectivity' that feminist scholars such as Rosi Braidotti and Adriana Cavarero activate to bring attention to subjectivities from a perspective diverging from the dominant Western, patriarchal paradigm. Braidotti suggests that thinking of care and being together is thinking of 'living being prior to inscription into a cultural code; prior to its being fit into a specific order' (Braidotti 1995, xvii). This is not the traditional sociological notion of the 'ethics of care', which can essentialise the role of caring into a normative, female stance. Rather, care is something that *is* a fact of our being singular plural *within* law, law as the trace of our originary sociality.

Care is not something to be acquired or activated by law. And neither is 'it' ascribable to one category of gender and not others. Such a classification moreover reinforces and naturalizes constructed categories of gender, race, class and so on. Thus, the responsibilities of all labour market participants include the responsibilities of care, not as a programme but as the ecotechnics of the world of singular plural, which form the social, which is what forms the need for an economic system and the tracing that is the law. Similarly, ecofeminists such as Salleh, Plumwood and Matthews link the exploitation of women with the exploitation of the natural environment, based not on biological determinism but the shared relationship of Other to the masculine patriarchal capitalist mainstream onto-epistemology (see Stevens et al. 2018). Salleh describes how in contrast to a recognition of ecological life and the circulation of sense, 'men's ungrounded restless search for the alienated Other part of themselves has led to a society where not life itself, but "change", bigger and better, whiter than white, has become the consumptive end.' (Salleh 2018, 32). This consumption, this hunger, has made life ecotechnical.

Notwithstanding the necessary work being done by labour law theorists and scholars to remedy the situation of marginalised work and workers within an existing labour law frame (Dukes; Fudge; Albin; Conoghan) deeper, or meta-level, analyses suggest that so long as our epistemological foundations remain unchallenged, labour law as embedded in a modern legal framework will not shift its value system to recognise 'feminised' labour and work in the home as equal to external, economically productive labour. Historically and culturally specific epistemologies have supported the development of 'masculinised economic knowledge, with its norm of competitiveness for growth,' which is 'privileged over alternative economic solutions' (Bruff and Wöhl, in Hozić and True 2016, 100). 'This mode of governance rewards masculine qualities of risk-taking, competitiveness, rationality, and a work ethic in the public sphere outside the home, while devaluing feminine qualities of caring, emotion, cooperation, and a work ethic in the private, household sphere' (True in Hozić and True, 45). These knowledges are based on economic values that are 'not just based on exploitation of wage labour [colonial etc], but the extraction of finite natural capital and the externalisation of cost of waste disposal onto nature' (True in Hozić and True 2016, 45). Zbyszewska traces this back to not only colonial expansion, but the commodification of resources through the enclosure of the commons and reforms that 'unmoored' labour 'from the land (and it's sustaining powers)' forcing it into the 'realm of market exchange as a means of survival' (Zbyszewska 2018, 13).

What remains external to market exchange – work that is carried out in the home and work that involves ecological reproduction away from, or in the shadow of, market-based economic production – continues to be marginalised. Perhaps this is due to the tenacity of the patriarchal system, where 'men, who may derive rather more ego gratification from the patriarchial status quo than women, are on the whole less motivated to change the system than women are' (Salleh 2018, 28). A separation between 'production and reproduction, generate conditions of structural vulnerability' (Diaz 2015) whereby those not participating fully due to age, gender, ability, race, geography, citizenship, in the singular, ostensibly 'global', economic market, including labour market, are made even more vulnerable than those who are already 'players' within the (precarious) market system. As ecotechnics diagnoses, environmental and ecological concerns have furthermore been subsumed into political economy, as nature has become the market (Zbyszewska 2018, 13). In other words, nature is seized by techne to 'economise' the environment and 'ecologise' the economy.

Bodies and ecologies

Following feminist ecologies, ecotechnical analysis focused on the *eco* turns the lens to consider what the mainstream liberal ideal, the rational economic man, subordinates. The answer is everything that allowed 'him' to function: the home, the environment, colonial expansion and resource exploitation (Federici 2008). Feminist ecologies recognise an inherent connection between the patriarchal domination of women and ecological destruction of the earth (Stevens et al. 2018, 122). Indeed, the pillar of neoclassical economic theory, the bedrock of liberal market economics and neoliberalism has been a fantasy of the rational economic man – a creation of the enlightenment followed by modern liberal thought. This rationale and philosophy informed the construction of modern law, including the parameters of labour law; its realm of possibility and potentiality. This is not limited to the ERA (the standard employee, engaged in an employment relationship with an employer), but extends to constitutional ideals that remain embedded in a nation-state/sovereignty/citizenship paradigm.

Federici argues that the twenty-first-century 'New World Order' is a process of recolonisation (2008, 102). This recolonisation has produced a 'planet of ghettos and a regime of global apartheid' (2008, 103), rather than what capitalism initially promised, which was a 'civilising' free market that would bring an end to 'famines, starvation, recurrent epidemics' (2008, 103). Widespread cuts to social services and spending on healthcare and education, in the UK part of austerity measures since 2008, has increased the burden on women. Women 'have been the shock absorbers of economic globalisation' (Federici 2008, 108). As states de-invest, women have to compensate with their labour. In spite of this overtime investment to the sociality, or because of this, women who are working in the home (either their own home or as domestic workers) and in caring capacities (often forced to negotiate work outside of the home for capital income in addition to caring responsibilities in the home) are reduced to the most economically vulnerable situations. Calling for the marketisation and commodification of women's work does not change the burden placed on these workers or the lack of value their work holds in the market economic system. The marginalised position of both femininity and ecology within the mainstream market economy demands that new forms of cooperation be recognised 'outside the logic of capital and the market' (Oksala 2018), and within a pluriversal onto-epistemology of being singular plural.

Our bodies, and caring for bodies, physical and natural, exceed the technologies of capital circulation. Attention to bodies as the site of sense circulating opens onto a bodily ontology. Body work refers to the work that is done around bodies that is messy, dealing often with 'human waste' and 'leaky bodies' (Shildrick 1997), often in private and hidden away. The body, like the experiences we place into predetermined normative categories, leaks out of the confines of the home and predetermined household and into the space of the 'irregular' 'migrant' and precarious legal subject at work. Indeed, body work is often carried out either by intimate (family) members, or the lowest-paid, 'low-skilled', foreign workers – people, workers, from the 'outside', excluded from 'public' citizenship in the territory that they live and work in. As care and care work has been commodified, the fact of the body remains as the visceral, tangible experience, eluding productivity and marketisation. That this physicality does not result in direct commodifiable product/ion denigrates the work of care in the face of the market and economic value: care work as body work deals with the 'negativities of the body – dirt, decay, decline and death' (Twigg 2000, 393). The work involved in body work is physical and emotional, for both carer and person being cared for, challenging modernity's notion that the body and the mind are, or can be, separate (i.e. Cartesian dualism). At this nexus of the material, physical body and the emotional demand of care and intimacy, bodies interrupt and exceed dominant Western conceptualisation of the autonomous individual, as well as market productivity. They are *sense* escaping technologisation, embodied. Consequently, bodies cannot be inscribed within a market system – working with/on bodies cannot easily, ethically, be valued as a commodity or product as the work given to the body, or more specifically given to another body, exceeds the market system. In other words, while the body circulates as people working (labourers in employment and work), the body itself exceeds the circulation of capital: it needs to be cared for, not merely bought, sold, or treated as a commodity, or as an input-output equation.

In a vivid example of how categories are not able to technologise the totality of our being and understanding of being, a meta-level analysis of how marketised labour and the globalised economic system has denied ecological labour and the circulation of sense is exemplified by the micro relationship that beings have with their own, and others, bodies.

Meso-level: labour, market and law

On a mesolevel, we observe how work that is largely ignored by employment law is work that has not fit into the frame of the standard employment contract and employee status within the Employment Rights Act 1996 (ERA). Neither do irregular forms of work fit into the industrial-production model where sector-specific collective bargaining units organised labour and labour rights. What is work, what counts as work, and what is the ambit of labour law and employment law is a question concerning many labour and employment scholars. As the previous sections demonstrate, this is not just a question concerning non-citizen migrant workers. Citizens workers in undervalued sectors – in particularly care work, but also work that is relegated to agency labour and/or zero-hour contracts – lack protection against abuse and legally embedded (structural) exploitation (Mantouvalou 2018). Poverty and in-work poverty rates are rising due to the prevalence and sole availability of precarious (i.e. casual, non-regular or zero-hours), low-waged work. As Van Arsdale notes in his study of temporary agency labour, 'the antiquated assumption that work is the solution to alleviating poverty is simply illogical in this era' (2016, 151). Within our current legal regime and employment model, employment law seems to be the only option to regulate work. However, if employment law does not extend itself to persons in precarious, exploited and vulnerable situations at work, what will? This section will review the relationship between labour law and the labour market, including the fragmentation of labour through increases in agency work and casualisation. Affecting migrant workers and citizen workers, the lack of security in work has led to a dramatic increase in in-work poverty in the UK (Barnard 2018).

Labour and employment law can function exclusively within a limited framework where, in spite of inclusive language, legislation differentiates labour relationships according to the contract of employment and 'employee' status (as per s. 230 ERA 1996). Limited definitions of employment relationships exclude certain types of work arrangements from the ambit of employee protections, even where this work is recognised within the labour market as waged labour. For example, as outlined in the previous chapter self-employment and independent contracting is not considered 'employment status' while in practice many work arrangements blur the line between self-employment and employment, as some judicial decisions have recognised (i.e. *Uber v Aslam* [2018], *Autoclenz* [2011]). Exclusion from statutory labour protection is often not attributed to labour law's shortcomings, but an individual choice whereby the absence of an employee-employer relationship ostensibly offers greater freedom and flexibility. This allows employment law to overlook the unequal exchange between the worker and the person soliciting the work, especially in conditions where many workers vie for one temporary job, or 'gig'. There is little freedom and flexibility for the worker who is dependent on an income. Nevertheless, the illusion of freedom and flexibility reaffirms the legally enabled deregulation of labour.

In spite of exploitative labour being recognised by the International Labour Organisation (ILO) as something to be prevented, these labour practices continue, encouraged by increasingly deregulated and competitive markets. A historically conditioned, specific distribution of labour law according to the formal labour market has acted to 'sustain citizens' privilege through asymmetrical policies, namely the colonial and neo-colonial division of labour ensuring privileged access to primary commodities in the process of industrial transformation' (Blackett 2011, 428). Labour and employment laws privilege domestic, regular, standard, labour and distinguish this from labour that is carried out by those considered migrant and/or those precariously relegated to positions of sub-citizenship. The conditions and parameters of UK employment law are assumed to be necessary if not quasi-natural. Section 230 of the Employment Rights Act 1996 (ERA) does not provide a definition of employee status, aside from outlining the prerequisite existence of a contract of employment. Case law, however, establishes a contract of employment using tests of mutuality of obligation, integration and control. To date, there is no existing alternative legal framework through which work arrangements outside the ambit of 'employee status' can be legally regulated. Increasingly, experiences within the labour market are at odds with legal recognition.

The labour market demand for globalised, cheap and disposable labour contradicts labour law's foundational and fundamental aims. Yet this impasse or gap in employment law protections (via the ERA 1996) is not troubling to the circulation of capital – rather, it enables capital accumulation by enabling a labour supply that is largely unhindered by the legal protection of employee rights. The lack of political attention given to strengthen employment rights protection in the UK demonstrates a clear government priority to 'foster and bolster the market' (Wacquant 2012) while deferring labour disputes and outright exploitation. Individuals who end up being wrongfully dismissed or discriminated against such that they lose their employment income can be left without recourse to reinstatement or compensation (see *Taiwo* and *Onu* [2016], following). In extreme cases, as in modern day slavery, labour disputes and labour exploitation are removed from employment law considerations and treated as criminal matters for criminal prosecution. As Fudge (2018) argues,

> the problem with the modern slavery approach to unfree labour is that it tends to displace labour law as the principal remedy to the problem of labour abuse and exploitation, while simultaneously reinforcing the idea that flexible labour markets of the type that prevails in the United Kingdom are realms of labour freedom.

Labour that is carried out in order to sustain and make possible capital circulation (i.e. work in the home, caregiving, artistic production and ecological preservation, the latter two often seen as hobbies, or 'volunteer' activities) is degraded. Exploitation in extreme circumstances may be criminalised, but in its mundane form this labour is merely expelled from labour law's ambit.

As the previous chapters have discussed, 'irregular' work that is excluded from employment law categories is not excluded from the labour market. In fact, such irregular and precarious work directly impacts the labour market by pushing down wages (see Fudge and Strauss 2013). In a globalised, competitive economic market that favours cheap, temporary, flexible production, agency work can be preferable for businesses looking to cut costs and boost profits. Labour law and labour markets together privilege a hierarchy of legal subjectivity in a subject/citizen/state/sovereignty paradigm, whereby lower-waged, lower-valued workers are necessary albeit only in their condition as low-waged and low-value. Non-waged work is even further devalued and is an absent presence in the circulation of capital, enabling capital while being excluded from recognition, as discussed previously. Non-marketised work, such as care work in private homes amongst family members, and ecological stewardship also benefit the sociality, but its value is obscured to the extent that this labour is denigrated for being outside labour market circulation. The market economic system, globalised through its predominance in national economies participating in global trade and finance, relies on the structurally, legally, embedded exploitation of labour (Mantouvalou 2018). In other words, labour practices that are reliant on the explicit exploitation of precarious and vulnerable workers occur in legal grey areas of national labour laws, but nevertheless in the labour market. For example, in the UK and worldwide, in sectors such as agricultural work, food production and processing, hospitality industry, waste and recycling plants, and domestic and care work (Routh 2016).

Commodified labour

Since the foundation of the International Labour Organisation (ILO) labour protections have rested on the assertion that 'labour is not a commodity', deeming that labour is not something that can be sold, consumed and traded like commodities in the globalised market. In other words, labour is not a product or activity produced for exchange and social-use value (Marx in Dragstedt 1976). Notwithstanding this claim, labour has been sold and traded throughout history. In other words, human labour has been treated as a commodity. While the transatlantic slave trade is the most vivid example of this, twenty-first-century employment agencies facilitate a current and legally sanctioned market of labour commodification, where workers and their labour are rented, sold and traded. Moreover, extra-legal or irregular forms of employment such as procuring live-in domestic labour from a different country without securing a permit (i.e. without a 'domestic workers in a private household' visa) or hiring temporary irregular migrant workers for seasonal labour, suggest that there is a market for *commodified* labour.

Judy Fudge identifies labour as a 'fictional commodity' (Fudge 2011, 121) because labour cannot exist as a commodity independent of an owner. This distinction is important to distil from debates within labour law where 'the *object* of regulation (a labour market problem of some kind or other here termed a regulatory dilemma) [is difficult to distinguish] from the *means* of regulation (particular institutional responses)' (Peck, quoted in Fudge 2011, 121). Labour market and market economic responses have engulfed labour studies into a self-referential circuit. Labour law is totalised into a specific form of regulation, although 'responding at a particular moment in time has come to be seen as *the* form, rather than *a* form, of labour law' (Fudge 2011, 121). Consequently, the labour market and recognition of marketised labour is only understood in response to the market economic system, such that international or national regulatory efforts to think of justice or (labour) rights can do so only with reference to market participation (e.g. the commodification of care work). The statement that 'labour is not a commodity', while true in that labour must be embodied and thereby exceeds commodification, is challenged within the realities of the twenty-first century workforce that is treated as a technical market more than a living sociality.

Renting work and employment agencies

The idealism for bridging the inequality of power between employers and employees, which fuelled much of twentieth-century labour law, is once again being called into question for its ability to respond to the needs of people working. In particular, there is a current, urgent demand for protection against abuses and exploitation across labour sectors and incomes, with the most vulnerable often being irregular migrants working in private, domestic homes. Notwithstanding work in private homes,[3] agency work is a significant labour 'sector' selling an increasingly precarious and cheap workforce. When a business or industry hires workers through an agency, the business itself reduces their

3 For an extreme example where labour is being sold, see Malay 2014.

costs: there is no need for a large human resources department, there are fewer payroll expenses, and workers can be hired and fired at will. Such flexibility enables businesses to respond to market fluctuations. In an extensive study on agency ('temp') work in the U.S., Van Arsdale heard employers justify relying on agency workers as job-producing: 'for every full-time job removed, two or three fragmented, flexible, part-time jobs are created' (Van Arsdale 2016, 3). In the UK, like the U.S., unemployment statistics do not count the cost of moving from one temporary employment to another, or the precarious, insecure, nature of these contracts. Therefore 'temporary work [creating 'temp slaves'] engenders deprived employment statuses' (Van Arsdale 2016, 3) while governments pride themselves, and even win elections, based on lowering unemployment rates and ostensibly creating jobs (The Economist 2018).

Corporate and non-corporate employment agencies act as 'privatised HR departments' (Van Arsdale 2016, 11) that provide flexible employment standards which are attractive to 'companies, investment and entrepreneurship' by sheltering employers from employee 'risks', such as trade union organising and general employment rights – dismissal, sick/maternity/paternity leave and so on (Van Arsdale 2016, 11). Meanwhile, the workers who find work in these temporary contracts are suspended, and often trapped, in uncertain, highly precarious work arrangements. From one day to the next, workers are not guaranteed any income, similar to workers on precarious zero-hour contracts. Agencies pay according to the job worked, or dispatch, not according to time at the agency itself. Furthermore, workers change from one sector to another and require broad skills in spite of typically being referred to as a 'low-skilled' labour force. According to Van Arsdale, 'the ability of agencies to pay their labourers solely for dispatch hours facilitates a supply of underemployed labourers in search of more work opportunities' (2016, 43). A hungry labour force crowds around employers and businesses who offer scattered crumbs and exploit the work of the crowding, competing and tired labourers. Where traditionally trade unions acted as organisations that by their collectivity prevented competition within labour sectors, common identity and union is destroyed when individuals compete daily for temporary jobs. Labour has truly been 'forced into the realm of market exchange as a 'means of survival'' (Zbyszewska 2018, quoting Polanyi). In other words, work has become techne, with only the most devalued forms of labour (i.e. care) exceeding technologisation.

Shifts in the UK labour force, including de-industrialisation and globalised resource extraction-production-manufacturing, have created new working arrangements within the 'formal' labour force as well as demand for more privatised forms of labour across a broader income bracket. Changes in agriculture such as mechanisation, large-scale farming versus smaller family farms and local agriculture, food processing and production via the internationalisation of trade and production of consumable goods, digitisation (technological IT support outsourced, see Gray and Suri 2019), a rise in short-term contracts, employment agencies and agency work due to more precarious market fluctuations and global reach of businesses (meaning that they may need to respond to the market by hiring and firing at short notice, or relocate to a different area or country) has resulted in a rapid decline in employee protections. Independent self-employment is legally recognised as a work arrangement that does not obligate the person paying for services to offer security or guarantee hours (i.e. wages) to the worker. This lack of mutuality of obligations rests on the belief that both contractual partners are equally free and flexible to withdraw from the agreement. This fundamentally does not take into account the power differential between the worker who is in need of or dependent on a wage, and the business, often multinational, that may believe it has a vast pool from which to select workers. Nevertheless, the Conservative government in 2019 continued to pride itself for decreasing unemployment rates (Gov.UK 2019b). Individuals with precarious contracts without stable or sufficient (living wage) income are considered, for statistical purposes, to be 'at work' and not unemployed, in spite of rising statistics highlighting in-work poverty – meaning insufficiently waged work (see Joseph Rowantree Foundation 2019).

Migration, precarious labour and the market

In 2013, then Prime Minister David Cameron stated that 'immigration and welfare are two sides of the same coin' (Cameron 2013). Migrants are blamed for labour market changes that result in higher pressures on social welfare systems and a perceived lack of social resources. However, government-led austerity measures since 2008 have resulted in cuts to public spending, severely limiting services such as housing benefits, social care provision, unemployment benefits (renamed jobseekers allowance) and pensions (Department for Work and Pensions 2019; Hayes 2017, 5; Slater 2016, 21–31). As Tom Slater writes, the Conservative governments since 2010 have 'transformed the 2007–2008 crisis of capitalism into a crisis of the welfare state' (Slater 2016, 26), resulting in a punitive regime under 'universal credit' and 'benefits reforms' (Gov.UK 2019c). The impact of these austerity measures surpass blame placed on a migrant workforce. According to a 2018 report by the Joseph Rowantree Foundation (JRF) on poverty in the UK, 'one-and-a-half million people were living in destitution in the UK at some point during 2017, including 365,000 children. Overall, 7% of people in the UK are in persistent poverty – 4.6 million people' (Barnard 2018). Child poverty has increased in working families, a problem caused by the high cost of housing and cuts to housing benefits. This report evidences that reducing the rate of unemployment, in other words increasing employment, does not reduce poverty. The report continues:

> The factors that tend to drive destitution are low benefit levels, benefit sanctions, and delays in receiving benefits (sometimes a lack of eligibility for benefits at all), harsh debt recovery practices, financial pressures due to poor health and disability, high costs for housing and fuel, and the rising cost of living. Extended restrictions on the benefits and support available

> to asylum seekers and European Economic Area (EEA) migrants also play a role for these groups.
>
> (Barnard 2018, 20)

An investigation by *The Guardian* in March 2019 found that austerity measures that cut spending to services since 2010 have significantly altered the quality of UK education, housing, local government, social care, NHS and the police (Butler et al. 2019). Consequently, citizen and non-national workers are affected by decentralised, deregulated market-focused labour regimes that have privatised responsibility for all persons, including workers, and their social welfare. If the social welfare and well-being of workers is not a market or industry priority, there is little accountability and few resources within government allocated to regulation and enforcement. Without regulation and enforcement, employers evade their duty to ensure individuals receive adequate wages, sick pay, access to health care, pensions or disability pay.

The UK government's focus on immigration policies as the cause of economic woe avoids addressing the consequences of a state-bolstered financial system on social welfare systems and quality employment. The deferral of responsibility onto the individual implies that the globalised economic market and market forces are somehow separate. The institutional response to immigration, in particular low-waged, low-skilled migrant labour, comes from within the market system that benefits from keeping this labour irregular and *invisible*. The labour market itself is 'fundamentally contested, and law does not simply regulate an already existing labour market but helps to produce employment and labour markets as social fields' (Anderson 2013, 79). Thus, while the market economic system is believed to provide justice and rights through 'free' market participation, the availability of cheap and dispensable labour in particular when citizenship rights are not recognised is more conducive to quick market growth through low employer and business costs. The twenty-first century 'new world of work' is characterised by financial pressure and accelerated production, prioritised above (costly) social protection for workers. Migration and the ostensibly global movement of workers 'serve to make labour vulnerable and controllable in very particular ways and to encourage precarity' (Medland et al. 2019). A hostile environment to migration coexists with internal borders barring citizenship from accessing social protection, as discussed in the previous chapter.

Dominant twenty-first century labour practices in the UK undermine the regulatory aim and historically specific (mid-twentieth century) mandate of labour law: namely to reduce the inequality of bargaining power in employment and promote the collective bargaining model of labour relations. The collective bargaining model, even now, can be seen to maintain a narrow focus on labour situated in workplaces, where workers are organised into unions or collective bargaining units to negotiate their rights and status with a clearly defined employer. Albeit since the 2016 Trade Union Act, the rights of unionised workers have been dramatically reduced and the right to industrial action complicated (Novitz 2017). The prevalence of more fragmented labour relations where employers-employees are not clearly defined, for instance Chapter two's discussion of subcontracted labour, and the breakdown of the industry model has caused labour lawyers to question the theoretical foundation (purpose) and future potential for labour law (Blackham et al. 2019; Zahn 2019; Arthurs 2011, 14–16, 20–22).

The late twentieth century witnessed responsibility for employment well-being and security shift from the nation-state and collective bargaining models based on worker associations to individual and private, even multinational, employment contracts (Freedland and Kountouris 2011). In the more current model, the individual is expected to depend on the market and personalised negotiation of the market for support (insurance, risk, benefits), rather than on state and/or collective action (Blackham et al. 2019; Rittich 2003, 167). The market is substituted for 'society' and the globalised economy is not an imagined site for collective support, but a free market of individuals. Moreover, the ideology of the market assures that 'the market will provide' if only individuals conform to its totalising presence. Conceptualisation of sociality has, largely through neoliberalisation, been dominated by conceptualising the market. Thus, unless we reclaim conceptualisation of sociality, the law that traces sociality traces the market and obscures the discrimination of those whose subjectivity is marginalised. This includes those whose contribution to the market is 'irregular', kept invisible from regulation, and precisely *as irregular* benefits the market.

Micro-level: living legal definitions

An ecotechnical analysis exposes how the technologies of capital, redeploying the nation-state and law, craft dwelling (ecotechne) through seizing life into the circulation of capital. Commodification through capital aims to negate the excessive labour that cannot be commodified, while at the same time benefits from its legally enforced invisibility, or irregularity. However, as law technologises, the response-ability of the being singular plural continues to respond as sense, as what relationality (in the eco, oikos, dwelling) bring forth, exceeding the technologies of law and capital. In Nancy's (2008) words,

> the transgressive, it is with the experiences that are marginalised by normativities, the people and the questions that don't-quite-fit-in that are beyond the bounds of comfort and conformity. This is where we touch the concretion of the world. This is where existence starts to make sense.

Importantly, this is not a judgement or appraisal whereby techne is negative and eco is positive: that which exceeds techne is not necessarily better, it simply *is*. Whilst the circulation of legal categories, frame and techniques of order serving capital accumulation can threaten, or act as if they were overwhelming, techne does not deny eco.

The employer-employee model on which modern employment law has been built is not broadly representative of contemporary labour market practices. This section will examine how some judicial decisions concerning irregular work and irregular migrants at work are adapting to changes and negotiating competing interests. However, legislative frameworks, statutory employee rights protections and Parliament show little signs of movement. On a micro-level, we can examine how through judicial decisions, employment law is being challenged; not to the extent, however, that employment protections are able to extend to all situations of labour exploitation. For instance, when applicants fail to meet the requisite anti-discrimination protected characteristics (*Taiwo* and *Onu* [2016] discussed later), or are voided by the doctrine of illegality (*Hounga v Allen* discussed in the previous chapter), or are in work arrangements that are not considered an 'employment relationship' (i.e. familial relationship: *Ajayi v (1) Abu (2) Abu* [2017]). Moreover, there is no easy legal action that can be taken to extend employment protection for persons who lack access to representation or legal aid, in particular workers in multiple casual jobs struggling to make enough money to survive, or migrants unfamiliar with the English language or English legal system.[4]

The 2011 Supreme Court decision, *Autoclenz Limited v. Belcher and others* [2011] marked a turn in favour of workers being able to hold employers to account for their responsibility to pay the entitlements outlined in the ERA 1996. In *Autoclenz* an expressed 'self-employment' contract was deemed to be a sham in light of the material practice of work followed by both parties to the contract (workers and employer). That the Supreme Court recognised the existence and business practice of 'sham self-employment contracts' suggests that there may be scope for judicial interpretation to challenge the exclusion of workers' rights as a result of decentralised and privately regulated employment practices. The case recognised that the terms and conditions of an employment contract may be drafted in a way that intentionally prevents workers from accessing protections. In *Autoclenz*, the judges used 'a strong purposive approach to ensure that those individuals most in need of protection can exercise fundamental social rights effectively' (Bogg 2012, 345). Even though the terms of the contract explicitly stated that the workers were self-employed, the actual provision of services demonstrated that the contract was in reality one of employment. In this case, the concern was holiday pay. In other scenarios, a

4 In *CN v The United Kingdom*, a woman from Uganda was found to have been trafficked into forced labour in the UK. This case in 2012 prompted UK Parliament to act on the Modern Slavery Act 2015, to align UK law with ECHR Article 4 prohibiting slavery, forced labour and indentured servitude. However, the focus on trafficking offenses and extreme conditions of slavery fail to take into account the daily abuses and structural exploitation that disadvantages workers in lower-income sectors (see Columb 2020; Mantouvalou 2018).

right to prevent arbitrary termination, for example, could be affected by sham contracts (Bogg 2012, 328). In a similar case, *Pimlico Plumbers* [2018] UKSC 29, ostensibly 'self-employed' workers (plumbers) were likewise recognised by the UK Supreme Court as being workers in practice, for the purposes of recognition under the Employment Rights Act 1996, the Working Time Regulations 1998 and the Equality Act 2010.[5] The Supreme Court came to this conclusion based on the evidence of the personal service the claimant Mr Smith provided to the company and the amount of control the company (Pimlico Plumbers) exerted over their workers.

Autoclenz and *Pimlico Plumbers* join a growing canon of case law concerning work in the 'gig economy' (notably also *Uber BV & ors v Aslam & ors* [2017] EWCA Civ 2748), where employers intentionally have drafted contracts that, by using the label of self-employment in the written terms of the contract, suggest that the business holds no legal responsibility and accountability (i.e. offering employment rights, such as but not limited to holiday pay, sick leave, and working time regulations, such as paid breaks and time off) to those working under the company label or platform. The judicial approach favoured by the UK Supreme Court has been to look at the actual relationship taking place (*happening*) over the written terms of the contract. This has enabled judges to intervene on behalf of otherwise precarious, irregular, workers. Yet the power of judicial interpretation can only go so far. In cases where an individual is illegal or is in 'semi-compliance' with the law because of insecure immigration status, the doctrine of illegality was applied and followed in the aforementioned *Hounga v Allen* [2014] and *Patel v Mirza* [2016]. The lack of parliamentary implementation of the Law Commission Report on the doctrine of illegality (Law Commission 2010) suggests the UK Supreme Court would not favour labour protection over the individuals' illegal actions, in particular where the subject can be seen to have benefited from the illegality. As discussed in Chapter 2, in spite of a decision that recognised Miss Hounga's exploited situation, *Hounga* [2014] did not negate the continuing possibility of enforcing the doctrine of illegality in cases of immigration illegality. The case instead focused on her situation of forced labour according to Parliamentary priorities combating modern slavery, namely the 2014 Modern Slavery Bill that became the Modern Slavery Act 2015. Since *Hounga*, *Patel v Mirza* [2016] suggested more context be considered when applying the doctrine of illegality. Yet *obiter* Lord Suption maintained that the 'integrity of the legal system' needs to be honoured and a 'range of factors test' cannot be followed at the price of consistency.

5 UK Supreme Court Press Summary: 'Mr Smith (i) was a "worker" within the meaning of s.230(3) of the Employment Rights Act 1996; (ii) was a "worker" within the meaning of regulation 2(1) of the Working Time Regulations 1998, and (iii) had been in "employment" for the purposes of s.83(2) of the Equality Act 2010.' www.supremecourt.uk/cases/docs/uksc-2017-0053-press-summary.pdf

In spite of progress for workers in the 'gig economy' and self-employment, judicial decisions concerning domestic (private) workers in private homes have been less proactive. Often concerning non-citizen workers, the abuse and lack of enforcement of employment contracts and work arrangements is exemplified in the cases of *Hounga v Allen*, discussed in Chapter 2 with regard to the affirmation of the doctrine of illegality rendering the employment contract and subsequent protections void, and the case of *Taiwo v Olaigbe*, *Onu v Akwiwu* heard together on appeal by the UK Supreme Court in 2016, and *Mruke v Khan* [2018]. In the latter three cases, the UK Supreme Court acknowledged that the abuse suffered by these women held in exploitative working conditions needed recognition and compensation. However, the Equality Act 2010's anti-discrimination provisions under employment law and the Modern Slavery Act 2015 lacked the jurisdiction to recognize the womens' legal subjectivity and remedy/compensate for their ill treatment. Here, the law was not able to respond to the exploitation they experienced, but rather affirmed the limit of law's reach at the existing statutory provisions for anti-discrimination and the protected characteristics.

Taiwo and Onu

Ms Taiwo and Ms Onu were, similar to Miss Hounga, brought from Nigeria to work in domestic, private households. Both women were independently employed to take care of the household and children. However, their right to employment in the UK (including their immigration status) was tied to their employers as per immigration rules on foreign domestic workers – workers in the UK via domestic worker visas cannot work for any other employer aside from the employer who brought them into the UK (Gov.uk 2019a). In both Ms Taiwo and Ms Onu's employment tribunal hearings, it was held that 'the reason for the employers' mistreatment of their employees was their victims' vulnerability owing to their precarious immigration status' (UKSC 2016 para 2). The Supreme Court, therefore, had to decide whether the two women suffered discrimination because of, or on the basis of, immigration status – which, under the Equality Act 2010, would constitute discrimination because of or on the basis of nationality (Equality Act 2010 s 9 (1) b).

Unlike Miss Hounga, Ms Taiwo and Ms Onu's immigration statuses were irregular, but not definitively illegal. While Ms Taiwo's entry into the country was legal via a domestic worker visa, the Olaigbes fabricated a contract of employment and failed to show her the contract or pay her for her work. Ms Taiwo's passport was taken from her and she was routinely abused physically and mentally. Ms Onu was employed by Mr and Mrs Akwiwu and, similar to Ms Taiwo, was brought to the UK on a domestic worker visa, with information falsified by the employers. Once Ms Onu was in the Akwiwu's residence, they refused to pay her for her work. Ms Onu was refused rest periods and annual leave. She was regularly threatened that if she tried to run away, she would be arrested and imprisoned. In both Ms Taiwo and

Ms Onu's experiences, their passports were taken and withheld by their employers.

According to the Employment Appeal Tribunal, Ms Taiwo's situation was 'systematic and callous exploitation' (UKSC 2016 para 4). Nevertheless, her ill treatment by her employer was held not to be due to her being Nigerian (race/nationality), but because she was a precarious migrant: precarious because her status depended on her employers, Mr and Mrs Olaigbe. On the basis that immigration status is not a protected characteristic under the Equality Act 2010 (Chapter 1, s 4), the Supreme Court rejected the appeals from both Ms Taiwo and Ms Onu. It was held that the rejection was 'not because these appellants do not deserve a remedy for all the grievous harms they have suffered. It is because the present law, while able to redress some of those harms, cannot redress them all' (Hale para 34).

Mruke v Khan

Ms Mruke (*Mruke v Khan* [2018]) was a Tanzanian national employed as a domestic worker. She was paid the equivalent of 33 pence an hour for her labour. Ms Mruke filed a claim of unfair dismissal and racial discrimination. Her claim for discrimination was unsuccessful based on the comparator test (Equality Act 2010), where the employment tribunal held that a domestic worker of comparable standing (not necessarily a British worker, but also not specifically black Tanzanian) would have been treated the same way. Referring to *Taiwo* and *Onu*, it was held that nationality and race were not the characteristics that led to Ms Mruke's ill treatment. Perhaps the cause was socio-economic circumstance or immigration status, neither of which are protected characteristics.

Existing provisions under the Employment Rights Act 1996, National Minimum Wage Act 1998 and Equality Act 2010, the statutory foundations of UK employment law, and the common law failed to extend themselves to these women in precarious work arrangements. Yet the shifting subjectivity of these 'irregular' workers was used to shape them into vulnerable *legal* subjects, where in the case of Miss Hounga the law was able to grant some compensation. She was deemed worthy of protection because her vulnerability was akin to the modern slavery being discussed in Parliament, and because she did not profit or benefit from her illegality. Her situation was not seen to condone illegal entry, but rather could be seen to condone employers abusing vulnerable workers. In the cases of Ms Taiwo, Ms Onu and Ms Mruke, the exploitation and abuse they experienced was recognised as being 'callous and systematic', but not due to a characteristic recognised as grounds for discrimination under UK law (Equality Act 2010). The limit of the law would have to be stretched too far to recognise immigration status, or even socio-economic marginalisation, as a characteristic in need of protection. This is in spite of the obvious vulnerability their precarious immigration and economic status created. The law deemed their immigration status beyond discrimination law, whereas their employers' abusive conduct was de facto protected by the law, by its being excluded from the law.[6] However, Ms Mruke's claim for unfair (constructive) dismissal was partially allowed, albeit the employment appeal tribunal questioned if the lack of minimum wage payment was indeed the reason for Ms Mruke leaving her employment based on the fact that Ms Mruke was unaware of the amount she was legally entitled to: 'We have to establish what was the reason the claimant had for terminating her employment? The claimant did not tell us and we simply do not know why she left' (at para 51). It was held that having knowledge of one's rights is not necessary for someone to terminate a contract that is fundamentally being breached to claim unfair dismissal, based on constructive dismissal.

Notwithstanding the movement in these judicial decisions, the statutory framework of employment law remains wedded to the employer-employee relationship as per ERA 1996 s 230 definition of 'employee' and written contractual terms that can deny mutuality of obligation existing between employers and workers. The lack of movement within the statutes and interpretation of UK employment law towards what is happening in the shifts and changes of the labour market consolidates the power of the employer(s) over workers. Political-economic emphasis on business growth in a globalised, fluctuating market economy means businesses have little incentive to invest in long-term labour development, especially when short-term profit can be made with temporary (agency, casual contract) workers. Thus, the technologies of standard legal categories continuously override the existence of labourers who need protection against an exploitative labour market, formal and informal.

Meta/Meso/Micro: against or within the labour market

Tackling the inequality of bargaining power between employers and employees was traditionally the rallying cry for labour law and labour regulation (Arthurs 2011). However, twenty-first century employment laws consolidate inequality and exacerbate precarity, especially for workers who are not working in traditionally defined labour sectors (i.e. without a single-employer, continuous employment, often without trade union representation). De-industrialisation in the UK through the 1970s–1990s, together with an increasingly connected 'globalised' market economy, caused traditionally working-class employment to shift to the service industry, which is now led by multinational firms such as Amazon, and outsourcing firms as mentioned previously – Serco, Sodexo, G4S. While labour disputes that are heard by Tribunals, or at the Court of Appeal or Supreme Court, suggest that a shift may be taking place towards recognising employment status in so-called 'gig economy' sectors, fragmentation, casualisation as well as the internationalisation of labour markets further

6 This is a further example of what will be discussed in Chapter 4, the no-*thing* of law that enables law to be nothing but part of ecotechnical circulation.

fracture workers in sectors that lack cohesion or representation. This is especially true in private employment arrangements.

Labour practices have significantly shifted the position of individual workers to the state, such that without status (social, economic, legal) workers are left to work in situations that are highly precarious and temporary; work previously reserved for a temporary, seasonal migrant labour force (Standing 2011; Anderson 2010, 313). International labour regulations and campaigns raise attention to atypical work and the forced labour of persons trafficked into industrialised countries. Inadvertently, these discourses can displace the experience of precarity onto those bodies excluded from citizenship, as if these experiences were not accountable to, or the responsibility of, domestic (UK) labour and employment laws (see Columb 2020). Moreover, the recognition of sham employment contracts or the rights of workers in the gig economy (see *Autoclenz, Uber, Pimlico*), while necessary to respond to changes in the UK labour market, do not herald a new era of labour protection across labour sectors or labour practices. Labour sectors and practices continue to rely on off-shore exploitative extractive industries, forced labour and indentured servitude in countries with even less labour regulations (i.e. China, India). Attention to exploitation in the UK labour market risks being narrow and exclusionary, as if we can disconnect all of what has built a 'globalised' 'industrialised' labour market from the ongoing reality of interconnected production and the material demands of technological advancements. Additionally, the UK case law suggests that there is a hierarchy of recognition and representation, where victories in the judicial system celebrate gig-economy jobs staffed primarily by male workers (taxi drivers, plumbers, carpenters), leaving precarious work primarily carried out by women (care work, cleaning, 'domestic' servitude) to be either relegated to individual cases of modern day slavery, or discounted as 'familial' work beyond the ambit of the law.

Micro-level decision making in UK courts reflect the macro-level hegemony of modern law, legal categories and economics, which, as masculinised knowledges, displace the experiences of women, migrants, and those racially, socially, economically excluded from 'Good' citizenship. This ultimately technologises, through employment law, the excessive labour as external to legal protection and the workers external to legal subjectivity. As external – irregular, invisible – these workers form part of the circulation of capital. Ecotechnics, however, suggests that we must not relegate them to some ethereal *sense of being* beyond capital but instead expose their presence and the contribution their labour makes. This exposure furthers the deconstruction of capital and processes of neoliberalisation by demonstrating that irregular labour is not absent or external to the dominant, formal market economic system. Thus, including irregular work into the techne (law) facilitating the circulation capital will not remedy, or stop, precarity and exploitation. Rather, what is needed is a conceptual break, a shift away from techne, to pay attention to what possibilities exist beyond the technologising force of capital.

The ethical imperative to respond to situations of subjugation and vulnerability can be placated, or silenced, by idealised market ends. So long as the market model continues largely unquestioned, it forms part of the solution. This means that the solution is forever incapable of addressing fundamental inequalities caused by an inherently imbalanced relationship between those that work because they need income, and those that have capital. The market is but one form of labour organisation and one that is itself fluid and malleable. Nevertheless, it is assumed to be the only framework. The single frame for labour law through the market is pervasive:

> we are [not simply] wedded to and driven to see the content of labour law in [terms of consumer protection for the vulnerable in the labour market] . . . we are also driven to answer questions about the scope of labour law in a certain way.
>
> (Langille 2011, 107)

When market economic growth is the priority, inequalities produced and sustained by lax labour regulations are excusable. Persons who are made vulnerable through precarious contracts and labour situations are firstly individually blamed for their own situation. Secondly, they are seen as regrettable casualties of economic growth. Their precarious work is justified for the sake of economic progress, as well as the income and economic growth they are believed to generate for a global economic community. The contribution to a global community here includes the economic benefit seen to be gained from a migrant labour force contributing remittance payments back to their home countries/countries of origin (Dustman and Mestres 2010, 62).

Because immigration tackles a familiar or tangible site of differentiation in the territorial border, low-waged labour is easier conceptualised as an immigration problem with competition created between citizen workers and foreign workers. Yet as a consequence of neoliberalisation and market priorities, immigration law and policy are incapable of addressing the market forces that underlie 'migration'. Discourses fixated on territorial borders bolster the fantasy of citizenship and obscure the manifestation of a privileged global market economic system that, through processes of neoliberalisation (redeployment of the state), threaten to become technologies that totally obscure the originary potential of being singular plural. By obstructing the *happening* of being singular plural (indeed, always happening because ecotechne is the simultaneous circulation of both, not one overpowering the other) the force of capital appears to be total and totalising, appearing to negate all possibility of life or understanding our being away from the market and capital accumulation.

Labour law, differently

To address the casualties of economic growth and create space for the beings made invisible by a seemingly overwhelming techne, some labour law scholars have argued in favour of a more sector-specific, localised labour law regime (Atleson 2002; Mundlak 2002). For others, the pervasiveness of cross-border industries and transnational or multinational businesses suggest the need for a reformed, stronger, international labour rights regime (Altson 2004). At least up until December 2019, legal obligations derived from EU membership mandate that consideration be given to EU Directives that permit the movement of labourers within EU member states. Concurrently, international labour regulations can only provide directives for the nation-state, not enforcement. Especially when national laws are driven by priorities of economic growth, international regulations are avoided in practice. The UK's membership in the EU has already been rejected by Brexit, building on years of intense criticism of the influx of EU-citizen workers and EU labour regulations that were met with scepticism if not outright antagonism (Hepple 2013). Paradoxically, resistance to international and/or EU regulations is justified not to enable a local regulatory labour regime, but by the need for the UK to participate more 'freely' in the global economic system. Increased employment is achieved by increasing labour market flexibility and private sector growth, not by providing better quality jobs to local, or citizen, workers – in spite of nationalist, protectionist rhetoric. More security in employment, cohesion in labour sectors, or rights at work are seen as too risky and too costly.

Ruth Dukes contends that labour law's inability to respond to current conditions of work is more specifically one of methodology (Dukes 2018, 408). Dukes suggests that labour law and the labour market must be recognised for their difference. When the labour market is the focus of all labour law scholarship, she argues, the potential of collective bargaining as a force against competition and marketisation loses its power (2018, 410). Collective bargaining, in the twentieth century, served to ameliorate conflict of interest between workers within a shared class. Precarious work arrangements have threatened this potential for 'class', if not sector, solidarity. Scholars (Zahn 2019; Dukes 2019; Van Arsdale 2016; Standing 2011) have demonstrated how workers, citizen and non-citizen, are being pitted against each other, perhaps in an effort to increase competition and create a sense of threat in joblessness (see Dukes 2019, 4). Labour law scholarship, Dukes argues, has a responsibility not to see the market and neoliberalisation as inevitable but to encourage the 'possibility and extent of shared interests' between workers. Divisions and inter-worker conflict, in particular between citizen and 'migrant' workers, has been constructed as if protection and resources for employee protection were finite. Yet there is no material reason, aside from capital accumulation by the business owners and multinational firms, that employee protection should be limited or reserved for a privileged few. Encouraging shared interest among workers could be similar to encouraging attention to what is created and creating in the relationality between people at work, including their motivations, their needs and their actions. As such, labour law can, given the meta, meso and micro factors considered, encompass a concern for our constitution as a sociality and plurality.

Dukes (2014) suggests labour law can be integral to the development of law's constitution and constitutional law, because of labour law's ability to intervene in situations of employment, work and economic participation beyond nation-state boundaries. These qualities of labour law support Arthur's affirmation that labour law is 'neither non-law nor a mutant form of law, but law incarnate, an experiment in social ordering that reveals the true nature of the legal system in general' (Arthurs 2011, 16). However, law incarnate cannot be theoretically pursued without situating labour law's *technical* complicity in processes of neoliberalisation. As a demonstration of ecotechnical circulation, labour law is orchestrated through the nation-state while practices of labour actively transgress bounded nation-state jurisdictions because market economic demands are transnational. Therefore, on the one hand the idea of labour law as law incarnate brings us closer to understanding how law might be thought outside the frame of the nation-state. Meaning, how the prevailing standard of labour law may be brought into relief as unrepresentative and therefore not universal because of the undeniable, and incommensurable, *eco* that exceeds the technical frame. On the other hand, in a move similar to Dauvergne's proposal of 'unhinging' sovereignty from the nation-state which will be discussed in Chapter 5, isolating ('unhinging') labour law away from the nation-state is not sufficient to enable us to de-link from capital circulation and market forces. An ecotechnical diagnosis does not deliver difference or alternative. Instead, ecotechnics can open onto a possibility and potentiality of ecotechne away from a total focus on the technological capital circulation.

Recognising that labour law and its constituting narrative alone has been unable to address the way that market dynamics influence labour standards more powerfully than legislation and legal tools intending to protect disadvantaged workers and address injustice, Supiot suggests attention be given to the core fundamental principles of the ILO since the 1944 Declaration of Philadelphia (Supiot 2001). The Declaration of Philadelphia, 1944, established the International Labour Organisation (ILO) within the United Nations, and has as its founding principle that labour is not a commodity. The declaration recognises that labour is elemental to our sociality. In other words, labour is key to how we are together as singular plural beings. As emphasised earlier, labour is what 'we do', as action, to maintain our common life. Meanwhile, the limited frame of recognition renders labour to be represented solely as labour market economic participation. Consequently, labour as basic human action is interpreted as productivity in the economic market. Human beings have been identified with their productivity, such that labour, especially in low-waged, low-skilled sectors has become a commodity, superseding the persons involved. Labour treated as a commodity denies the significance of labour to social production and re-production, and the circulation of commodities as only one facet among many in our lives. Supiot's call to return to the principles of the ILO reflects an effort to bring attention to labourers as persons whose rights and dignity, according to the UN, need to be protected and honoured. The

ILO aims to support countries to achieve full employment and affirms that 'all human beings, irrespective of race, creed or sex, have the right to pursue both their material well-being and their spiritual development in conditions of freedom and dignity, of economic security and equal opportunity' (International Labour Organisation (ILO) Declaration of Philadelphia, 1944, II (a)). Supiot, moreover, describes labour law as 'social hermeneutics' (in Christodoulidis et al. 2010, 217). Labour law, when considered an issue of basic foundational social relations, is constitutional. Labour law's constitutional significance dispels a distinction between the political public sphere and the workplace, often assumed to be private. A constitutional approach to labour law identifies vulnerability and powerlessness as something that affects all citizens and workers. This widens labour law's scope beyond the workplace and employer-employee relations to have a social function (Supiot in Christodoulidis et al. 2010, 217).

There are strengths to Supiot's attention to the sociality of labour. Yet Supiot does not recognise the EU's inability to create and enforce substantive rights, particularly for those who are without *practically* recognized citizenship privileges. This limits the applicability of Supiot's new norms (Ewing in Christodoulidis et al. 2010, 220). Moreover, the lack of constitutional doctrine in the EU has been pointed out as rendering discussions of constitutional duties futile (Rödl in Christodoulidis et al. 2010, 244). Without a fundamental critique of the demands within a neoliberal market economy, together with a more honest appraisal of the EU's imagined community constructed according to exclusionary racial and ethnic lines, Supiot's contention that international financial institutions and worker organisations would be able to discuss social justice and local experiences ignores the systemically embedded function of precarious, irregular labour in the neoliberal 'globalised' economic market. The international legal regime and the persistent difficulty to discuss labour law's complicity in the labour market – and what de-coupling labour law from the labour market would entail – suggests the imperative to think of new and more fundamentally transformative approaches to precarity and vulnerability in labour. A broad social role for labour law, moreover, can detract attention away from the labour market and the economic reasons that irregular labour situations and precarious work, including precarious migrant labour, are maintained. If labour law as constitutional remains within a legal framework that relies on the recognition of rights to be based in a nation-state system then the systemic, technical ways that economic policies condition a deregulated labour market beyond the nation-state can be ignored.

Thinking of labour law alternatively is only possible insofar as we fundamentally re-evaluate what is considered to be labour, work and labour market participation. Labour law has developed with a purpose of enabling workers to seek equality and/or justice in the workplace and arguably the labour market. The structure of the workplace and labour market are currently predisposed to prevent access to labour protections for workers in the labour market, particularly for those in low-skilled, low-waged work. Regulations are seen to inhibit economic growth and financial progress. However, labour law and indeed labour and law independent of each other are not isolated practices or independent sets of rules. Law is no discrete, material *thing*. Labour law has within its ambit a task to rethink, and arguably to redefine, how the limits of labour and work are constituted and reproduced, primarily and fundamentally before the market. While Supiot (2018) identifies that currently the 'rule of law is replaced by law "shopping", subordinating the law to economic calculations rather than vice versa,' the task for labour law – and law more generally – is to reclaim its role as tracing the limit of sociality, as will be discussed in Chapter 4. Indeed, labour law's transformative potential persists because of labour's productive and reproductive capacity that reaches across multiple borders, including but not limited to the dominant market economic system (Blackett 2011, 436). In spite of its dominant employment law form, UK labour law is informed by practices of employment, cultures of work and economic markets, as well as notions of justice, fairness/equality (Equality Act 2010) and rights (Employment Rights Act 1996). Labour law also concerns the link between production and reproduction, the social as overarching the economic. The paradox of law is played out in the demand for flexibility, productivity and business efficacy, and fairness, regulation and justice for workers as well as the sphere of ex-commodification, where work and labour are reproducing systems of market control and regulation as well as its excess: life beyond – or in spite of – the market. The ecotechnics of labour migration, moreover, emphasise the movement conceptually beyond nation-state borders and legal regimes that sustain capital circulation and sense: the sociality of being singular plural. A critique that questions what is meant by sociality may be the way to address why persons in irregular situations continue to be present in spite of legislative protections.

Rethinking labour law is not a project to create new forms of labour or new forms of being. Labour law is rethought in order to give attention to what is already happening within the ecotechnics of labour, which processes of neoliberalisation and the market capitalise on while legal structures and vocabularies struggle to keep up. In assessments of the financial crisis of 2008, employees were seen to have too much protection versus workers. This dual segmentation of the labour market created employment as if it were the problem, rather than turn attention to the financial system (Dukes 2018, 8). Migration discourse, and the precarious standards of work that an emphasis on migration obscure, acts as a repository of the labourers that are excluded from employment law categories and denied participation as 'Good Citizens' in the community of value (Anderson 2013). These workers are nevertheless included; in fact, they are a regular and invaluable (cheap) presence in the labour market and economic production. The question linking together the preceding observations is what is the future of labour law with regard to protecting all workers against exploitation and precarity, regardless of citizenship and immigration status? Discrimination laws are insufficient to deal with this question (*Taiwo, Onu, Mruke*), as are often outdated and epistemologically limited philosophical debates of justice, rights and human freedom. People at work are regularly, routinely, exploited. People 'get by', they survive and continue through their determination to work for a living notwithstanding mundane exploitation.

A shift within the field and approach of labour law, as suggested earlier, cannot happen without dismantling the regulatory power of the labour market and categories of employment law, based in contract law principles via the employment contract. This shift is methodological, epistemological and ontological. Proposals to expand the definition of labour to recognise persons working in precarious situations allow the constructed primacy of the labour market system to continue unquestioned. However, a shift from the traditional, standard frame of labour to a different orientation does not only mean engaging in deconstructive questioning. The very practice itself is 'anxiety-inducing' (Freedland, quoted in Langille 2011, 107–108), not least because this fundamental (ontological) questioning touches upon our very relationship to law and to our way of understanding sociality and social relations. It uproots traditional labour law, which was intended to mediate inequality for workers in disadvantaged bargaining positions. A new approach would deeply question labour law's complicity in maintaining the disadvantaged positions and structural exploitation of workers in precarious arrangements against an archaic industrial model. This is unsettling in its conceptual de-linking from already threatened and dwindling statutory protections. Fudge suggests that nothing less than a new imaginary is required to address the regulatory dilemmas, inclusions and exclusions, which result from the limited scope of labour law (Fudge 2011, 136). A new imaginary involves addressing the embedded contingencies that inform labour law and employment, while keeping within the frame of analysis the real situations of workers and employment practices. It involves fathoming the ecotechnics of labour circulating beyond established onto-epistemological norms that are the functioning space of, seemingly totalising, capital.

Labour law functions as law incarnate via its diverse applications and significance. Labour law acts in response to the labour market, which responds to a neoliberal market economic system. The labour market – demand and supply – differentiates subjectivity, where some people are maintained in precarious labour situations when their work is not valued equal to an ideal citizen labourer in a full, standard employment relationship. The market, however, is not an entity itself. The nation-state and citizenship are subsumed to the ideology of a market economic system that works in tandem with the architecture of the nation-state that practices differentiated citizenships to the benefit of (short-term) economic growth. Nevertheless, labour law is positioned to engage critically with the privilege of economic productivity and growth. While some suggest labour law should be merged with broader social welfare concerns, justice and social rights (social security law), labour law is also specifically concerned with employment, work, productivity and economic participation. In other words, value. This specificity enables labour law to speak to the privilege and totalising presence of the market as it has conditioned work and labour to be limited to labour and employment that is recognised within the labour market. The market is, like citizenship, a fantasy, and includes-by-excluding the value and ecotechnical contribution of social production and reproduction. Labour is, under this lens, a 'mass but not collective activity', where 'the lower you are on the economic scale, the less formal your relation to the economy, the more alone you are in the project of maintaining and reproducing life' (Berlant 2011, 167). A right to work and earn wages is espoused as a fundamental element of social inclusion and citizenship. For example, the previous chapter highlighted how UK immigration law privileges 'high skilled' workers through the point-based system (PBS). Consequently, unauthorised work, non-market labour, unpaid work, or undeclared work, including precarious or undefined work, is a basis for exclusion, marginalisation and sub-citizenship. Yet this type of worker continues to be in demand, and what is excluded ultimately participates inside, to loop back and bolster the very structures that are ostensibly exclusive.

Supiot, in 2018, rightly stated that: 'labour laws are designed for a world that no longer exists'. The movement of people providing labour (labourers) and the shifting demands, or fluidity, of the labour market challenge regulatory efforts and alternatives emerging from the same traditional labour law narrative. Irregular labourers are an elusive category beyond existing methodologies of labour law – both in terms of employment law and traditional theories of labour which were largely addressed to industrial production. The demands of market productivity, dwindling national (domestic) labour protections, and global market economic growth enact differential legal subjectivity inside the ecotechnical circulation of capital and social being. Labour, its form and its reflexive critique, circulates in a world that is ecotechnical, but scholars struggle with understanding the techne of law away from the market and capital. Yes, the circulation of labour is both capital circulation and sense that exceeds it, but how can labour law understand work as *eco*?

By identifying the potential for labour law to be understood beyond the standard or conventional employment relationship model, labour law scholars are raising issue with the fallacy of the market. The fallacy of the market creates precarious labour as the demand and supply of workers and 'global' migration. So, the question is how do we avoid merely reproducing the techne by deferring this demand onto more and more invisible bodies? At the root of this question is the ostensible naturalness and necessity of the market and capital. Yes, the world is ecotechnical whereby the technologisation of sense into forms of intelligibility is inevitable, but is techne necessarily capital? Is every seizure of sense necessarily concretised as capital circulation? Is the action of labour always, naturally, contributing to the accumulation of capital? We experience *eco* (eco-nomy, eco-logy, eco-techne) as a sense of being, being singular plural, distinct from the experience of order/law (*nomos*), form/ground (*logos*) and craft/technology (*technē*). Therefore, can we not experience the technologisation as something other than the seizure of life as capital calculation and accumulation? Arguably we already do, by our very being singular plural and the experiences and relationality that emerge from this. Moreover, work that is by its very action excessive of categories and commodification (care, reproductive labour, emotion) is carried out not solely at the behest and for the purpose of capital. Yet how to bring this experience into light? Can technologies of law shift to value non-marketised, non-commodified labour?

The example of care work entering the formal labour market through its commodification demonstrates that the incorporation of labour into the market is not a clear solution to protect precarious, vulnerable workers. If labour were to be addressed only through the market for its role in market efficiency, then labour law could conceivably be extended to protect 'socially valuable work,' as Supiot argues (Supiot, quoted in Fudge 2011, 126). However, this brings us back to the concern that labour law is meant to (a) bring non-marketised work into the market economic or (b) expand labour law beyond the market to social economic production. Both proposals have consequences beyond individual rights for workers. The proliferation of legislation to protect care workers or precarious work, for example, may reinforce the confluence of labour law with the labour market, aiming, unsuccessfully, to push atypical care-based work into a predetermined frame which then recognises employment for some, but not others (see prior *Hounga, Taiwo, Onu, Mruke*). Moreover, extending protection to care workers does not address the underlying determination of what makes one's labour intelligible and valued in the dominant market economy over the sociality valued as the sharing out of persons in the singular plural. The notion that non-market labour is less worthy due to its lack of direct market productivity must be subverted and challenged if the situation for workers is to change. Recognising these contingencies is not a matter of strain and intellectual labour. Contingencies that have been an 'absent present' (Marks 2009, 14), such as the dependence of the market on labour marginalised into legal grey areas and consequently the tension between remedying precarious statuses and maintaining access to cheap labour, can be questioned and resisted (Marks 2009, 12). The apparent necessity of prioritising the market economic system is in tension with social realities and basic human needs; this tension is ecotechnics. Thinking of labour and migration reveals activity, as well as processes of neoliberalisation, that are part of the paradox of law, as well as the ecosociality *happening* in forms and sectors of work externalised by the normative frame.

It is difficult to escape the circulation of the market and neoliberalisation. The sociality of singular plural beings together is not an alternative to neoliberalisation, rather ecotechnics reveals the co-appearance and formation of the limited economy. Processes of neoliberalisation *happen* through the movement and groundlessness of our bodily ontology, only as the being singular plural amassing of bodies happens removed from (in spite of) predetermined legal categories. This movement complicates efforts to pinpoint law's precise limit or purpose in migration and labour because the processes of neoliberalisation as ecotechnical constantly overreach legal limits, notably when immigration laws and labour laws are transgressed. If law is understood as the tracing of a sociality, then the political and juridical systems of governance that mandate legislation and inscription of law are removed from law itself; the systems of governance do not define law, they instrumentalise a fantasy creation of it. Law as we know it exists alongside other creations, other possibilities (explored in more detail in Chapter 5).

Conclusion: ecotechnical labour and law

The primary concern of employment regulation in the UK can currently be identified as ensuring growth and flexibility for business development (Davis and Freedland 2007, 234). Conveniently, the UK's economic struggles are blamed on immigrants. Since the economic crisis of 2008, rising unemployment, joblessness and poverty caused by austerity measures in Britain shape precarity and insecurity (Hattenston and Lavelle 2019; Mason et al. 2019). Concerns of economic downturn and rising unemployment, when discussed in media and public policy debates, rarely correlate with analyses of the globalised movement of cheap labour or the dominance of a particular globalised economic market (Campbell 2019; Hall et al. 2013, 8). An eco-technical analysis at meta, meso and micro levels draw attention to the way that processes of sociality continue within the functions of labour, law and the market, merging all three 'levels' together. Giving attention to those who are made irregular through the practice of employment and immigration law illuminates the limits of employment law and employment rights that underlie law's universal claim. Moreover, law's (false) universal claim assumes that law can encompass everybody, and that a failure for law to have this scope is 'random, accidental and arbitrary' (Marks 2009, 20).

That political, economic and judicial decisions must serve and support the market, and 'keep the market happy', is seen as a necessity for government. The priority of the market suggests that our society, the social, is coterminous with the market economic system, which is manifest in the nation-state. The law, as practiced and developed under the nation-state as a regulatory instrument that provides order and enforces social norms, has no alternative reference under the limited contingencies of the global economic system but to be subservient to the market. The market economy is dependent on a market society where all the elements of industry – labour, land and money – are required to be part of the market. These elements become recognisable (*are made to make sense*) when subordinated to the market and understood within a marketised ideology (Polanyi 2001, 74). In other words, the economic market and processes of neoliberalisation are seen as the only possibility, and law is feebly used to plaster over the market's voracious appetite for precarious, cheap labour.

The ecotechnics of labour migration, productivity and the *making sense* of our being in common in economies here and now, in spite of immigration controls and other regulatory systems that seek to differentiate and separate, illuminates the possibility for labour law to look beyond the division of private versus public, or non-market versus market labour. Labour law has the potential to be a site for rethinking value not based on a new or alternative ideology (of justice, rights or citizenship), but through thinking of what we do, how we labour, in our very being in-common. The function of the economic market system is built on the dysfunction of the labour force and weak labour laws. The process of de-familiarising the market economic system as well as the notion of citizenship that is intricately bound up in it is necessary to expose the prevalence of instability and precariousness, as embedded in the nation-state, citizenship and the labour market. Far from the contrary public perception, this precariousness and instability is not the fault of individuals (i.e. migrants) or immigration controls. Precariousness is not only a regular state of the neoliberal market system, as will be discussed further in Chapters 4 and 5, it is the material experience of being in the singular plural. The universality of the individual 'I' as the autonomous liberal subject (Good, 'regular' Citizen) is a myth. The material experience in the sociality does not constitute individuals in independent spaces as created by liberal thought. The material experience, being singular plural, when we try and conceive of it away from categories of recognition and belonging, is messy. It lacks a familiar foundation, and thus even the thought of such experience and being is unstable and precarious. This disruption is, however, unavoidable because the stability and security that is presented by modern liberal philosophy as the ideal is itself incommensurable with the ecotechnics of being.

Ecotechnics is unstable. Being is constantly transgressing the categories that attempt to frame what, or who, is the Good Citizen, and the 'full' legal subject. Moreover, the categories (and their onto-epistemological foundation) are incommensurable due to the historical specificity of our understanding of being. Modern philosophy has been built on a colonial, racialised and gendered notion of the 'I': the autonomous, individual legal subject and citizen. The 'I' is arguably central to modernity, as Hegel affirmed, since Descartes, whose work set the philosophical question as one concerned with the individual mind and body (Dussel 2003, 15). However, Dussel highlights foundations of the individual 'I' as rooted in a distinction from the colonial non-European other (Dussel 2003, with reference to the writing of Ginés de Sepúlveda (+1793), 22–23, 27). According to Dussel, 'the entirety of Modernity, during five centuries, would remain in this state of "lethargy" of *ethical political unconsciousness*, as if "asleep", without "feeling" toward the pain of the peripheral world of the South' (Dussel 2003, 27). From this lethargy political and legal subjectivity has evolved to reinforce the primacy of the Good Citizen-subject. The 'I', or ego-logics, are found in the current construct of the Good Citizen, which leaves the 'others' (gendered, racialised, ableised) as Failed or sub-citizens. The citizen-subject reaffirms the (idealised) autonomous being, as one that is thought to relate to, and represent, a universal political and legal system.[7] Ideologically, this interweaves our embodiment with the market. 'I', as the basis of modern thought, is contingent on excluding from modernity's fold what is outside recognition within 'I': those 'others' who are deemed not-quite-there, backwards, underdeveloped, primitive, collective/communal and *irregular*. However, the embodiment of labour is not simply, or only, a market force, as caring vividly illustrates. Our participation and circulation within marketised capital is not totalising – within this circulation we have not abandoned autonomy, because autonomy is nothing but the experience of alterity in the being singular plural. The following chapter expands on this as related to our modern conceptualisation of law. Social forces influence law, but the social is itself combustible. Law has to be malleable, but it can never be anything but a techne.

As ecotechnics, labour migration discourses highlight what is happening on the ground, ecologically, within practices of employment and work (market economic participation), where labour and employment has for many people become an experience of precarity, instability, vulnerability and uncertainty. This includes the experience of participating in the economy of sociality excluded from market economic value. The condition of precarity in the labour market is assumed to be unavoidable and attributable to the individual (and the individuals' family in the case of care needs), not the market economic system, which claims 'globality' but in experience is specific and limited. UK employment law is based on a model of a single-employer-employment contract, one that is not reflected in the labour market of our 'globalised' market economy, nor the labour (as *eco, sense*) happening beyond the market. The dynamics of twenty-first century markets and shifting labour demands complicate assumptions of citizenship and economic participation. This challenge is rooted deeper than considering complications caused by transnational, 'global' markets and underlying onto-epistemological frames of thought. Thinking of employment, migration and law as ecotechnical can release our thinking from the confines of citizenship and, in labour law, the fixation on the contractual employment relationship. Yet this paradigmatic shift can only happen if value, economy, sociality, ecology and law are rethought. The next chapter considers law, in particular the techne of law, in more detail.

References

Albin, Einat. 2018, in *Philosophical Foundations of Labour Law*. Virginia Mantouvalou, Hugh Collins and Gillian Lester (eds). Oxford: Oxford University Press.

Altson, Philip. 2004, 'Core labour standards' and the transformation of the international labour rights regime' *European Journal of International Law* vol. 15, no. 3, pp. 457–521.

7 In Hegel and in Kant, but who build on Socrates and Plato, the citizen is held up as the role for men in community, society and world (Derrida and Dufourmantelle 2000).

Anderson, Bridget. 2013, *Us & Them: The Dangerous Politics of Immigration Control.* Cambridge University Press.

Anderson, Bridget. 2010, 'Migration, immigration controls and the fashioning of precarious workers' *Work, Employment and Society* vol. 24, no. 2, pp. 300–317. Doi:10.1177/0950017010362141

Anderson, Bridget and Isabel Shutes. 2014, *Migration and Care Labour: Theory, Policy and Politics.* London: Palgrave Macmillan.

Arendt, Hannah. 1958, *The Human Condition.* Chicago: University of Chicago.

Arthurs, Harry. 2011, 'Labour law after labour' in *The Idea of Labour Law.* Guy Davidov and Brian Langille (eds), pp. 13–30. Oxford: Oxford University Press.

Atleson, James. 2002, 'The voyage of the neptune jade: Transnational labour solidarity and the obstacles of domestic law' in *Labour Law in an Era of Globalisation: Transformative Practices and Possibilities.* Michael Fischl, Karl Klare and Joanne Conaghan (eds), pp. 471–487. Oxford: Oxford University Press.

Barnard, Helen. 2018, 'UK poverty 2018' Joseph Rowantree Foundation www.jrf.org.uk/report/uk-poverty-2018

Berlant, Lauren. 2011, *Cruel Optimism.* Durham, London: Duke University Press.

Blackett, Adelle. 2011, 'Emancipation in the idea of labour law' in *The Idea of Labour Law.* Guy Davidov and Brian Langille (eds), pp. 420–436. Oxford: Oxford University Press.

Blackham, Alysia, Miriam Kullmann and Ania Zbyszewska (eds). 2019, *Theorising Labour Law in a Changing World.* Oxford: Hart Publishing.

Bogg, Alan. 2012, 'Sham self-employment in the supreme court' *Industrial Law Journal* vol. 41, no. 3, pp. 328–345.

Bogg, Alan, Cathryn Costello, ACL Davies and Jeremias Prassl (eds). 2015, *The Autonomy of Labour Law.* Oxford: Hart Publishing.

Bogg, Alan and Tonia Novitz. 2014, *Voices at Work.* Oxford: Oxford University Press.

Braidotti, Rosi. 1995, 'Foreward' in *In Spite of Plato: A Feminist Rewriting of Ancient Philosophy.* Adriana Caverero (ed). New York: Polity Press.

Briskman, Linda, Deborah Zion and Bebe Loff. 2012, 'Care or collusion in asylum seeker detention' *Ethics and Social Welfare* vol. 6, no. 1, pp. 37–55. Doi:10.1080/17496535.2011.575383

Busby, Nicola. 2011, *A Right to Care? Unpaid Care Work in European Employment Law.* Oxford: Oxford University Press.

Busby, Nicola, Douglas Brodie and Rebecca Zahn (eds). 2016, *The Future Regulation of Work: New Concepts, New Paradigms.* London: Palgrave Socio-Legal Studies.

Butler, Patrick et al. 2019, 'Not just schools: Five public service areas struggling with cuts' *The Guardian* 8 March 2019, viewed 28 September 2019 www.theguardian.com

Cameron, David. 2013, 'Immigration speech' Government UK 25 March 2013, viewed 28 September 2019 www.gov.uk/government/speeches/david-camerons-immigration-speech

Campbell, Denis. 2019, 'Both labour and tory migration plans "would worsen NHS staffing"' *The Guardian* 4 December 2019, viewed 5 December 2019 www.theguardian.com/

Christodoulidis, Emilios et al. 2010, 'Dialogue & debate: Labour, constitution and a sense of measure: A debate with Alain Supiot' *Social Legal Studies* vol. 19, no. 2, pp. 217–252.

Collins, Hugh, Gillian Lester and Virginia Mantouvalou (eds). 2018, *Philosophical Foundations of Labour Law.* Oxford: Oxford University Press.

Columb, Seán. 2020, *Trading Life: Organ Trafficking, Illicit Networks and Exploitation.* Stanford: Stanford University Press.

Conaghan, Joanne. 2018, 'Gender and the law' in *Philosophical Foundations of Labour Law*. Hugh Collins, Gillian Lester and Virginia Mantouvalou (eds), pp. 271–286. Oxford: Oxford University Press.

Curry, Mann et al. 2001, 'Abuse of women with disabilities: An ecological model and review' *Violence Against Women* vol. 7, no. 1, pp. 60–79.

Davidov, Guy and Brian Langille (eds). 2011, *The Idea of Labour Law*. Oxford: Oxford University Press.

Davis, Paul and Mark Freedland. 2007, *Towards a Flexible Labour Market*. Oxford: Oxford University Press.

Department for Work and Pensions. 2019, *Pension Credit Toolkit* Government UK, viewed 28 September 2019 www.gov.uk/government/publications/pension-credit-toolkit/pension-credit-toolkit-advice-and-guidance-for-stakeholders

Derrida, Jacques and Anne Dufourmantelle. 2000, *Of Hospitality*. Stanford: Stanford University Press.

Diaz, Natalia Quiroga. 2015, 'Decolonial feminist economics: A necessary view for strengthening social and popular economy' *View Point Magazine* 31 October 2015, viewed 28 September 2019 www.viewpointmag.com

Dragstedt, Albert. 1976, *Value: Studies by Karl Marx*. London: New Park Publications, pp. 7–40.

Dukes, Ruth. 2019, 'Critical labour law: Then and now' in *Research Handbook on Critical Legal Theory*. Emilios Christodoulidis, Ruth Dukes and Marco Goldoni (eds). Cheltenham: Edward Elgar.

Dukes, Ruth. 2018, 'Introduction to special issue, labour laws and labour markets: New methodologies' *Social & Legal Studies* vol. 27, no. 4, pp. 407–413.

Dukes, Ruth. 2014, *The Labour Constitution*. Oxford: Oxford University Press.

Dussel, Enrique. 2003, *Beyond Philosophy: Ethics, History, Marxism, and Theology of Liberation*. Maryland: Rowman and Littlefield Publishers.

Dustman, Christian and Joseph Mestres. 2010, 'Remittances and temporary migration' *Journal of Development Economics* vol. 92, no. 1, pp. 62–70.

The Economist. 2018, 'Britain's unemployment is ultra low, but its wages are ultra measly' 6 September 2018, viewed 28 September 2019 www.economist.com/

Federici, Silvia. 2008, 'Precarious labor: A feminist viewpoint' viewed 28 September 2019 http://inthemiddleofthewhirlwind.wordpress.com/precarious-labor-a-feminist-viewpoint/

Freedland, Mark and Nicola Kountouris. 2011, 'Legal characterisation of personal work relations' in *The Idea of Labour Law*. Guy Davidov and Brian Langille (eds), pp. 190–207. Oxford: Oxford University Press.

Fudge, Judy. 2018, 'Modern slavery, unfree labour and the labour market: The social dynamics of legal characterization' *Social & Legal Studies* vol. 27, no. 4, pp. 414–434. Doi:10.1177/0964663917746736

Fudge, Judy. 2014, 'Feminist reflections on the scope of labour law: Domestic work, social reproduction, and jurisdiction' *Feminist Legal Studies* vol. 21, no. 3, pp. 1–23.

Fudge, Judy. 2012, 'Making claims for migrant workers: Human rights and citizenship' unpublished conference paper, Migrants at Work Oxford University, 22 June 2012.

Fudge, Judy. 2011, 'Labour as a fictive commodity' in *The Idea of Labour*. Guy Davidov and Brian Langille (eds), pp. 120–136. Oxford: Oxford University Press.

Fudge, Judy and Kendra Strauss (eds). 2013, *Temporary Work, Agencies and Unfree Labour: Insecurity in the New World of Work*. New York, London: Routledge.

Gov.UK. 2019a, 'Domestic workers in a private household visa' viewed 15 December 2019 www.gov.uk/domestic-workers-in-a-private-household-visa

Gov.UK. 2019b, 'UK sees record employment as unemployment falls below 4 per cent' viewed 15 December 2019 https://www.gov.uk/government/news/uk-sees-record-employment-as-unemployment-falls-below-4-per-cent

Gov.UK. 2019c, 'Universal credit' viewed 28 September 2019 www.gov.uk/universal-credit

Gray, Mary and Siddharth Suri. 2019, *Ghost Work*. Boston: Houghton Mifflin Harcourt.

Hall, Stuart, Doreen Massey and Michael Rustin (eds). 2013, 'After neoliberalism: Analysing the present' in *After Neoliberalism? The Kilburn Manifesto Soundings*. Chadwell Heath: Lawrence & Wishart.

Hattenstone, Simon and Daniel Lavelle. 2019, 'Britain has a horrific homelessness crisis' *The Guardian* 19 November 2019, viewed 5 December 2019 www.theguardian.com/

Hayes, Lydia. 2017, *Stories of Care: A Labour of Law*. London: Palgrave Macmillan.

Hepple, Bob. 2013, 'Back to the future: Employment law under the coalition government' *Industrial Law Journal* vol. 42, pp. 203–223.

Hozić, Aida A. and Jacqui True. 2016, *Scandalous Economics: Gender and the Politics of Financial Crises*. Oxford: Oxford University Press.

International Labour Organisation (ILO). 1944, *Declaration of Philadelphia*, II (a). Geneva: International Labour Organisation.

Jongkil, Jeong et al. 2012, 'Exploring the current status of call centres offshoring research: A research agenda and future directions' 23rd Australasian Conference on Information Systems, 3–5 December 2012, Geelong.

Joseph Rowantree Foundation. 2019, 'In-work poverty' viewed 15 December 2019 www.jrf.org.uk/work/in-work-poverty

Kotiswaran, Prabha. 2011, *Dangerous Sex, Invisible Labour: Sex Work and the Law in India*. Princeton, NJ: Princeton University Press.

Langille, Brian. 2011, 'Labour law's theory of justice' in *The Idea of Labour Law*. Guy Davidov and Brian Langille (eds), pp. 101–119. Oxford: Oxford University Press.

Law Commission, 'The illegality defence' March 2010, viewed 28 September 2019 www.lawcom.gov.uk/project/illegality/

Lutz, Helma. 2017, 'Care as a fictitious commodity: Reflections on the intersections of migration, gender and care regimes' *Migration Studies* vol. 5, no. 3, pp. 356–368.

Malay, Michael. 2014, 'Buy a discount maid at Singapore's malls' *Al Jezeera* 27 June 2014, viewed 28 September 2019 www.aljazeera.com/

Mantouvalou, Virgina. 2018, 'Legal construction of structures of exploitation' in *Philosophical Foundations of Labour Law*. Hugh Collins, Gillian Lester and Virginia Mantouvalou (eds). Oxford: Oxford University Press.

Mantouvalou, Virginia (ed). 2015, *The Right to Work: Legal and Philosophical Perspectives*. Oxford: Hart Publishing.

Mantouvalou, Virginia. 2006, 'Servitude and forced labour in the 21st century: The human rights of domestic workers' *Industrial Law Journal* vol. 35, no. 4, pp. 395–414.

Marks, Susan. 2009, 'False contingency' *Current Legal Problems* vol 62, no. 1, pp. 1–21.

Marx, Karl. 1844, *Estranged Labour* www.marxists.org/archive/marx/works/1844/manuscripts/labour.htm

Mason, Rowena et al. 2019, 'Fears of child poverty may rise to record 60-year high under Tories' *The Guardian* 26 November 2019, viewed 5 December 2019 www.guardian.co.uk

Medland, Linda et al. 2019, 'The "future" of work? A call for the recognition of continuities in the challenges for conceptualising work and its regulation' in *Perspectives on Work Faculty Research Group*, Law Research Paper Series #001. Bristol: School of Law, University of Bristol.

Morin, Marie-Eve. 2012, *Jean-Luc Nancy*. New York: State University of New York Press.

Mundlak, Guy. 2002, 'The limits of labour law in a fungible community' in *Labour Law in an Era of Globalization*. Joanne Conaghan, Michael Fischl and Karl Klare (eds). Oxford: Oxford University Press.

Nancy, Jean-Luc. 2008, *Corpus*. Trans., Richard A. Rand. New York: Fordham University Press.

Nancy, Jean-Luc. 1997, *Sense of the World*. Trans., Jeffrey S. Librett (1st edition 1993). Minnesota: University of Minnesota Press.

Novitz, Tonia. 2017, 'Collective bargaining, equality and migration: The journey to and from Brexit' *Industrial Law Journal* vol. 46, no. 1, pp. 109–133. https://doi.org/10.1093/indlaw/dww042

O'Brien, Hettie. 2019, 'The ghosts in the machines' *The New Statesman* 7–13 June 2019.

Office of the High Commissioner on Human Rights (OHCHR). 2015, *Behind Closed Doors: Protecting and Promoting the Human Rights of Migrant Domestic Workers in an Irregular Situation*. New York, Geneva: OHCHR, viewed 28 September 2019 www.ohchr.org/

Oksala, Johanna. 2018, 'Feminism, capitalism, and ecology' *Hypatia* vol. 33, pp. 216–234. Doi:10.1111/hypa.12395

Parliament, UK. 2015, 'Gender pay gap' UK Parliament https://publications.parliament.uk/pa/cm201516/cmselect/cmwomeq/584/58410.htm

Peck, Jaime, Nik Theodore and Neil Brennar. 2012, 'Neoliberalism resurgent? Market rule after the great recession' *The South Atlantic Quarterly* vol. 111, no. 2, pp. 265–288.

Picchio, Antonella. 1992, *Social Reproduction: The Political Economy of the Labour Market*. Cambridge: Cambridge University Press.

Polanyi, Karl. 2001, *The Great Transformation: The Political and Economic Origins of Our Time* (2nd edition). Boston: Beacon Press.

Rittich, Kerry. 2003, 'Core labour rights and labour market flexibility: Two paths entwined?' in *Labor Law Beyond Borders: ADR and the Internationalization of Labor Dispute Resolution International Bureau of the Permanent Court of Arbitration*, pp. 157–208. The Netherlands: Kluwer Law International.

Routh, Supriya. 2018, 'Embedding work in nature: Anthropocene and law' *Comparative Labour Law and Policy Journal* vol. 40, no. 1, pp. 29–60.

Routh, Supriya. 2016, 'Informal workers' aggregation and law' *Theoretical Inquiries in Law* vol. 17, no. 1, pp. 283–320.

Salazar Perreñas, Rhacel. 2014, 'Migrant domestic workers as "One of the family"' in *Migration and Care Labour*. Bridget Anderson and Isabel Shutes (eds), pp. 49–64. London: Palgrave Macmillan.

Salleh, Ariel. 2018, 'Deeper than deep ecology: The eco-feminist connection' in *Feminist Ecologies: Changing Environments in the Anthropocene*. Lara Stevens et al. (eds), pp. 25–33. London: Palgrave Macmillan.

Shildrick, Margrit. 1997, *Leaky Bodies and Boundaries: Feminism, Postmodernism and (bio)ethics*. New York: Routledge, Psychology Press.

Slater, Tom. 2016, 'Revanchism, stigma and the production of ignorance: Housing struggles in austerity Britain' *Research in Political Economy* vol. 31, pp. 23–48.

Standing, Guy. 2011, *The Precariat: The New Dangerous Class*. London: Bloomsbury.

Stevens, Lara et al. 2018, *Feminist Ecologies: Changing Environments in the Anthropocene*. London: Palgrave Macmillan.

Supiot, Alan. 2018, 'A labour code for the 21st century' *Le Monde Diplomatique* May 2018, viewed 28 September 2019 https://mondediplo.com/2018/05/17-labourcode

Supiot, Alan. 2001, *Beyond Employment: Changes in Work and the Future of Labour Law in Europe*. Oxford: Oxford University Press.

Twigg, Julia. 2000, 'Carework as a form of bodywork' *Ageing and Society* vol. 20, no. 4, pp. 389–411.

Van Arsdale, David. 2016, *Poverty at Work*. Leiden: Brill Publishing.

Wacquant, Loïc. 2012, 'Three steps to a historical anthropology of actually existing neoliberalism' *Social Anthropology* vol. 20, pp. 66–79. Doi:10.1111/j.1469-8676.2011.00189.x

Zahn, Rebecca. 2019, 'Trade unions, the gig economy and the feminisation of work: Lessons from the past?' in *Theorising Labour Law in a Changing World*. Alysia Blackham et al (eds), pp. 107–124. Oxford: Hart Publishing.

Zbyszewska, Ania. 2018, 'Labor law for a warming world? Exploring the intersections of work regulation and environmental sustainability: An introduction' *Comparative Labor Law and Policy Journal* vol. 40, no. 1.

Case Law

Ajayi v (1) Abu (2) Abu [2017] EWHC 1946

CN v The United Kingdom [2012] Application no. 4239/08

Hounga v Allen [2014] UKSC 47

Mruke v Khan [2018] EWCA Civ 280

Nambalat v Taher & Anor: Udin v Pasha & Ors [2012] EWCA Civ 1249

Patel v Mirza [2016] UKSC 42

Pimlico Plumbers Ltd and Another v Smith [2018] UKSC 29

Reyes v Al-Malki [2017] UKSC 61

Siliadin v France, App No. 73316/91, Judgment of 26 July 2005

Taiwo v Olaigbe and another; Onu v Akwiwu and another [2016] UKSC 31

Uber BV & ors v. Aslam & ors [2018] EWCA Civ 2748

4 Law as ecotechnics

The previous chapters have explored how legal categories and discourses in migration and labour reaffirm dichotomies of legal versus illegal, citizen versus non-citizen, worker versus self-employed, precarious versus ostensibly secure. Labour migration analyses and critique, moreover, circulate in closed conditions of possibility, where contingencies of recognition, status and value remain bound to the nation-state. Yet privileged belonging in a nation-state, in other words reaping the benefits of citizenship, ignores formal legal categories. Belonging in the community of value and having one's work recognised as productive work (e.g. work that contributes to the economic system) are privileged experiences based more on socially and ideologically constructed frames than one's ability to secure legal recognition or status.

The *sense* of what is happening with/in labour migration, *sense* understood via Jean-Luc Nancy as the alterity of the being singular plural, goes unnoticed (or is ignored) where experiences are pre-empted by categories that define belonging. Sense – paying attention to the *happening* of beings coming together – exposes the fact that at the heart of any 'common' is presence that is always precarious and irregular. But this is not the same as the precarity and irregularity that is experienced as a result of the techne of capital – the cold, calculated seizure of life. Sense happens simultaneously with, but in excess of, the techne; it is *eco*, home, *oikos*, the basic unit of sociality. The ecotechnics of labour migration law, or seeing labour, migration and law as ecotechnics, suggests that so long as our thinking of community is concerned with establishing definitions and borders to identify, name and solidify experience and presence, then hope for those whose presence is denied or denigrated is incapacitated. The techne seizes sense into categories of intelligibility that translate as capital, for the sake of capital accumulation. The purpose of an ecotechnical diagnosis is not to deny techne, nor to deny how form circulates as capital. Neither is my purpose to make law 'differently'. Rather, the purpose and value of ecotechnics is to expose and resist the totalising presence of law where law is posited and problematised as if it were an absolute authority indistinguishable from the nation-state and market (neoliberalisation). Seen as *ecotechnics*, law maintains *eco* where it is recognised for its relationship with sociality, originary and presence, as well as the techne. My work explores what this means for precarious, 'irregular' labour migration: its form, discourse and experience. The alienating experience of categories and modern law's framework can only but open onto a different *sense* of the world.

In this chapter, I introduce theories of law as aporetic. Law as in/determinate traces sociality. Aporetic law brings to light the inherent tension, or incommensurability in law as order, rules (juridical) and the ever-elusive pursuit of justice in being 'with' (existential). Positivist jurisprudence, in other words mainstream modern legal thought, obscures the incommensurability of law by attributing law with a ground (e.g. the rule of law), as if law itself was some*thing* within which modern, liberal, secular being (state, citizen) can take root. Through the ecotechnics of precarious labour migration I suggest that law, as tracing sociality, be disentangled from liberal ideology to encompass all singularities in the being singular plural. Opening onto sense is possible in law but for the epistemological hegemony of law as embedded into processes of neoliberalisation facilitating the concretised technologisation of life.

The attempt to 'think differently' or to shift perspectives or paradigms of thought is one that has haunted theorists. Indeed, post-structuralist and Marxist thinkers have identified that what we write, whatever we wish to express and represent, is rooted in particular historical contingencies that perpetuate normative violence, guided by spectres of the colonial matrix of power, or at the very least spectres of previous philosophies (Dussel 2014; Quijano 2010; Marks 2009; Derrida 1994; Butler 1992; Nancy 1991).[1] Scholars of de-coloniality draw attention to the centrality of the 'I' commanding ego-logical thinking that has guided our understanding and articulation of being since the Enlightenment, if not before (Mignolo and Escobar 2010; Quijano 2007). Critical studies that expose the monopoly of onto-epistemological thought undertake a Sisyphean task, not least because our communication (writing, knowledge production and exchange) is itself rooted in modern, enlightenment vocabularies.

In this book, the urge to think differently to create a space for a different approach to labour and migration arose from a specific frustration with the discourse surrounding migration. In particular, the movement and employment of persons in low-waged, 'low-skilled' labour glaringly reveals the inefficacy of legal remedies, as the previous chapters have described. Not only in the UK, there is a dangerous disconnect between legal instruments aimed to curb migration and the increase in work that is 'illegal' 'informal' and outside the scope of

1 Notably, *Spectres of Marx* (Derrida 1994); Nancy (1991), the chapters entitled 'Literary communism'. Enrique Dussel writes even more specifically a critique of the historical (colonial) foundations of modern thought, see Dussel (2014). Judith Butler writes of the 'contingent foundations' of thought (constructing 'the subject', 'gender', 'sexuality') and the claims, or task, of postmodernist and post-structuralist thought (see Butler 1992).

labour regulation (see Columb 2020). While the UK's membership in the EU was blamed for the influx of 'non-British' workers in the UK (especially since free movement became available to Eastern Bloc countries post-2004), post-Brexit employment demand will not be met by 'British workers' alone (see Campbell 2019). Presumably labour markets will look to further deregulate employment, and without EU regulations overseeing working time, agency work and equality at work, cheap labour will be extracted not only from the most vulnerable citizens, but also from the formal and informal employment of migrants from around the world. The material reality of persons migrating, with different immigration statuses and nationalities, across territorial borders to work in low-waged, low-skilled, low-regulated labour sectors will continue, at least so long as capital accumulation remains the priority of governments and businesses. Thus, the differentiation of 'citizenship' within a nation-state, enabling populations to be cheap and expendable, will continue. Without a remedy or alternative found within existing policies and legal-political solutions, the demonisation of outsiders ('migrants') and the precaritisation of work will continue. Meanwhile, the capital benefit derived from systemic differentiation and exploitation ensures that the status quo is maintained.

Migration and work, before the law

In discourses of migration intersecting with work and labour law, as discussed in Chapter 2, people's experiences are evaluated as deserving or not. The discourse implies that those moving and working must compete for limited recognition and protection as if protection was finite and scarce. Political resistance to extending legal protection suggests that if gaps found in immigration and employment law were addressed, this would still not rectify the failure of employment and immigration law frameworks to recognise 'irregularity' in migration and labour. Moreover, political relationships to law and legal structures that until recently seemed fairly fixed and honoured, at least in the Anglo-American world, have shifted. For example, in the U.S. Donald Trump regularly speaks against members of the judiciary and justice agencies that he personally disagrees with, with no regard for the practice of respecting office, authority, or the rule of law principle that 'no one is above the law' (Haberman and Rogers 2019; Ford 2019; Savage 2019). This was echoed clearly in September 2019 in the UK, when the Supreme Court deemed Prime Minister Johnson's action of proroguing Parliament unlawful, to which Johnson insisted that he 'disagreed' and that he will not be 'deterred' (BBC News 2019). Earlier that same year, Sajid Javid's actions revoking Shamima Begum's citizenship were publicised before it was known whether or not he had, as Home Secretary, the power to revoke her citizenship – potentially rendering her and her child stateless. The ecotechnics acting in labour migration have exposed a technical seizure that is far less legalistic and more capital driven. This reveals how law is not only fallible but also malleable: wielded when convenient and avoided when opportune by those in positions of power. For example, the rhetoric of 'taking back control' (Brexit, see Wolf 2019) through the exclusive project of nationalism technologises the fear of foreign invasion and identity loss. The techne, the cold calculation of capital, allows for the movement of workers and the exploitation of their labour to remain *as irregular,* while the eco, although seized by the techne to uphold the fantasy of the nation-state, nevertheless exists as the experience of people (being singular plural) struggling to make sense of their communities, identities, labour and belonging.

A retreat back to the nation is currently the loudest public response to twenty-first-century manifestations of globalisation. Yet within this retreat to the nation, existing categories of law fall short of providing a satisfactory resolution for the shifts experienced in employment. While advocacy efforts may instrumentalise legal categories to extend to those marginalised or excluded from the nation-state (often through the language of human rights), widening legal categories is not a guarantee of improved recognition for specific individuals. As the labour market adapts to a globalised demand for casual, flexible workers, the neoliberal nation-state is redeployed to prioritise capital accumulation. Thus, legal recognition, protection and rights at work become privileges only available for a select few. In the UK, for those recognised as employees in a standard employment relationship under the Employment Rights Act 1996 (ERA). Moreover, the focus on the ill treatment of 'migrant' workers who are in suspended subjectivity *as irregular* – juxtaposed to citizen workers, who may be entitled to work, but work that is often inadequate for survival (in-work poverty) – suffers from a commitment to principles already shattered and widely inaccessible. Namely, the idea that citizenship and regular immigration status will afford an individual at work legal rights and protections against being exploited for their labour. Guaranteed employment status, job security, minimum wage in casual flexible work, access to employment tribunal in case of employment relationship breakdown, are privileges ('employment rights') ostensibly enjoyed by persons with legal migration status. However, these employment rights, as discussed in the previous chapter, are largely absent from labour sectors such as care work and jobs outsourced to agencies or corporate services offering zero-hour or self-employment contracts. Irrefutably there are individuals stuck in legal limbo working without recognised legal immigration status, a very small minority of whom would be able to appear on the legal stage like Miss Hounga, Ms Taiwo, Ms Onu and Ms Reyes. A lack of secure immigration status defines people's existence as 'deportable' (DeGenova 2002). Yet the scale of abuses, exploitation and irregularity in the systems, policies and practices of border crossing, immigration, labour and employment, sanctioned at the highest level of government, have become normal. Normalised to the extent that the subjects of labour and migration discourse are not necessarily those subjected to migration and employment law.

While labour migration (people crossing territorial borders for work) is historically constant, the phenomenon of labour migration has captivated political attention across Europe and North America over the past ten years not least during the heightened so-called migration crisis into Europe from routes crossing the Mediterranean Sea in 2015, and the Brexit political chaos in the UK since 2016. Responses to migration suggest that the circulation of sense is opening onto its own closure: xenophobic, nationalist and populist seizure of politics. While the fear and insecurity experienced by people may be itself a sense (eco) of unknown interrupting their fantasy of security in the nation-state, this fear is technologised by politics and political agendas to concretise that very ephemeral illusion of security and home. Rather than be an opening onto an alternative, different, possibility of being singular plural, the precariousness experienced in the twenty-first century is capitalised as nationalism. The instrumentalisation of national legal structures practice and enforce a limited, exclusive belonging for people existing in the same sociality with those excluded.

As the previous chapters have demonstrated, the actions of migration and labour open onto realities not-yet-settled or determined: how we move, how we work, produce and reproduce sociality is circulating as eco precisely where it cannot be seized by techne. Creativity and relationality (being singular plural) is unpredictable and physical, materially experienced as sense. While modern law attempts to provide grounding, the mobility of existence precedes law and in doing so, *creates world*. From the cellular composition of our physical bodies to our physical migrations, shifting political identities, our thoughts, ideas, perceptions, senses – the world is motion. While ecotechnics can simplistically seem itself like an inevitable predetermination, observing that the environment is consumed by technological expansion, the ecological circulation of sense seized by the technologisation of meaning is not inevitably capitalist and neoliberal. Neither is ecotechnics itself consumed and obliterated by the seizure of techne. Our modern Western epistemological homogeneity obscures a vocabulary of being where we can be aware of what is going on: bodies are simultaneously creative and destructive, experiencing dislocation, dis-localisation, consumption and degradation, in what Nancy terms 'a double suspension of sense' (Nancy 2008, 105). This experience is not a panacea; rather it can indeed be the very real experience of fear and insecurity which then welcomes a techne that gives form, structure and meaning. For instance, in the aftermath of the UK general election in December 2019, it was noted that one of the reasons for the high voter support for the Conservative party may have been related to both the sense that the leadership would offer predictability and a direct approach: 'no nonsense' regarding Brexit (Mueller 2019). Predictability and directness within the 'known' techniques of governance appease a sense of groundlessness and precariousness.

Nevertheless, our beings as bodies, travelling, moving, working, experience the limit of language, legal regulatory tools and definitions. The violence of current processes of neoliberalisation has become normalised if not naturalised (Marks 2009) by technical categories that prescribe recognition and render the excess of these categories 'irregular' in order that the market economic system may benefit from their labour. But the 'irregular' are regular beings existing in sociality; a sociality that exists, ecologically and socially. Language, regulatory tools and categories are incapable of grasping, or pinpointing, how we relate to each other in the world. The technical imperative of sociality, interpreted by the dominant political and juridical structures that order and regulate our sociality, insufficiently frame the work of bodies into categories according to a liberal, ego-logical ideology embedded in the mythology of the nation-state and the fantasy of citizenship.

Theories of law: incommensurability

It is on the level of constituting sociality, in the midst of, or as inseparable from, market forces, that we can begin to interrogate law – what it is, who it serves, and how it may respond and change. Law as existential law can be seen not as a substance in and of itself, but as tracing the limit of the sociality. Existential law refers to what exists in the aporia of order and justice as it impacts existence. Law understood in this way is responsive to the material experience of beings working, living and thus, being.[2] The ecotechnics of labour and migration law circulate the power that traps, confines and conforms life as material experience and the sense of the material experience that escapes signification, but nevertheless informs law. Living materiality does come with an ethical demand that is a consequence of our existence 'with' – being singular plural – beyond the technical processes that concretise sense. The ethical demand is being response-able to experiencing sociality in the alterity 'with' singular plural beings: to be *presence* in the world, as the world. Nancy suggests, 'there is no difference between the ethical and the ontological: the "ethical" exposes what the "ontological" disposes' (Nancy 2000, 99). Attention to movement as ecotechnical exposes that it is *irresponsible* to remain within existing paradigms of migration and labour, where the law – as it is conventionally juridical and embodied in UK statute (Immigration Act; Employment Rights Act) – is imbued with an imagined capacity to adapt to the sense of circulation in work that is transnational, emotional and transgressive.

Law is failing migration and labour in its orchestration of, and its complicity in, and its complicity in the technological circulation of market forces embedded in the nation-state that benefit from maintaining 'juridical twilight zones' (Lutz 2017). Meanwhile the sense that circulates in excess of techne is deemed 'irregular' for its transgression of, or inability to fit into, legal categories and frameworks. Existential law, as part of ecotechnics, suggests that ecosociality

2 In Peter Fitzpatrick's work this is the beyond of law, or the excess. For Foucault, the transgressive. In thinking of law as no *thing*, and thus as the sense and not the signification, one could move this analysis into psychoanalytic thinking and in particular discussions of law and Lacan (see Aristodemou 2014).

exposes what juridical law is configured to deny or silence. This is not to suggest that we can do away with juridical law and the nation-state; the technological seizure of law is part of ecotechnical circulation. That law enforces a limit is inevitable. What is *happening* in, and experienced as, the nation-state and its legal system undeniably facilitates capital accumulation, but as constituting sociality in the being singular plural – all singularities are presence in the law that traces sociality. Eco-social being transgresses the hegemony of egological onto-epistemology, not as an outside or other, but in the plurality that constitutes law. Thus, law is able to respond.

Law plays a key role within the web of explanations for our being (singular plural) and our sociality as the experience creating our world. Firstly, law is aporetic. Law exists as rules and orders; structures are inscribed as laws, legislation, codes and judgements/judicial decisions. Law, moreover, supports infrastructures of exploitation, power and dis/advantage. But at the same time, the processes that pursue justice involve interpretation and decision making, contingent and contextualised by the persons exacting the law. Secondly, in its basic role or bare task, law traces the originary sociality (Nancy 1993, 30).[3]

Aporetic law

Jacques Derrida, in *Force of Law: The 'Mystical Foundation of Authority'* describes law as the 'element of calculation, and it is just that there be law, but justice is incalculable' (Derrida 1992, 244). He contends that law necessarily exists in tension with justice, which is 'an experience of the impossible' (244). Law carries the potential to respond to a call for justice, while at the same time law as the limit, the 'force of law', can never do justice to justice. Derrida and Nancy share this approach to law and justice, where justice involves an ongoing search for a way to speak that would 'do justice to what is or what occurs' (James 2012, 42). In Derrida's words, 'deconstruction is justice'; justice is an experience of aporia (Derrida 1992, 243). While in Nancy's work, 'justice can only reside in the renewed decision to challenge the validity of an established or prevailing just measure *in the name of the incommensurable*' (Nancy 1993, 75). Justice in the name of the incommensurable is the inability to secure a ground, or a firm basis from which the subject can be fixed (Fenves in Nancy 1993, xxiv). Here, thinking of justice is not about seeking a concept or word to encompass 'justice' or to situate it between concepts. Rather, justice is abandonment, where we are abandoned to groundlessness – the freedom from strict determinacy.

Law understood as tracing the sociality, wherein the abandonment of justice happens, does not precede the sociality. Rather law, as incommensurability,

3 Law as a trace of the limit, comes from Nancy: 'We could also say: "existence is law," but if law, in general, essentially traces a limit, the law of existence does not impose a limit *on* existence: it traces existence as the limit that it is and on which it resolves' (Nancy 1993, 30).

is between inscribing the limit of sociality each time and moving the limit to respond to the mobility of existence. Sociality refers to the social happening of law, the shared economies of production, reproduction and exchange happening as originary every time, incapable of predetermination. But law cannot and does not define the totality of sociality, law is no-*thing* (Nancy 2003, 138, 212). Yet law takes place and happens as an imperative precisely because there is no determinate foundation or core. The movement within law is both its form and its fluidity; in other words, the aporia. However, based on the dominance of determinate categories and their pursuit, law is always (albeit not inevitably) being prescribed and predetermined by those who enjoy recognition, and therefore authority, within the community of value: Good Citizens, full legal subjects, privileged in the modern Western philosophical paradigm.

When law is conceptualised in this way, we no longer look solely to how we might improve legal categories. Law is not some*thing* to be applied, used and instrumentalised, nor is it some*thing* that contains its own power within itself. Law, instead, is a trace response of the singular plural beings that are relating and through this relation constitute a limit. Within the current circulation of beings, capital production and economic market systems, the limit operates within a specific ideological paradigm that names privileged legal subjects while obscuring the participation of others. Yet 'law' as a constituting limit and the force of this limit is not limited to these particular vocabularies and ideology. In fact, the indeterminacy of some judicial decisions with regards to 'irregular' migration and labour/employment demonstrates that law, by what it ultimately permits, traces ecotechnics more so than it firmly re-enforces techne through rigid frameworks of existing legal categories. We see this through the inconsistency of legal decision making and decisions that have extended legal recognition to those that otherwise would be denied protection, such as *Hounga* [2014], *Zambrano* [2011] and *Autoclenz* [2011].

Labour migration law illuminates a tension between juridical and existential law.[4] Juridical law, adhering to legal instruments and artefacts such as immigration regulation and employment legislation, deems the presence of persons without clear immigration and employment status irregular or illegal. Existential law suggests their presence in the sociality of the territory (if not the state) constitutes the need for recognition as beings in the plural.

4 A tension between juridical and existential law is not inherent to law but is a condition of law's authors instrumentalising the nation-state and market economy. We are abandoned to law because of the loss of control, meaning that because we cannot control the movement of sociality and being, categories, limits and exclusions are inevitable. Freedom, and opening onto freedom is the only way to be because there is only being, not determination (Nancy 1993, 30). Law (juridical) is not founded by freedom because it brings order, it pins down and contains, and thereby denies freedom. But the commandment can always be violated because there is more than the framed being-as-a-subject under law's authority (in other words, there is existential law).

Such recognition would be 'just' insofar as it recognises the *happening* or *existence* of the sociality being singular plural: originary sociality. In conventional Anglo-American jurisprudence, taught as if it were the definitive legal jurisprudence, the gaps of juridical law are intellectually 'filled' with an existentialist pursuit of 'justice' 'ethics' or 'morality' based on a historically and socially contingent determination of what such justice and morality are based on. For instance, Rawls (1999) developed his theory of justice understood from behind a 'veil of ignorance' that rests on liberal notions of sociality and equality. His renown theory, in spite of heralding a universal possibility for understanding justice, ignores structural inequalities affecting people according to gendered, racial, ableist, socio-economic discrimination and diverse worldviews, histories and traditions (see Forrester 2019). Similarly, the classic debates between positive law and natural law made famous by scholars of jurisprudence (including H.L.A. Hart, L. Fuller, J. Finnis and R. Dworkin) reaffirm a foundation of law within a sovereign entity, be it the representative of the populous (democratic or appointed), the divine, or nature. These jurisprudential debates that have come to define legal theory and philosophies of modern law are 'committed to establishing the unity and self-identity of law' (Davies 2017, 27). As such, they provide a circular definition of law, wherein law is defined by itself (see Davies 2017, 25–29). Discussions of rights and democracy circulate within an epistemological frame that does not question its own foundation in a modern, liberal, Enlightenment order, whereby exclusive rights are inherited by virtue of one's action as human and participation in a predetermined 'public'. International law's canon, even beyond the specifics of Anglo-American jurisprudence, is based in the historically situated and culturally specific work of scholars such as Grotius, Vittoria and Kant (see Anghie 2005). In contrast, the simultaneity of existential law that ecotechnics harkens to is neither metaphysically transcendent nor based on modernity's espousal of equality, rights and justice. Existential law, instead, is what deals with existence: being created as world, ongoing and in motion. In other words, in the singular plural. And the singular plural is, by definition, plural and diverse. Existing is precisely what bodies are about, as weight, as presence, as happening, not according to what they *should* be or should do (Nancy 2008, 101). Bodies, however, are not exclusive beings in existence. The being singular plural encompasses all singularities as existence, and thus as world.

Law, a technology without doubt, develops as a consequence of processes whereby singular beings come together (plural) to form sociality. Through law, in-appropriable experience is inscribed as a limit. This in-appropriable experience is presence, and it is material. The technics and the ecology of existence reveal an experience of defamiliarisation because it is external from what is taken, assumed, to fit a predetermined frame. Thus, while it is complicated to speak about the 'eco' or ecosociality, it pertains to exactly what escapes signification but what is *lived* and *happening*.

Law-as-incommensurable can appear to fall short in the face of the tangible exploitation experienced in labour and migration. However, the key argument of this book and the point of drawing on ecotechnics is that the discourses of migration, contestations of citizenship, processes of neoliberalisation and the precariatisation of labour are experiences that cannot be remedied from within the same paradigm that have created the mess in the first place. Labour migration as ecotechnical interrupts the notion that if we adhere to a strict, progressive narrative, where law serves as the final arbitrator of recognition and justice, there will be an end or a 'return' to normalcy. Subsequently ecotechnical circulation renders law incapable of being conclusive; such techne would deny the circulation of sense and being. Seeing law in this way does not discount other analyses that search for short-term solutions within the juridical to speak to immediate, specific needs. However, when we consider the phenomenon of labour migration as a whole, which persists in spite of legal and advocacy attempts to address 'irregular' migration and labour, grappling with the ecotechnics of these politics is an unknown but crucial conceptual step.

Modern law

Law plays a key role in constituting and legitimising communities, communities that have in the modern era been identified through the framework of the nation (Buchanan and Pahuja 2004, 137, 143). The nation-state – the governance structure together with the imagined community of the nation – has been understood to, in turn, prescribe the law (Butler and Chakravorty Spivak 2007). The nation served, and continues to serve, as a foundation for the modern legal system and modern theories of law, through what Quijano (2010) refers to as the colonial matrix of power. The law constitutes and legitimates nations, and the nation-state enables legal systems to order and regulate populations, through legislation and the common law. Concurrently, law is connected to notions of justice, which reveals incommensurability between a juridico-ethical pursuit, and the order of law as a regulatory regime. Moreover, as discussed in the previous chapters, identity and belonging to the nation-state is consolidated by what it is not: the foreigner, the non-citizen. Law, therefore, in its paradox is open to the possibility of what is beyond the confines of the nation-state border and that particular historically specific ideology, maintaining its own negation as part of its formulation (see Leung 2015). In other words, while the nation-state structure is reaffirmed by law and through law, law also allows for its content to extend beyond its constitution in what can be described as a merger of juridical and existential law in the *happening* of law.

It is impossible, ultimately, to keep the identified juridical and existential aspects of law distinct from one another – juridical law and existential law co-appear (Nancy 1991, 28).[5] Juridical and existential law co-exist and are happening within the ecotechnical circulation of the world. In this case, when law intersects with the experience of people migrating and working. This particular perspective on law – juridical and existential law co-existing – is a theoretically based examination of law's presence and role. The practical experience of relating to juridical law imposing legal subjectivity, however, is not irrelevant to this discussion. There are experiences that are enforced as an acceptable part of juridical law and others that are condemned, or criminally punished within law's ambit. For example, in Italy in the summer 2019, an action that contravened Deputy Prime Minister Salvini's mandate to close Italy's borders to refugee migrants was not immediately condemned by the Courts and legal system (Euronews 2019). Carola Rackete's actions in June 2019 disregarded a law by Italy's then interior minister Salvini, by docking a boat of rescued migrants in the Italian port of Lampedusa. The ambiguity between Italy's juridical law versus international maritime law, as well as the prerogative of existential law, meant that her actions were simultaneously celebrated and condemned. Celebrated, Rackete was a brave ship captain who saved the lives of those stranded aboard her ship, after being rescued from the Mediterranean Sea. Condemned, she was a rogue actor who defied not only Italian law, made by a democratically elected leader (Salvini) whose commitment to closing Italy's borders in a mandate to 'protect' Italy against foreigners gained him popularity and support, but European border security (see France 24 2019).

The paradox of law suggests that although juridical law is guided by categories that provide order and definition from a foundation of modernity and colonial expansion, these categories can only offer a limited order due to an ever-shifting existential law. Existential law, however, has little tangible materiality without the power, or force, of juridical law. This paradox practically causes the ambiguous legal grey areas where persons are considered 'migrant' and placed in irregular legal situations. For example, it may seem unjust (and contrary to existential law) to deny protection for Miss Hounga [*Hounga v Allen* 2012; 2014] based on the abuse she suffered at the hands of her employers. However, her presence in the UK was in contravention of immigration law. The doctrine of illegality exists so that illegal acts do not go unpunished and thereby make a mockery of the legal system [*Hounga v Allen* 2012]. Existential law mandates that there be a law recognising those living and working in a given territory. The limited frames of recognition instrumentalised by juridical law and bound by citizenship prevent openness to all bodies living and working in a given territory.

The tension of juridical and existential law is seized by neoliberalisation and the economic market. Law is instrumentalised in the nation-state system and

5 What is exterior or external to definitions and categories of law nevertheless informs and makes law. But further, to say law 'itself' is to make it go out of 'itself' because law cannot be contained 'in' a 'self' (Derrida 2004, 299).

market economy to allow for the unregulated exploitation of non-citizens: 'irregular' or 'illegal' migrants. The complicity of law with the state and economic market is not, however, inherent to law itself. Rather it is a condition of law's authors. Law itself, juridical and existential, is no-*thing* until it is given value and meaning by those who speak it and are subjected to it. For example, in the case of *Hounga*, to deny an 'illegal' migrant recognition and 'protection' from the law of the nation-state is consistent with legal custom and rules. The doctrine of illegality exists to ensure the sanctity of the legal system by not rewarding illegal conduct. However, to deny a person, in particular a young girl, protection against abuse, exploitation and violence is also an affront to the law and calls into question not only the sanctity but the efficacy of the judicial system as a harbinger of justice. Thus, in Miss Hounga's case in 2014 she was recognised as being a victim of 'conditions akin to modern day slavery' and received compensation for this, instead of the initial employment law claim made against her employer for breach of employment laws (unfair dismissal, withholding wages, failure to pay minimum wage).

Another example of law's juridical force in tension with its existential possibility involves Serco, a for-profit, multinational 'public sector provider', discussed in Chapter 1. Serco was contracted by the UK Home Office to provide housing for asylum seekers. In 2018, Serco, rolled out a 'Move On' protocol in Glasgow. In Glasgow, as elsewhere in the country, when an asylum seeker's claim is denied and other options of lawfully staying in the UK are denied or exhausted, these persons are deemed to not have the 'right to remain' in the UK. The 'Move-On' protocol essentially responds to Home Office refusals by denying failed asylum seekers access to previously provided housing by changing the locks on their homes, thus rendering these individuals (including families) homeless. In 2018, a legal case was brought to the Court of Session (Scotland's Supreme Court) on behalf of two asylum seekers in Glasgow who received an eviction order. The case disputed the legality (contravention of the Human Rights Act 1998) of the Move-On Protocol and was widely supported by housing associations and refugee advocacy groups throughout the UK (Miller et al. 2018). In April 15, 2019, the Court confirmed the legality of the protocol, affirming property law rights of the landowners and Serco's contract with the Home Office to provide housing for asylum claimants. In June 2019, Serco once again gave notice that the protocol would be rolled out in Glasgow. Serco's press statements, both in 2018 and in June 2019, expressed that they are responding to being placed in an 'impossible position' being 'neither a welfare agency, nor a charity' but having to bear the financial costs of asylum application refusals carried out by the Home Office (Serco 2018).

Indeed, Serco is a for-profit company. Their interest in winning the contract with the Home Office is financial, market driven. In a direct illustration of this, Serco in June 2019, maintained that they are doing their legal duty by upholding the (juridical) law: the doctrine of illegality would maintain that without the Right to Remain, persons living in the UK are doing so 'illegally'. To facilitate their prolonged presence would be 'making a mockery of the law'. The Move-On Protocol is legally sanctioned action, protecting taxpayers' money from the financial burden of housing illegal migrants. Nevertheless, Serco acknowledged the violence their protocol enacts against the sociality of persons living in Glasgow (the existential law), evidenced by their commitment to donate £150,000 to homeless charities in Glasgow. As a demonstration of ecotechnics performed by Serco, the only way that a for-profit company can interact with the violence they enacted onto the 'happening' of persons in the city is by recirculating financial capital back into the market: donating £150,000 to help the problem, homelessness, to which they directly contributed. In other words, Serco's only interest in the people they displaced is through re-investment into capital circulation and economic transactions in the market, not the sociality happening and existing beyond capital. The cold circulation of capital is thus responding to the sense exceeding the capital concretisation, and the sense exceeds the capital circulation where bodies are expelled from housing through legally sanctioned decisions rendering persons 'deserving' or 'undeserving' of participation in the community. The people evicted still exist – but as rejected, homeless.

Ecotechnics: nothing outside

Law as ecotechnics can be understood as tracing the movement generated through the coming together that happens in the *originary sociality*. Thus, law cannot be reduced to analysis and critique solely as a fixed entity arbitrating order and justice, or what is legal versus illegal, according to a techne of order and rights. An interrogation of the factors at play in the global circulation of capital as labour, through an ecotechnical approach, provokes an altered thinking of law. My aim is not to make existing legislation or legal practices more just or open. It is the form itself that I problematise. If our critique demands that law be some*thing* 'better' – when 'it' itself is fictitiously constituted as a *thing* and a totality – then the happening of beings relating in the world, where the law is shaped by and shapes events and economic interrelationships is obscured. Ecotechnics offers a way to see law as vitally connected to the *happening* of a sociality where otherwise law is only a means to serve market ends. Beings participate together in shared economies of production, reproduction and exchange. This includes law as a part of its constitution, but law does not, and cannot, define the totality of sociality because this sociality is in motion. Existence is mobile.

Incommensurability is also a starting point for understanding being singular plural. Being 'with' affirms incommensurability as the only grounding for existence possible to conceptualise from within the normative, dominant, modern onto-epistemological framework. As incommensurable, therefore, it is not a ground (James 2012, 37). Consequently, as argued previously, the law is no-*thing* but for being infused with signification and meaning from what is inscribed as law. Meanwhile, law takes place, it *happens*, as an imperative (Nancy 2003, 138). Through this imperative, law enables a sharing which is 'always incomplete, or it is beyond completion and incompletion' (Nancy 1991, 35). This sharing is not cohesive or coherent, but it is sharing as a consequence of our being singular plural. This 'sharing' (sharing of the incommensurable) is where the law addresses itself to an opening. This opening is an incomplete sharing which opens to freedom, to that which is beyond: the alterity, pluriversality, of the singular plural.

The technique of economic activity has been made intelligible via a market economic system. However, processes of neoliberalisation are constantly in movement responding to and engulfing bodies-at-work as labourers: casual/temporary/employees, within shifting labour market demands as Chapters 2 and 3 described. These labour relationships transcend categories that order identities through the nation-state. Ecotechnics opens onto processes of neoliberalisation where the critiques of political and juridical approaches are unable to capture movement beyond, or in excess of categories and frameworks. Neoliberalisation moves beyond the inscribed labour market that operates within a nation-state. Within this system, workers are maintained as vital for their precarious and dispensable position: workers are vital because they are precarious, and precarious because they are vital to an ostensibly free market, globalised, economic system – in spite of the fact that this circulation of labour and capital is neither free nor geographically global. When persons come together, the ecotechnics of labour markets and economic exchanges is the happening of capital and social reproduction. Yet labour markets and economic exchanges are identified only through already limited economic experiences and subjectivities, all the while purporting to be 'global' and 'free'.

Ecotechnics suggests that the originary sociality of singular plural being forms economies of sociability, as well as a need for a limit and an order. This is the paradox of law: a need for law clashes with the ecology of sociality, which presently is known through, and because of, the technologies of modern law and neoliberal economics. Being singular plural is the techne that is the bodies-at-work, which in their originary sociality create the need for categories and order. At the same time, this sociality and co-appearance goes beyond the categories that give shape to an ever-elusive demographic of irregular migrant labourers. The 'irregular' 'migrant' 'labourers' are people sustaining themselves, their livelihoods and working within and beyond labels of citizenship, legal status and legal recognition. And law, as a concretisation of national mythologizing can only continue in its failure to respond. A dynamic and plural conceptualisation of this *happening* is needed in order to open and shift away from the dominant framework that cannot conceptualise beyond modernity's (neo) liberal paradigm.

Simplification of being

Being singular plural – the singular being that is a being because it is 'with' (plural) – challenges us to think through the foundational constructions of being, or foundational ontological questioning. When we think through the constructs that have, throughout history, shaped and formed our way of imagining being, it may become difficult to conceive of what is not a construct of this same ideology of being. How can we ever understand *being* without the imposition of historically, culturally specific interpretations? Viveiros de Castro argues that we, rooted in modernity as our postmodern inheritance, suffer from a 'simplification of ontology' which has 'led to enormous complication of epistemology' (2004, 484). Seeming to establish that we are 'human' individuals (from Descartes, through Kant, to Rosseau and so on), we struggle over ourselves to seize knowledge, to label, identify and control how we know. Indeed, Kirby argues that the 'Cartesian logic remains necessary to our sense of self, our belief that we exist'. The fact that we make decisions, 'presumes this self-possession' and is necessary to the idea of the human-species (Kirby in Fritsch et al. 2018, 123). Opening onto pluriversality is not a suggestion that we get rid of existing thought; but the unqualified privilege of individual ego-logics embedded in the nation-state, citizenship and legal subjectivity needs to be confronted in order that we may see what knowledges have been silenced. Being is not simple: conceptualising cosmologies and relationality between life and non-life has suffered from a Western, Christian monopoly at the expense of other diverse ontologies (Viveiros de Castro 2004). Seeing migration and labour as ecotechnics and drawing out the sense of 'eco' is difficult not simply because we are restricted by language and vocabularies. It is not an exercise of trying to strip away history. In recognising the contingency of constructions of being against the experience of being, we are left with the bare materiality of being as the basis of law and sociality: all we have is what is happening in material, lived, felt, experience. In Viveiros de Castro's words, 'at the heart of the matter, there is no stuff; only form, only relation' (2004, 484). The challenge remains open as to where ecotechnics takes us – and what direction, what focus or experience the being singular plural draws out, as opportunity, not prescription. Already postcolonial and decolonial studies, and feminist legal research open onto silenced knowledges. Feminist labour law scholars, discussed in the previous chapter, endeavour to mobilise different contingencies of value and work, away from a definition of work limited to waged labour towards valuing the social reproductive labour and unwaged work traditionally carried out by women. The hegemony of masculine definitions of economy, economically productive work, and value engendered the assumption that work done in the home – caring, cleaning, nurturing – is the unpaid responsibility of a woman (the mother) or the low-paid hired worker assumed to be treated as 'family' due to the nature of her work. Work that is of 'high value' is work that earns a large wage in the capital market ('public' 'external' sphere). Work that is of 'low value' is work that is not profitable; does not bring about a large wage and equally does not contribute to external, market economic productivity, such as caring for the severely dependent or disabled (i.e. non-economically productive individuals).

Ecotechnics brings attention to the circulation of techne and the circulation of the eco. On the one hand, the circulation of technology and capital and on the other hand, the circulation of ecology, of being and *sense*. This *sense* exceeds definition because it can never be captured. It is what is lived, it is *happening* as a material, sensual experience – not predetermined, and not intelligible or recognisable through set frameworks and vocabularies. Ecotechnics, and seeing the world as ecotechnical, is necessary because the experiences and multiple forms of discrimination and marginalisation (gender, sex, race, nationality, ability) cannot be transformed to enable persons to have equal recognition within the standard, normative framework. The normative frame has been exposed as built on a fantasy; the modern liberal dream where citizenship is a ticket to protection, security and freedom ('taking back control') is not real. In spite of enabling citizenship or regular status through regularisation programmes or citizenship laws, citizenship remains contested even for those who 'have' it. A panacea of labour law protection does not exist. The marketized economic system chisels away at protections that inhibit the supply of cheap labour, while labour as active life, away from the market, exceeds the formula of state protection and capacity.

Moreover, 'life' cannot be 'protected' from within a paradigm that is based on a limited and historically contingent subjectivity. Multiple interests, economic and philosophical, rely on the suspension of regular subjectivity. The differential treatment of persons, sometimes of those within the country of their birth, continues regardless of migration status. Assumed to be a non-citizen, the figure of the migrant allows the modern philosophical tradition to continue as if it were attainable together with the neoliberal economic market system. Indeed modern philosophy and the economic market have been embedded since colonial expansion (Quijano 2010). Meanwhile, the discrimination and exclusion embedded into the market economic system ('global') is offset, as if it were an issue of migration and non/citizenship or individual failure.

The world economy, or capitalism, is not an 'economy', in that there is no line between economy and politics, or economy and law, or economy and society. Such distinctions are false imaginaries (Nancy 1997). What is referred to now as 'economy' is not contained, but instead is a 'global structuration of the world as the rearticulated space of an essentially capitalist, globalist, and monopolist organisation that is monopolising the world' (Nancy 1997, 101). The ecotechnical nature of the global economy threatens to overcome everything with technologised sense, to explain and thus give meaning to our active being in the world – our labour. The eco (environment, ecology) is utilised as if the techne (technology, techniques) were natural and necessary, when technology (as form, technique of order, category and law) and technological advancements as capital are constructed, historically specific and contingent. Moreover, ecotechnics demonstrates that a totalisation, encompassing our entire sense, is impossible. Ecotechnics opens onto 'the infinity of sense' as being that which escapes the totalisation and concretisation of the techne – precisely because 'techne' is not 'eco'. Labour, as fundamental to our being and relation, opens onto this sense through the materiality, the physical embodiment, of life.

Bodily ontologies

The experience of body, as bodies, is always exterior – we can never know from the inside of our body what 'we' are as a physical being. For this reason, our singularity and singular experience is not enough, even just for 'ourselves' (see Derrida 2004). The eco-technical circulation of capital is founded on the basis that capital is a market of bodies. If we take as a starting point that bodies are the materiality of the world, then the bodies coming together form the concretisation of circulation: capital, economics, law. But capital does not form bodies or the sense of being singular plural. Singular plural being, as sociality, is in constant motion determined in as much as it constantly exceeds determination. Moreover, being singular plural is not limited to bodies, but includes the circulation of all singularities. Thus, circulation, as 'happening', is incommensurable and escapes containment at the point at which it is contained. This is, of course, similar to the discussion of law: law, as juridical, is the limit of a sociality expressed through rules, principles and order. However juridical law cannot exist without existential law, juridical law alone would be rules without justice, and existential law alone would be ephemeral and lacking material substance. Bodily ontology rests only in the paradox of constant movement, where all there is *is* the encounter of bodies coming together as singular plural beings. In the coming together then we cannot expect law to serve as definitive ordering, but rather as a temporary gesture, albeit electric, from what is 'seen' and 'said' to what is 'still to be seen' and 'spoken'. Law then speaks not from a position of fixity, but from a position of the (k)not (Nancy 1997): untying the claims of the market, the proto-political and neoliberal and tying the un-tieable materiality of bodies.

Conclusion: being before law

The technological manifestation of sense makes the world work through economics, politics, culture, communication, knowledge, consumption, reproduction, health, mobility and so on. The global is a techne; globalisation is a technological circulation. All that happens above, beyond, below this techne is the *eco*: eco-logy. The sustenance that is elemental to survival: air, water, food, raw materials, as well as the circulation of air, heat, water, earth that maintains our atmosphere and environment. The fluidity of contemporary practices of labour and migration enable, concretely, the neoliberal market economic system to flourish due to the availability of deregulated labour and employment arrangements that are themselves in the shadow of the law. The *ecotechne* that is how persons live and work together makes concrete the modern 'globalised' market economic system and the current framework of the labour market. The labourers who work in precarious employment are the materiality, signified as irregular while their presence exceeds their formal exclusion. Materiality, 'the affect-medium in which objects endure (appear and fade away)' (Mules 2006, 22) is neither a distinct instance nor a set definition. Like a body (human, animal, plant) materiality resists itself as a singular expression because it is a happening of being in a form and presence. Thus the materiality of physical labourers who are able and ready to work in low-waged, low-skilled, bottom-end labour, and respond to the demand for cheap, precarious flexible workers in the UK not only allows the labour market and economic system to continue, but depends on the legal framework to omit and obscure the regulation of exploited labourers. They are not permitted into the community, in spite of their physical presence and contribution to the (global) labour market.[6]

The ecotechnics of being (living) in the twenty-first century has the potential to alter the terrain of the concepts that guide our political, juridical and economic world: citizen, subject, sovereignty and community. These terms dominate political and philosophical thinking. Yet this proto-political-philosophical order is an imagined foil to the nation-state which permits the nation-state to structure exclusive legal recognition and interpretations of law while being constituted by purportedly inclusive labour markets that subject everyone to its frame via claims of a global economic order. Conventional approaches identify subjects as citizens using a linear logic: if 'a' plus 'b', then 'c' (a + b = c). Hence, if we are human beings living in a nation-state then we are citizens with rights and protections. Being singular plural confounds linear logic and rests upon the complexity of material being in the world, as the messiness of bodies inscribed and *ex*scribed in various legal subjectivities that both include and exclude particular movement and labour.

From ecotechnics, opening onto eco-*sociality* causes us to revisit the citizen and the subject at its core. A singularity, known in the plural, is as important to the plurality of other singular beings as the plurality is to the singular being. Moreover, the singular being in the plural is not a citizen or a subject before being signified as one. Even as a citizen or a subject, the sense of my singularity remains as well as the undeniable singularity of physical bodily form. A body cannot be melded with an/other. I am at my limit in relation to other bodies, other singular beings, who themselves

6 The pursuit of, or longing for, an 'authentic community' is a historically specific product of Western-modern thought, attributable to philosophers such as John Locke and the social contract, or Immanuel Kant (Nancy 1997, 109). This 'authentic community' has produced inclusion and exclusion in the 'community of value', administering who has rights in the, or as the, authentic community to be protected by law versus those who do not have these rights and do not belong in the community. However, this is not to say that the gesture, or desire to experience 'authentic community', is also wedded to a liberal ideology. The language or vocabulary through which we communicate limits our lived experiences of sociality (being singular plural) into pre-formulated categories that, with their historical contingencies, fall short of capturing experience which can also be deemed as *something or some experience* 'authentic'.

are always a singularity.[7] 'You' touches 'I' and 'I' touches 'you', neither to become one or the other, nor to know one because of the other (Derrida 2004). But between 'us' is space that creates both 'I' and 'you': the being with. This *happening* pursues a comprehension of being that is a radically different premise from the modern western philosophical paradigm where 'I' starts from being recognised as some*thing* some*one* under a sovereign community, as a subject and citizen of nation-state and law. But we cannot rest here. If we think about migration and labour and law in this way, we think away from pre-existing categories. But then what of the existing law and the force of the law, including its violence? If law is what traces the ecotechnical circulation of capital, and of bodies, it is still a part of our sociality and a result of the sociality. Law does not externally define the sociality but is a technique of intelligibility: a technique that is employed by those in positions of power to make intelligible and impose their 'community of value' as if it, through the nation-state, were universal and natural. Within sociality, power immediately determines how the law traces the plurality and the limit of the plurality. We cannot escape this determination even through calls for justice. Justice is part of the lexicon of modern law, and reinforces falsely universalising notions of equality, access and fairness, which remain contingent on the nation-state, citizenship and market economic values such as socio-economic status. Thus, within the resistance to determination we must also resist thinking of law as ever capable of addressing the totality of our existence. If law is the trace of sociality, it must come from the sociality itself, which is the very pluriversal movement that continues to circulate (ecotechnics) as the alterity and techne, wherein those who claim authorship over the law (power) would not be in power without the labourers and migration that maintain economic circulation and systems. Citizenship would not be privileged were it not for the non-citizen, or migrant; the regular does not exist without the irregular. Authority therefore is contingent on obscuring the interconnection of production and reproduction with economic market prosperity, in other words, hiding sociality *happening*. Rethinking the citizen, subject and community therefore involves uprooting these 'false contingencies' (Marks 2009) without knowing what revealing their grey areas will spark. Furthermore, this 'revealing' is only new insofar as we turn our attention to what *is already* happening. There is nothing new, nothing created or constructed.

Our thinking of labour migration is confined to thinking of whose community membership is granted or withheld, and a particular definition and

7 Further, the singular plural cannot be configured as a dialectic of you versus I, or I versus you. Nancy interrupts a dialectic with the singular plural as what touches on the limit of our (individual) thinking; the singular plural is not dialectic, it is simultaneous (Pryor 2004).

understanding of 'community'. Labour and migration circulate in closed discursive conditions of possibility, where contingencies remain bound to the nation-state and citizenship. The *sense* of what is happening (the alterity of the being singular plural) goes unheard in community as it is fixed and constituted. Thinking of sense, or paying attention to sense, brings us towards the fact that abandonment is at the heart of community: any 'common' is at once present and fragmented. The community, like law, is no*thing*. The only possibility of justice, therefore, is 'the exposition of finitude and abandonment in community' (Pryor 2004, 274). So long as our thinking of community is concerned with establishing definitions and borders to identify, name and solidify experience and presence, then justice is definitively incapacitated. In place of a universalising claim for law or the opposite denial of law, 'we are then left with a radiant paradox: the *law guarantees the outlaw*, it guarantees the exception to the exception; indeed it becomes their condition of possibility' (Leung 2015). The task here, therefore, is not to make law 'differently', but to expose and resist the totalising presence of law where law is posited and problematised as if it were an absolute and total authority intertwined with the nation-state and market (neoliberalisation). Law maintains 'eco' where it assumes a relationship with sociality, originary and presence. The challenge is not to lose sight of law as a regulatory limit that articulates the definition of an ecosociality, all the while maintaining eco as that which escapes. Again, this is what defines law as incalculable, incommensurable: it is both a movement and a fixed limit. Law is furthermore incommensurable with being defined as some*thing* just as our sociality is incommensurable with the singular, the singularity, of plurality of being. The radiant paradox of law, if it grapples with a process of sociality as ex-istence rather than assuming law is fixed or stagnant (either in its notion of justice or regulation), subverts the false contingency where law occupies a total presence as a predetermined authority mediated through the structure of the nation-state and citizenship, or through extra-national, post-national governance.

Structural violence and with it the politics of exhaustion is the condition of our times (Guild and Ansems de Vries 2018). Resisting the structures that reinforce current experiences of irregular migration and irregular labour can seem hopeless. To respond to this exhaustion, the ecotechnics of labour migration does not provide a formula for what *ought* to happen instead. Within ecotechnics, sense exceeds concretisation, suggesting that what is *happening* in the ecosociality of beings coming together in spite of, or because of, market forces happen (ex-ist) and carry a potential beyond the categories of critique. People are moving, they are working and relating. That this movement is not solely a movement capitalised by the market is difficult to retrieve from the 'trap of productivity' (Zbyszewska and Routh 2019, 262). Yet the potentiality in our existence as singular plural shifts towards valuing the *eco*sociality as a site for law. This is a shift that can be enacted through our writing and analysis. Such a shift, albeit anarchic in its potential,[8] opens onto possible difference away from the structural violence that defines our present.

References

Anghie, Antony. 2005, *Imperialism, Sovereignty and the Making of International Law*. Cambridge: Cambridge University Press.

Aristodemou, Maria. 2014, *Law, Psychoanalysis, Society*. Abington: Routledge.

BBC News. 2019, 'Supreme court: Suspending parliament was unlawful, judges rule' *BBC News* 24 September 2019 www.bbc.co.uk/news/uk-politics-49810261

Buchanan, Ruth and Sundhya Pahuja. 2004, 'Law, nation and (Imagined) international community' *Law/Text/Culture* vol. 8, pp. 137–167.

Butler, Judith. 1992, 'Contingent foundations: Feminism and the question of "postmodernism"' in *Feminist Theorise the Political*. Judith Butler and Joan W. Scott (eds), pp. 3–21. New York, London: Routledge.

Butler, Judith and Gayatri Chakravorty Spivak. 2007, *Who Sings the Nation-State?* New York, London, Calcutta: Seagull Books.

Campbell, Denis. 2019, 'Both labour and tory migration plans "would worsen NHS staffing"' *The Guardian* 4 December 2019, viewed 5 December 2019 www.guardian.co.uk

Columb, Seán. 2020, *Trading Life: Organ Trafficking, Illicit Networks and Exploitation*. Stanford: Stanford University Press.

Davies, Margaret. 2017, *Law Unlimited*. Oxon: Routledge.

DeGenova, Nicholas. 2002, 'Migrant "Illegality" and deportability in everyday life' *Annual Review of Anthropology* vol. 31, no. 1, pp. 419–447.

Derrida, Jacques. 2004, *On Touching – Jean-Luc Nancy*. trans., Christine Irizarry. Standford: Stanford University Press.

Derrida, Jacques. 1994, *Spectres of Marx*. trans., Peggy Kamuf. New York, London: Routledge.

Derrida, Jacques. 1992, 'Force of law: The metaphysical foundation of authority' in *Deconstruction and the Possibility of Justice*. Drucilla Cornell, Michel Rosenfeld and David Carlson (eds), pp. 3–67. New York: Routledge.

Dussel, Enrique. 2014, 'Anti-cartesian meditations: On the origin of the philosophical anti-discourse of modernity' *Journal for Culture and Religious Theory* vol. 13, no. 1, pp. 11–52.

Euronews. 2019, 'Sea watch captain Carola Rackete released by Italian Judge' *Euronews* 2 July 2019, viewed 28 September 2019 www.euronews.com/

Ford, Matt. 2019, 'Trump's war on the rule of law is reaching the breaking point' *New Republic* 9 April 2019, viewed 28 September 2019 https://newrepublic.com/

Forrester, Katrina. 2019, *In the Shadow of Justice*. Princeton, NJ: Princeton University Press.

8 What I mean by 'anarchic' will be developed further in Chapter 5. However, as a brief introduction, I refer to recent work on anarchist theory, such as *PostAnarchism* (Newman 2015) and *Changing Anarchism* (Purkis and Bowen eds 2012), where anarchic thinking 'calls for a repositioning of the individual within global flows and the need to respond to complex ethical and strategic problems' (Purkis and Bowen 2012, 5). This is a departure from classic traditions of anarchism that affirmed the individual in particular through individual freedom and liberty (Kropotkin, Proudhon). Thinking anarchically involves pluriversal thinking and is, by definition, open rather than prescriptive.

France 24. 2019, 'Exclusive interview: Carola Rackete Sea Watch 3 Capitain' *France 24* 24 September 2019, viewed 28 September 2019 www.france24.com/en/

Fritsch, Michael, Phillipe Lynes and David Wood. 2018, *Eco-Deconstruction: Derrida and Environmental Philosophy*. New York: Fordham University Press.

Guild, Elspeth and Leonie Ansems de Vries. 2018, 'Seeing refuge in Europe: Spaces of transit and the violence of migration management' *Journal of Ethnic and Migration Studies* vol. 45, no. 12, pp. 2156–2166.

Haberman, Maggie and Katie Rogers. 2019, 'Trump attacks whistle-blower's sources and alludes to punishment for spies' *New York Times* 26 September 2019, viewed 28 September 2019 www.nytimes.com

James, Ian. 2012, 'The just measure' in *Jean-Luc Nancy: Justice, Legality and World*. Benjamin Hutchens (ed), pp. 35–46. London, New York: Continuum.

Leung, Gilbert. 2015, 'Law' in *The Jean-Luc Nancy Dictionary*. Paul Gratton and Marie-Eve Morin (eds). Edinburgh: University of Edinburgh Press.

Lutz, Helma. 2017, 'Care as a fictitious commodity: Reflections on the intersections of migration, gender and care regimes' *Migration Studies* vol. 5, no. 3, pp. 356–368.

Marks, Susan. 2009, 'False contingency' *Current Legal Problems* vol 62, no. 1, pp. 1–21.

Marks, Susan. 2011, 'Human rights and root causes' *Modern Law Review* vol 74, no. 1, pp. 57–78.

Mignolo, Walter and Arturo Escobar (eds). 2010, *Globalisation and the Decolonial Option*. New York: Routledge.

Miller et al. 2018, 'New test case launched against Glasgow refugee evictions from Serco homes' *MSH Legal* 31 August 2018, viewed 28 September 2019 www.mshblegal.com/

Mueller, Benjamin. 2019, 'How labour's working-class vote crumbled and its nemesis won the vote' *The New York Times* 13 December 2019, viewed 16 December 2019 www.nytimes.com/

Mules, Warwick. 2006, 'Creativity, singularity and techné' *Angelaki* vol. 3, no. 1, pp. 83–84.

Nancy, Jean-Luc. 2008, *Corpus*. trans., Richard A. Rand. New York: Fordham University Press.

Nancy, Jean-Luc. 2003, *A Finite Thinking*. Simon Sparks (ed). Stanford: Stanford University Press.

Nancy, Jean-Luc. 2000, *Being Singular Plural*. trans., Robert Richardson and Anne O'Byrne. Stanford: Stanford University Press.

Nancy, Jean-Luc. 1997, *Sense of the World*. trans., Jeffrey S. Librett (1st edition 1993). Minnesota: University of Minnesota Press.

Nancy, Jean-Luc. 1993, *The Experience of Freedom*. trans., Bridget McDonald. Stanford: Stanford University Press.

Nancy, Jean-Luc. 1991, *The Inoperative Community*. Minnesota: University of Minnesota Press.

Newman, Saul. 2015, *Postanarchism*. Cambridge: Polity Press.

Pryor, Benjamin. 2004, 'Law in Abandon: Jean-Luc Nancy and the critical study of law' *Law and Critique* vol. 15, pp. 259–285.

Purkis, Jonathan and James Bowen (eds). 2012, *Changing Anarchism: Anarchist Theory and Practice*. Manchester: Manchester University Press.

Quijano, Aníbal. 2010, 'Coloniality and modernity/rationality' in *Globalisation and the Decolonial Option*. Walter Mignolo and Arturo Escobar (eds), pp. 22–32. New York: Routledge.

Quijano, Aníbal. 2007, 'Coloniality and modernity/rationality' *Cultural Studies* vol. 21, no. 2–3, pp. 168–178. doi:10.1080/09502380601164353

Rawls, John. 1999, *A Theory of Justice*. Cambridge, MA: Harvard University Press.
Savage, Charlie. 2019, 'The supeona and contempt fight between trump and congress, explained' *The New York Times* 2 May 2019, viewed 28 September 2019 www.nytimes.com/
SERCO. 2018, 'Statement by Serco on Asylum Seeker Accomodation in Glasgow' viewed 28 September 2019 www.serco.com/
Viveiros de Castro, Eduardo. 2004, 'Exchanging perspectives: The transformation of objects into subjects in Amerindian ontologies' *Common Knowledge* vol. 10, no. 3, pp. 463–484.
Wolf, Martin. 2019, 'The Brexit delusion of taking back control' *The Financial Times* 26 March 2019, viewed 15 December 2019 www.ft.com
Zbyszewska, Ania and Supriya Routh. 2019, 'Challenging labour law's 'productivity' bias through a feminist lens: A conversation' in *Theorising Labour Law in a Changing World*. Alysia Blackham, Miriam Kullmann and Ania Zbyszewska (eds), pp. 245–264. Oxford: Hart Publishing.

5 Home/nation

Eco/techne

Migration discourses, immigration laws and policies, and labour/employment laws emerge from specific onto-epistemological foundations. The European, (neo)liberal, ego-logical conceptualisation of being and knowledge has shaped modern law and legal categories, such that these laws and categories seem normal, if not natural (see Chapter 3, Marks 2009; Dussel 2014). Illuminating labour migration law as ecotechnics, however, deconstructs these discourses and categories to open onto the simultaneous circulation of capital and sense within 'irregular' migration and precarious labour. That 'the world is ecotechnical' suggests that the techne, technologisation and technique, of the world is only possible because of that which exceeds it: *eco*, our dwelling, our sense of being, of home. This does not mean that 'eco' is completely technologised, but neither is it separate from the circulation of technologies, capital progress and accumulation, that concretise sense of being into normative categories. As such, the migrant is not external to sociality, nor to the nation-state; the precarious labourer is not external to employment law, nor to work and the labour market; law, as an aspiration, as rules and order, is not external to capital, power, nor the pursuit of justice within a sociality. All of this is our world, and our world is ecotechnical.

Our modern legal system is embedded in the nation-state and vice versa. While modern law privileges the rational, autonomous individual (contracting party), the nation-state creates and enables legal subjectivity. Neoliberalism and processes of neoliberalisation define a particular co-dependence of the nation-state and the globalised economic market, a system supported and facilitated by the modern legal system. This system ostensibly provides us, beings, with identity and our participation is valued through economic productivity (output/labour) and consumerism/consumption. Yet the categories and constructs bolstering the nation-state and law towards the function of a neoliberal economic system prevent us from thinking of what we already have in, and as, originary sociality. Originary sociality is what is happening in, around, because of and in spite of, predetermined categories. Originary sociality is law creating, as the elemental manifestation of being singular plural. In other words, *eco*, that which escapes signification in ecotechnics, is the *sense* that circulates as the possibility of sociality. This eco is difficult to pin down, and perhaps consequently, receives less attention than techne. Of course, it is difficult to discuss 'that which escapes signification'. Nevertheless, peeling away the constructedness of categories founded in modern ego-logics and the neoliberalised nation-state (ostensibly existing in a 'global' market that prescribes value according to capital gain), we open onto ecotechnics. Giving weight to 'eco' (as in *oikos*: dwelling, ecology) we conceptually depart from the primacy of, and obsession with, the market economy, ostensibly global and embedded in the nation-state. Paying attention to eco, not at the expense of techne, reveals a revivified, pluriversal (rather than universal) onto-epistemology. Through this eco-lens, society, being (working, moving, coming together as singular plural beings), and thus, economy and/as ecology, can be – must be – conceptualised differently.

Thinking of eco leads us to question what is our dwelling, our existence, in plurality? Not in the metaphysical sense, but rather, what is the actual, practical ecology of our ecotechnical world? This question leads us to think, critique and analyse the nation-state not as an institutional regime but as a form laying claim to home and to a sense of being together. This sense has been technologised as belonging in a nation-state. Home, deconstructed, brings us to consider what it is that we have in common: indeed, 'our' ecology. The foremost political, economic and social challenges of our present era are the 'crises' of labour and migration, but also ecology and the climate. While it may at first seem tenuous to connect the ecotechnics of labour migration with ecology, if our world is ecotechnical, and our world – as people labouring and moving – is rethought from the very basis of our being singular plural as *eco*, then our world (labour migration law included) is our ecology.

This chapter considers what is prohibiting, or obstructing, openness to eco. I do this by interrogating the tenacity of the nation-state as an ideology and as an imagined foundation. My drawing attention to 'eco' is not to deny the technologisation that happens, but existing critiques and debates often circulate within the techne at the expense of giving attention to the potentiality within the sense of how we dwell (eco). Hereafter eco is given weight (not form) by being thought of as an openness to originary sociality, a sociality of being singular plural that precedes determination and signification. Focusing on the nexus of ideas of law, home and hospitality, ecotechnics presents a challenge to the fallacy of the nation as a place of belonging and, as discussed later, home.

Protectionist migration discourses and limited employment protection manifest a belief that community, nationhood and citizenship need to be contained and maintained. The fear of losing a sense of national identity bolsters normative laws that configure the autonomous, economically active individual as the key constituent of the state. This ultimately encourages the social, political and legal exclusion of those rendered less desirable or less valuable; that is, expendable. The ecotechnics of migration and labour reveal the circulation of predetermined categories that facilitate capital accumulation built on the differentiation of 'Good' citizens versus 'Failed' or 'not-quite' citizens. Simultaneously globalisation claims totalising identities under the pretence of shared being. Yet this supposed shared being in a 'global' or 'cosmopolitan' conceptualisation has no ground but for a return to (or reaffirmation of) the nation-state. Meanwhile, beings relate as singular plural in excess of all such categories/titles. The *eco* of being, the circulation of sense as the world creating itself, continues no matter what distinctions and exclusions are enforced through terminology.

The first section of this chapter will look at the nation-state, nationalism and the idea of law, including two 'alternatives' to the nation-state: Dauvergne's rule of law unhinged from the nation-state, and Benhabib's cosmopolitan citizenship. In particular, notions of universalism, cosmopolitanism and hospitality will be interrogated. The next section discusses the idea of home and hospitality as an aspiration of the nation, following onto the third section, which continues the deconstruction of this aspiration by revisiting the idea of community or common in sociality, drawing on feminist, decolonial and post-anarchist scholarship to explore what exceeds being technologised into 'nation' or 'community'. Eco*sociality*, as the 'dwelling in common', is used in this chapter to refer to this sociality that is the sense emergent through the circulation of sense in ecotechnics. Ecosociality is not a term to replace ecotechnics. Rather, ecosociality aids us to rethink the craft of dwelling through sociality. Through rethinking, constant questioning, we open onto an anarchic onto-epistemology, a creative presence, responsive to the singular plural, where singularities are not limited to human, animal or even living beings, but everything that circulates in our ecology, creating world.

Ecotechnics, the nation-state and law

The current actions of migration and labour, of people moving across territorial borders and the widespread precaritisation of work, unravels the mythologies of nation-state and nationhood. In the European Union (EU), European nationalist parties (ironically) share a common goal of protectionism by being 'anti-immigrant', manifest as 'ethnonationalist xenophobia' (Rydgern 2018, 2). The irony of their shared attempts at distinctiveness suggest that they seek consensus within a European nation-state system while explicitly being anti-Union. Leading European right-wing nationalist political parties include Le Front National – France; UKIP – UK; Legal Nord – Italy; Fidesz-Christian Democratic Party – Hungary; Vox – Spain; Freedom Party of Austria; Law and Justice – Poland; Progress Party – Norway; and Alternative for Germany (although without seats in Parliament, said to be gaining popularity in late 2019). Reinforcing ethnonationalist identities, as opposed to civic nationalism (Bar-On in Rydgern 2018, 22), these parties together rally against a 'migrant' threat. More particularly, they protest the spectre of Islam ostensibly challenging an (archaic) idea of pure European Christianity, otherwise assumed to be pure Europeanness (Rydgern 2018). But what are these political parties, and the movements supporting them, protecting? Nationalist protectionism in the twenty-first century does not secure a country's economic success and growth: migrant labour is vital for 'domestic' economies to thrive in the twenty-first century globalised financial economic system. Rhetorically boasting of restoring an authentic, ethnic community in the face of resented institutional (liberal, bureaucratic, secular) elitism, European nationalist political parties' champion nostalgic myths of ethnicity and illusions of racial and religious homogeneity (Gilroy 2019; Rydgern 2018, 1). Yet the European project itself, as currently embodied in the European Union, builds upon historically intertwined nationalities and diverse, intermixed, peoples on the territory of Europe. Thus, the perceived current crisis facing European countries – international migration threatening national integrity, including job security – can only garner incongruent responses.[1] The rallying of nationalist fervour is furthermore troubling where nationalist parties simultaneously cut social services and state support by waging war on bureaucracy ('political establishment') and the institutional, liberal democratic process, with a disregard for both citizen and non-citizen populations (Krastev 2017).

The emotionally charged political performances proclaiming national identity consequently reaffirm the only 'ground' epistemically available: the nation. The fallacy of the nation as a site of a 'common' to be reinforced against 'migrants' emboldens political actors and their supporters to oppose persons considered 'irregular' or foreign. The emotion that fuels the idea of distinct nationhood springs from a need that is more intrinsic than the desire for a homogeneous community. This passion interwoven with anti-globalisation sentiment harkens back to a mythical, pure state of being through genuine (ethnic, origin-based) belonging. Meanwhile, the twenty-first century nation-state is a cyclical ideology that promises such belonging while demanding fragmentation, individualism and atomised identity to pursue the accumulation of capital for the sake of the nation, even though capital exceeds the nation (through processes of neoliberalisation see Peck and Theodore 2019; Peck 2013). Within this complex system, the nation-state ideal is offered as the normal, natural and solitary possibility. The nation-state fictitiously binds beings into a fallacy of belonging and collectivity, as if claiming a home – a proper space of belonging – were possible. Where capitalism is without ground and the 'global' is nonsensical, or at least difficult to comprehend, retreating to familiar categories and identities reaffirms a

1 Is it the idea of a white, Christian Europe they are 'saving'? Is it distinct nationalities: Italy for Italians, Austria for Austrians, Finland for the Finns, Britain for Brits? Who are these true patriots when Italy has only existed as a nation since 1861, Austria emphasises German language skills as a prerequisite to state support, ethic Finnish settlements extend across northern Russia, and the descendants of true Britons can only be found in Wales, Cornwall and Brittany (France)?

fantastical foundation. Thus, ethnonationalism's appeal to a pure belonging in nation, culture and identity has found currency in the twenty-first century. The familiar enemy in the 'migrant' (in particular, where this migrant body is black and Muslim) have historically threatened an ostensibly Christian Europe (Kallis 2018). Rhetorically aspiring towards reclaiming 'nation' as a secure, predictable home offers a ground for, and resolution to, the precarity people are experiencing.

Capital circulation benefits from, and is sustained by, the suspended, or limited, subjectivity of labourers (cheap, deregulated labour). Ironically, these are the very bodies nationalism ostensibly protects itself against. While the 'nation' proclaims inclusive belonging for citizens, its viability in globalised economic markets is contingent on the fragmentation of the persons physically present, albeit included as excluded. Normative legal categories embedded in the nation-state threaten failure for anyone who slips out of line (Anderson 2013). Furthermore, a globalised world is, essentially, 'anti-world' rendering any opening ('eco') as an opening onto a marketplace, immediately already technologised as capital accumulation. Indeed, global capital circulation navigates the nation-state, but on a larger scale with access to a larger supply of 'irregular' labourers in suspended subjectivity (Cheah 2009, 90). Meanwhile, 'migrant' 'irregular' bodies give nationalist movements a figure to demonise and exclude, while bolstering the imagined gravity (Fitzpatrick 2008, 71) or 'heft' (Macklin 2007) of citizenship. These migration discourses, and the panic they elicit, obscure the mechanisms of capital that condition exploitation, social fragmentation and ecological destruction for all beings, no matter who is considered a citizen and who is considered a foreigner. Thus, while the aspirations of the nation that are manifest through populist nationalist movements can appear to be incongruent with the aspirations of global capital through neoliberalisation, the differentiation reinforced by ethno-nationalism ensures a supply of precarious labour. The cheap labour garnered from workers 'willing to work for less' supports a downward pressure on wages that benefits short-term capital accumulation on a 'global' scale. This is a labour supply that, by their exclusion from the nation (either in legal status or exclusion from the 'community of value' as discussed in Chapter 2), are not deemed worthy of protection. Hence, their labour remains cheap and exploitable – 'willing' being their only option to gain work. Labour needs to be irregular in order to be cheap, thus nationalism's selective recognition, or privilege, coexists with and indeed facilitates neoliberalism's pursuit of deregulated work.

The radicalisation and mobilisation of ethnonationalism in Europe, and around the world, is all the more complicit with the globalisation of finance and commodities (global economic market) when we consider how labour migration within Europe and beyond is not a new phenomenon. In what is now the UK, since the fifteenth and sixteenth centuries peasant populations were contained through 'compulsory service' and vagrancy laws that controlled migration – migration that was caused by dislocation due to changes in land ownership through processes of land-grabbing and enclosures (Anderson 2013, 15, 23). Colonial expansion gathered labourers, acquired land, and set about 'civilising' and 'modernising' peasant populations. The labour migration that took place 'internationally' (i.e. away from Europe) was the movement of settlers, colonisers, slaves for cheap manual labour, and the expansion of colonial authority via governance by landowners and representatives of colonial governments (Gilroy 2019, 2004). Beginning in the sixteenth century, but continuing well into the nineteenth century, rural to urban labour migration and industrialisation shaped the regulation of movement and mobility within and across territories. The technology of work in expanding urban settlements was furthermore enabled by colonial expansion and imperialism, resource extraction and the centralisation of labour.

Leaping to the twentieth century, labour migration, particularly in Europe and North America, was defined by persons fleeing violence (war) and the need for cheap labour to rebuild post-war economies. Post-war re-industrialisation depended on labour, while the consolidation of nation-states was needed to maintain control over populations and borders to reinforce the authoritative power of the nation-state within the 'international' (see Sassen 2008, 15, 138). A double movement reinforced the nation-state and bounded citizenship to facilitate a social welfare state at the same time that post-war dislocation meant that people were not only in motion (refugees, displaced persons) but in demand as post-war labourers. Moreover, post-colonial movements in former European colonies facilitated more migration within the Commonwealth, for example, for labour, education and resettlement opportunities. The Windrush Generation in the UK is an example of this migration (Hall 1998). In the twenty-first century, violence again has caused profound international displacement as people flee war, poverty, profound climate and environmental changes, causing a lack of possibilities to secure their livelihoods. Environmental disasters and climate changes have compelled people to flee to other territories and countries, where fires, rising sea levels, tsunamis, hurricanes, earthquakes and volcanoes have made their homes inhabitable. This migration conflicts with the protectionist impulse to keep populations bounded, such that only citizens (nationals) have access to a nation-state and thereby the laws, jobs and, in cases where such a system exists, social welfare protection from the state. While it may seem that nationalism and xenophobia contradict a continuing demand for cheap labour, increasingly the technologisation of goods and services allows for cheap labour to be found 'off-shore', outsourced away from workers recognised to have a physical presence in the nation-state – both literally and figuratively (see Chapter 3). Political and media discourses focus on anti-immigration movements, migration pressures including the need to open borders for humanitarian reasons. Cheap labour, however, is made invisible, both through technological means (internet communication and mobility) and disenfranchised local populations whose labour is made, and kept, invisible.

The presence of people, beings and bodies, working and moving across and against the confines of the nation-state and legal categories is ecotechnical. Yet the nation-state organising people coming together, moreover the nation-state understood through classical notions of *demos* and *polis*, is not originary sociality, or sense, in the way that I have understood and explored ecotechnics. There is little creativity where belonging is predetermined within an imagined, albeit carefully controlled and constructed, state. In spite of the artificial construction of borders and territory, immigration laws and policies, employment law, social welfare regulations and criminalisation of poverty are examples of the very real control that is exercised by governments onto the people – their lives and bodies – within a designated territory. Nevertheless, the circulation of sense happens in spite of the market, formal citizenship and legal (state) recognition. In short, sociality happens in spite of, not because of, the nation-state and its borders, laws and designations.

The nation-state and its legal system do not form the 'eco' of ecotechnics. But vitally, eco is not a 'thing' that can 'be' formed. Understanding ecotechnics starts from 'everydayness' instead of abstract thought (Devisch 2013, 116). While eco is the home and belonging that the nation-state lays claim to and law ostensibly arbitrates (eco-nomos), eco always escapes techne by 'render[ing] inoperative every appeal to an authentic original togetherness' (Devisch 2013, 116). Ecotechnics exposes the awkward and insufficient techne of a normative 'return' to the 'proper', as in the nation-state through citizenship and national belonging. Such a normative return, as if circulation had a starting or end point, has been explored by Berlant as a cruel optimism (Olusoga 2019; Berlant 2011). Indeed, the hope that order will be restored for a 'citizen', or if a non-citizen migrant gains legal status, is doomed to disappoint. Ecotechnics reveals that there is no restoration possible, only creation from the singular plural. Thus, ecotechnics discloses an 'ecology of unhomliness' (Philippopoulos-Mihalopoulos 2011, 7). The fallacy of the nation, together with its embeddedness with neoliberalisation and capital progress, is exposed when we observe beings together in the world, as the world. The *unhomliness* does not aim to align us to a pure nature; the purity imagined by Enlightenment thinkers (in particular, Kant) does not exist either in modernity or in nature. Ecology is messy and disorderly, as is life. Unaligned, chaotic, transgressive: this is the *economos*, law of dwelling, law of home.

As discussed in Chapter 1, originary sociality does not refer to a chronological 'origin' or an original togetherness that can be found in the traditions of a nation. Instead, originary sociality is what is *happening*: the coming together of our bodies as bodies that function, work, create, and reproduce. Bodies are co-originary with sense, because they are happening. Bodies (human, animal, nature) tangibly enact being in relation to juridical and existential law (see Chapter 4). Which is why when the material practices of being come up against juridical law, in other words when the law denies recognition or subjectivity, for example to 'illegal' migrants (see Chapter 2), or criminalises actions attempting to save life such as Sea Watch 3 (see Chapter 4), then the law is tracing the limit of constructed, predetermined sociality, not the sociality of beings in the plural happening here and now.

Law-as-wedded to the nation-state is not a law that responds to sociality since the nation-state is a fallacy built on an attempt to make a foundation for being and identity when no ground exists. Existence, as that which exceeds signification in techne, is precisely un-grounded. Therefore, the law-as-wedded to the nation-state could even be considered not as law, but an ideologically specific system of order and control. Or, if considered as law, this law is then only one possibility for law's existence, among many. Such a critical perspective on law is not unique. Legal pluralism as well as deeper, more creative critical questions exploring law's multiplicity and pervasiveness have constituted a subfield in critical legal studies and socio-legal studies (see Davies 2017; see also 'lawscapes' Philippopoulos-Mihalopoulos 2014). While the dominant interpretation of law within classical Anglo-American-European jurisprudence is that law is a system of rules embedded in the nation-state, critiques of law as quasi-theological (Fitzpatrick 2008), plural and social (Darian Smith 2013) or atmospheric (Philippopoulos-Mihalopoulos 2014) continue to challenge traditional jurisprudential thought. Joining authors who push their legal critique to shift onto-epistemological paradigms of thought by engaging interdisciplinary and embodied thought (Philippopoulos-Mihalopoulos currently being a creative and prolific example), I remain cautious of what has now become a mainstream 'critical analyses of law' and proposals of legal alternatives (as opposed to alternative legal thinking, see de Sousa Santos 2014). Critical analyses of law that ultimately stay within 'the law' as a thing, a form to be attained or achieved *better*, reaffirm a persistent belief in law's potential ability to provide resolution: to provide a ground. Especially in migration scholarship that imagines citizenship beyond the nation-state, such as a world without borders, alternatives intended to transform the international 'global' space and its relationship to migration and labour can nevertheless reinforce law as an ends meant to provide a resolution to the struggle.

I will now consider two proposed theories that present alternatives to illustrate this further: Catherine Dauvergne's unhinging the rule of law from the nation-state, and Seyla Behabib's cosmopolitan citizenship.

Unhinging the nation-state

In response to protectionist and restrictive immigration laws and policies, Dauvergne (2008) suggests unhinging the law from the nation-state. This, Dauvergne argues, would allow the law and the legal form (the rule of law) to operate independent of the state. Citizenship, as a measure of membership in a territorially defined political community, would lose its claim to identify and differentiate legal subjects. Rights and accountability would be juridical and international (Dauvergne 2008, 169–190). Dauvergne (2008) develops this proposal in light of the 'global crackdown on extra-legal migration' (2) in response to the perceived loss of control of states over policy initiatives. This perceived loss of control has only increased into the 2010s with the 'migration/refugee crisis' and Brexit questioning the power of European Union regulations over national domestic laws. States derive power from 'the global' to organise identity and economic production. If the state is no longer the arbitrator of one's legal subjectivity, as Dauvergne suggests, then one could be a 'global citizen' without membership in a particular nation-state. But one would still have rights, particularly labour rights, protected similar to what other scholars have referred to as cosmopolitan citizenship, discussed later. This protection, Dauvergne argues, would prevent the ongoing situation where illegality is created in part by a lack of comprehensive migration policy and a widespread lack of implementation of refugee protocol commitments. However, in spite of her awareness that international governance is hierarchical and hegemonic, Dauvergne's alternative reaffirms traditional frameworks of a hierarchical law, albeit disembedded from the nation-state.

By placing faith in an extra-national law, Dauvergne assumes that law is some*thing* that can exist apart from the nation-state. The faith in this some*thing* of law suggests law can be used as an extra-national power to govern or contain human interaction and sociality, namely labour. Dauvergne contends that if migration laws were international, they would allow for equality amongst nations and their citizens, as well as those excluded from citizenship. Accordingly, she purports that globalisation opens onto the rule of law's emancipatory potential where law, unhinged from the nation-state, holds the capacity to include the excluded (Dauvergne 2008, 175, 181). Yet such a commitment to the rule of law as a potential to mediate migrants internationally fails to problematise historical exclusions within the practice of law, including the evident financial benefit of a legally excluded labour force. Notwithstanding the limits of the rule of law as a concept (see Bix 2006). Furthermore, Dauvergne does not consider that the 'international' itself is based on the hierarchical arrangement of sovereign power that relies on the membership of citizens organised into a nation-state. Those who speak in the name of the international have the power to dictate the terms and conditions and to subject others to their authority, within a statist regime. What is more, power in the 'international' reaffirms nation and citizenship as privileged belonging (Dussel 2014; Butler and Chakravorty Spivak 2007; Anghie 2005). Thus while 'unhinging law and the nation-state' would conceptually shift the boundaries of migration law as a legal practice, the question of where to locate legitimacy remains (Dauvergne 2008, 183). While legitimacy does not need to be found in the nation-state, if law is the tracing of the limit and not an entity or governing body itself then the tracing must reconstitute the sociality based on who (bodies, beings) is participating in the sociality.

In order for the law, the tracing, to depart from the existing statist order a profound re-examination of sociality is necessary. Sociality understood as what is happening, existing, and not what is legally sanctioned, or formally recognised as happening. The previous chapter referred to the actions of Carole Rackete and Sea Watch 3 rescue in the Mediterranean Sea in July 2019. Following Rackete's actions, the *Guardian, New York Times* and other news outlets featured stories and interviews with other individuals who, fully aware of the restrictions and risks that ultimately their actions would be deemed illegal, were actively supporting and assisting migrants to the shores of Italy, into U.S. territory and providing housing, safe passage and assistance in France, Greece, and the U.S.[2] The actions in support of non-citizens (migrants) suggest that unlike more complex indicators such as electoral polling and attending rallies, the daily lives of persons coming together are affected not only towards violence and exclusion, but relationships of support and even care. In spite of institutional refusal to sanction these emergent sites of sociality, they persist in happening. These socialities are engaged, existing, relationships that illustrate the freedom that people have, not the freedom they wait to be granted from an external law (see Newman 2015).

An alternative law found in un-hinging from nation-state sovereignty does not pursue the question of law and sociality at a foundational level. Therefore, Dauvergne's proposal continues to be based within a framework that reaffirms a faith in the ability of law to withstand separation from the nation-state by being some*thing* independent (Dauvergne 2008, 188). Dauvergne presupposes law as a *thing* that, when instrumentalised in the nation-state or by some supranational legitimacy, grounds sociality. Yet sociality happens. Moreover, sociality is captured and constructed by both law (embedded in the nation-state) and the market. Law orders sociality; it does not produce it. While it is conceivable that the law and jurisprudence would manifest justice and order differently if these concepts were not embedded in the nation-state, market (capital) forces guide recognition and legal subjectivity through eco-nomos/ economics – which conceivably would continue in spite of the nation-state. The significant presence of the global market economic system cannot be ignored for the sake of theorising an emancipatory potential of law. While some rights may be recognised, as Chapters 2 and 3 demonstrated through the cases of Miss Hounga,

2 The examples of socialities emerging in spite of, perhaps because of, the technologisaton of border controls, anti-immigration and migration discourses include Sicilian fishermen risking prison to rescue migrants (Tondo 2019); MSF resuming operations in the Mediterranean Sea in spite of continuing attacks from European states (von der Burchard 2019); a French farmer who helped migrants was recognised by the court as showing 'fraternity' (Clarisse 2018); a community group, No More Deaths, in Arizona have been volunteering for over 15 years providing water and rescue for people attempting to cross the border, risking prosecution and jail (Jordan 2019); and retirees (physicians, nurses and others) working in convents and monasteries providing shelter, emergency medical care, clothing and food for migrants travelling across the U.S. (Jordan 2019b). Sea Watch and Carole Rackete, among others (see Mediterranearescue.org), acting in contravention of orders from European states are a further example of this.

Ms Taiwo, Ms Onu and Ms Reyes, subjectivity is forever incomplete for those whose limited subjectivity is sought from within the techne of capital that ultimately benefits from their 'irregularity'.

Cosmopolitan citizenship

A second proposed alternative of radical transformation of the international in its relationship to migration and labour deemed irregular, is Seyla Benhabib's disaggregated or cosmopolitan citizenship. Benhabib (2006) explores the notion of cosmopolitan citizenship in the context of calls for distributive justice. She refers to a Kantian notion of cosmopolitanism (Kant 1795). According to Kant's design of cosmopolitan citizenship, foreigners have a right to membership and to be naturalised in a given territory. From this, Benhabib proposes a 'discourse-ethical standpoint' where the sovereign of a democratic nation decides between the principle of rights and a schedule of rights in order to best address the needs of the population they oversee (Benhabib 2006, 18). Such a cosmopolitanism is a 'philosophical project of mediations' (Benhabib 2006, 21). Benhabib has faith that the twenty-first century is characterised by the emergence of cosmopolitan norms, norms that are supported by moral justifications for modern attributes, such as territorial borders and political membership. While proposing to challenge existing frames of recognition and citizenship Benhabib's theory nevertheless reaffirms citizenship-as-belonging, albeit citizenship on a larger scale that moves beyond the bounded territory of the nation-state.

Conceptually, the paradigm of the nation-state, as central to recognition, is not disentangled from ideas of citizenship and membership in a universal community. The paradigm remains. Moreover, the suggestion that a cosmopolitan *proper* exists somewhere, external to the nation, has elsewhere been referred to as a proto-political community (Lindahl 2009). The belief in a proto-political community expounds the myth of a cosmopolitan citizen who is not granted membership in the nation-state, yet still finds belonging in the universal. However, in this theoretical construction, again, no consideration is given to capital accumulation or the labour market economy. The 'cruel optimism' (Berlant 2011) underpinning notions of cosmopolitanism and cosmopolitan citizenship denies the practical inefficacy and continuing epistemological hegemony of universal 'globality', e.g. the ostensibly global, ostensibly inclusive, community.

While Benhabib does imagine beyond the limits of the nation-state, citizenship remains the ultimate goal and symbol of *individual* identity and belonging. A similar belief in the importance of citizenship is reflected in proposals for the regularisation or legalisation of statuses (Cholewinski 2009). Undeniably in the immediate short-term, being granted citizenship where one otherwise is an undocumented migrant is beneficial to reduce the immediate threat of deportation. However, as the previous chapters have demonstrated, citizenship does not lead to a panacea of rights and privilege. At the intersection of migration and labour, the normalisation of precarious working conditions and situations such as 'in-work poverty', evidence that legal status and formal citizenship do not remedy sub-citizenship or subjugated, precarious employment (JRF 2019; Barnard 2018). 'Irregular' status and precarious work, as cheap and deregulated, continue to benefit the market economic system and for this reason it is not in the interest of capital to remedy exploitative systems (i.e. labour and migration laws). Cosmopolitanism allows for the perpetuation of a myth that persons can be denied the privilege of citizenship under the assumption that their 'exclusion' from the 'community of value' will be included in the proto-political community (cosmopolitan, international human rights regime). This is similar to the belief that somewhere, somehow, the law will provide. Indeed, the international is still ordered through citizenship, for example the treatment of migrants across the world and the choice of nations to ignore the international refugee convention principle of non-refoulement, increasingly with impunity (see EU-Turkey Joint Agreement, discussed in Columb 2020). Meanwhile, the predetermined 'international' community, like the nation, is unresponsive to the originary sociality of beings, cosmopolitan or otherwise. Evidently, to exist is not enough; one needs legal status and economic value to belong in *the* community.

Benhabib's cosmopolitanism, in spite of claiming to be open for everyone – all humanity under a cosmopolitan citizenship – remains rooted in the structure of the modern nation-state as the mediator of rights and granter of status to the individual. Cosmopolitan citizenship, or as referred to by Benhabib, 'disaggregated' citizenship, obscures how the purported exclusion of some, at the boundary of the nation-state, forms and gives identity to one bounded nation-state against another bounded nation-state. The citizen is recognised in contrast to the non-citizen in the international order. In the 'international' order there is no space for the 'non-citizen', or stateless person. Claims of cosmopolitan citizenship elide the actual experience of being excluded inside, of sub-citizenship and marginalisation within the system of the nation-state. Within the nation-state, immigration and labour laws are used to manage and regulate the movement and rights of individuals. Some persons are marginalised into unofficial situations of sub-citizenship or simply not given the power to speak as subjects in spite of their labour contributing to capital accumulation. In the face of globalised economic markets and labour mobility 'citizenship is an aspiration to persist' (Dauvergne 2008) in the nation-state: an aspiration to persist as a recognised subject in the limited, hegemonic, techne of being within a particular paradigm of recognition. The techne being the legal ordering which, in spite of proclaiming universality and globalism, produces and reinforces spheres of inclusion, exclusion and exploitation.

In response to concerns for the recognition and protection of migrants' rights, scholars beyond Benhabib have explored the potential for denationalised, or post-national, citizenship. The EU, and within this the idea of a European community, was one such an imagined haven of post-national citizenship (Soysal 1994). It is through this potential that Benhabib argues that legal recognition (rights) should not rely on national citizenship, but on citizenship as a global, cosmopolitan belonging. Using the EU as her primary point of reference, Benhabib proposes that a discourse-ethical standpoint, recommended as a perspective for Europe, is a double gesture that extends itself beyond itself and thus has the potential to include those excluded. Benhabib uses the language of hospitality to describe the 'mediation between the ethical and the moral, the moral and the political' (Benhabib 2006, 158). However, her distinction of ethical, moral and political implies a normative standard that new claims for membership need to meet and satisfy before they can be validated or included (Honig in Benhabib 2006, 110). Benhabib again reaffirms a faith in a universality as a principle from which claims are judged. This implies an overarching logic that conditions the categories, or limits, of the universal. The foreigner, or the one labelled as a migrant, is always 'marked as particularly in relation to European universality' (Honig in Benhabib et al. 2006, 110). Rights claims concern the foreigner's relationship to the fixed universal encompassed in the myth of the EU. 'They' are foreign to 'us', the international, universal European. While the European Union may represent success for the inclusion of some through its supranational citizenship-potential, Benhabib's claim that it represents a 'remarkable evolution of hospitality' (Benhabib 2006, 36) or a new type of transferrable, post-national cosmopolitanism denies the present realities of persons, citizens and non-citizens, relegated by a nation-state-centric legal governance regime to legal grey areas. EU projects fund the reinforcement of Fortress Europe, including FRONTEX border control and Association Agreements with EU border countries, such as Turkey, Ukraine and Libya (see Statewatch 2019). These projects and international agreements aim to maintain the sanctity of Europe by keeping undesirable, so-called non-Europeans (black, non-Christian, migrants) out, or at least without claim to European citizenship (Guild and Ansems de Vries 2018).

It is, moreover, ironic that the EU is used as an example of post-national citizenship: the European Union was not designed to transcend the nation. The EU is an economically and socially motivated union of separate sovereign nation-states. According to Jacqueline Bhaba, already in 1998 it was evident that

> the concept of European Union citizenship, designed in part to address the rights deficit within Europe, has not so far created a base of fundamental rights capable of trumping state interests. Instead, EU citizenship functions primarily as an exclusionary concept directed against non-Europeans.
>
> (Bhaba 1998)

The EU is defined by its exclusionary border, in spite of the inclusion of rights provisions within the Lisbon Treaty for those *inside* the Union. It is the

European Court of Human Rights (ECtHR) under the Council of Europe that recognises legally admitted visitors and/or residents and allows claims to be brought forth to the European Court, for example *Siliadin v. France* and *CN v UK* (see Chapter 2). The ill treatment of 'irregular' migrants at work can be held to be in contravention to the ECHR, specifically article 3 prohibiting torture, degrading or inhumane treatment, and article 4 prohibiting slavery, servitude, forced or compulsory labour (ECHR 2010). However, these provisions do not easily extend to cases where one is without legal status or when residency and/or employment are insecure within the EU (again, see *Siliadin*). The external borders of the EU are constituted such that if one is not a Union citizen then EU hospitality and disaggregated citizenship, as celebrated by Benhabib, is of little practical consequence.

In spite of the supranational economic structure of the EU and provision for the freedom of movement, citizenship in the EU is regulated by individual nation-states through unique processes of naturalisation and national immigration laws. EU citizenship enables mobility and labour rights within EU nations signed onto the Schengen agreement as of 2004 the Directive on the right to move freely (European Parliament 2004). However, persons deemed undesirable, predominantly but not exclusively non-citizen with precarious legal status, can be removed in spite of their work and residence. For example, in 2010 there was a broad, legally sanctioned expulsion of Roma workers (EU nationals) that were deemed to be in France 'illegally' (Cahn and Guild 2010). The European community's decision to cease funding the Italian *mare nostrum* programme in 2014 further exemplified the limit of European hospitality and the stark lack of recognition of the humanity of persons beyond European citizens.[3] In 2015, the ongoing criticism of Greek and Italian immigration controls revealed the policing of Europe's external borders, particularly at the border with North Africa, encouraged the outright refusal of refugee claims and the containment of persons in camps akin to prisons (Trilling 2018). In 2016, the EU-Turkey Joint Action Plan illustrated the refusal of European countries to open onto a hospitable, humane, welcome of migrants desperate to flee violence in Syria, Afghanistan, Yemen and North Africa (Somalia, Sudan, Eritrea and Ethiopia). In June of 2019, the arrest and subsequent acquittal of Carole Rackete illustrated the Italian government's refusal to allow boats to dock on Italian (EU) shores, such that they threatened legal action against any who assisted non–EU citizens to gain 'illegal' access to Italian territory. Statewatch Observatory continues to monitor the actions by European governments prohibiting, or failure to act in support of, migrants and asylum seekers seeking to enter European territory (Statewatch 2019).

3 European nations pride themselves on the 'universal' protection of human rights, through the ECHR (European Council of Refugees and Exiles 2014).

Universalism, cosmopolitanism and hospitality

Neither Dauvergne nor Benhabib's alternative proposals take into account the experiences of people moving across territorial borders to participate in labour markets, formally and informally. Consequently, theories of 'unhinging the nation-state' and 'cosmopolitan or disaggregate citizenship' fall short of interrogating the limits of universalism and hospitality that are experienced by those who are relegated to legal grey areas or sub-citizenship, yet still undeniably part of the *ecotechne* of capital accumulation. Universalism refers to a foundation, which contradicts its ability to be universal. A claim to universalism implies overcoming statism and notions of citizenship. Claiming universalism would mean opening up to, or abandoning ourselves to, a void; a void which cannot but be, literally, universal (Kirkby in Fritsch et al. 2018, 230). The claim to universalism, however, is itself 'far from empty; rather it is flush with yearning for innumerable possibilities/imaginings of what was, could be, might yet have been, all coexisting' (Fritsch et al. 2018, 232). Until a conceptual, paradigmatic leap is made to be *un*-comprehending of the universal as a void – but one that holds all possibilities – any acts claiming the 'universal' are understood through a statist project and rely on citizenship to organise membership. Additionally, the claim for cosmopolitanism, rather than an open inclusive notion, can become a 'technically delivered accountancy for the powerful' (Douzinas 2007, 225). While Benhabib aspires towards a conceptualisation of 'mediation between the ethical and the moral, the moral and the political' (Benhabib 2006, 158), this, ultimately, is limited to a predetermined framework. Under the pretence of a mediated 'universal' or 'cosmopolitanism', the categories of 'ethical', 'moral', and 'political' are not questioned as originating in a limited epistemology. Benhabib assumes that these are *the* logical categories through which to speak about rights, citizenship and migration, specifically the rights of non-citizens or new citizens.

Both Dauvergne's and Benhabib's theoretical analyses of citizenship and the nation-state prompt alternative ways to think about law, migration and labour. These alternatives reaffirm the presumed necessity, almost naturalness, of the nation-state and its legal structure, even while claiming a new rule of law or a universal cosmopolitanism. Their alternative theories overlook that labour markets benefit from sub-citizenship and precarious labour. Cosmopolitan rights or the rule of law unhinged from the nation-state seem to deny that peoples' experiences in working and crossing territorial boundaries are caught up in processes of neoliberalisation and labour needs; both labour demand and the need for people to earn a livelihood and sustain themselves and their dependants. Citizenship is assumed to be the only way to order our identity and belonging, as if the nation-state were the only possible governance structure that our scholarship must either instrumentalise or refuse. As alternatives, the idea of citizenship and the idea of the rule of law remain ensconced in an idealised structure of the state and its institutions, obfuscating possibilities of thinking beyond foundational, ideologically prescribed presumptions. Yet in practice, ecotechnically, people work and move in spite of the nation-state.

Thinking alternatively about migration and labour cannot deny the world is ecotechnics: we cannot deny that capital circulation and accumulation is happening at the circulation of beings in the world. The unexamined idea of citizenship, that this is something that must be protected and maintained as an exclusive privilege, is embedded in the processes of capital accumulation that benefit from a sub-citizen, irregular labouring population. Similarly, work that is marginalised within the dominant labour market and its ascriptions of value, such as care work and work carried out in the home, is embedded *as marginalised* in capital circulation. Ecotechnics reminds us that we cannot move away from capital circulation, just like we cannot think away the eco that exceeds capital concretisation and technologisation. Eco-technical circulation is our world; we have nothing else. Thus, our analysis must reckon with techne and eco as we think beyond the tenacity of embedded concepts and categories that seize meaning and order to our being singular plural.

Frantz Fanon argued that dislocation is figuratively experienced as the uncanny occupation of oneself as a divided subject (Fanon 2008). The experience of dislocation, uncanniness, division and, ultimately, homelessness, is not only experienced in the (post)colonial body. Our world understood as being ecotechnics, where our 'entire system of intimate joining is exposed as technics' (James 2014, 121) is a world of unhomliness. We are, and ergo our world is, experienced only ever as dislocated from the foundations, epistemological and emotional, that we are conditioned to believe in and aspire towards. Dislocation is not split between two or more, it is dislocation from the ground and an abandonment to existence. Significantly, this abandonment is not loss. Rather it is opening (eco) onto what exists as experience, not the categories and constructs used to filter or process experiences. Part of the experience, existence in the eco is the being singular plural. Legal-political frames have been used in an attempt to articulate (form, reform) this relationship according to more ethical or inclusive formulations.

Hospitality and home: ecotechnical circulation

Benhabib discusses the European project and cosmopolitan citizenship as a site for hospitality. Hospitality, as a foundational political and theoretical concept, has somewhat gone out of vogue in the securitisation panic turned migration crisis characterising the recent decade of the twenty-first century. Nevertheless, the profitable 'hospitality industry', which worldwide is largely reliant on precarious, low-waged workers, capitalises on selling 'hospitality' over 'service' (see also Roslofsen and Minca 2018). Hospitality, to be hospitable, requires having a home, a base, as a nucleus from which hospitality can be extended. The state, purportedly 'home' for citizens, claims to be protecting such a nucleus when hospitality is denied to foreigners, immigrants and strangers.

Ironically, the preconditions of being hospitable – having a home – encourages a protectionist and xenophobic retreat to the home: protecting and withholding openness in the name of maintaining the home as one's own (see Derrida and Dufourmantelle 2000). If the home were open, unprotected, it would not be a home able to be opened. Ultimately, any hospitality that is offered from the home is limited and conditional because it depends on having a home that is yours and not the other's, i.e. not the foreigner's in need of hospitality. Without conditions and boundaries, 'my' home space, like 'my' distinct identity, would no longer be my own. It would lose its specificity by being 'everyone's'. Hospitality, in proximity to hostility, therefore, can only be understood as the in-between, the threshold of home that at the same time has the potential to unravel and destroy home.

Hospitality, in its traditional Kantian form, is conditional, and reinforces citizenship-based exclusion: 'conditional hospitality concerns itself with rights, duties, obligations, etc. It has a lineage tracing back to the Greco-Roman world, through the Judeo-Christian tradition, and to the political philosophies of Kant and Hegel' (Westmoreland 2008, 1). Those who are citizens in the host state hold the prerogative to refuse hospitality (from *hostis*, also etymologically linked to hostility), or withhold welcome. This implies a limited hospitality that is conditional on the existence of a limit from which to offer, to open, hospitality (Derrida and Dufourmantelle 2000). Within the modern nation state, the legal and economic systems that are 'global' constitute the 'irregular' 'migrant' labourer as if these persons were permanent foreigner-outsiders inside the state. In asking to be 'regular' rather than 'irregular', or to be secure rather than precarious, the so-called irregular migrant labourer begs a hospitality that is unrecognised and denied in manifestations of state-regulated migration. The fear is that the foreigner becomes a permanent guest. The foreign-other might become a permanent visitor without the possibility of reciprocating hospitality in their own home, while the place where they 'ask to be hosted' can never become their proper home because they have come from 'outside' the origin-ethnic-nation.

Without a home territory to return to, or without demonstrating a requisite homage towards the nation-state through Good Citizenship or participation in the elusive 'community of value' (see Chapter 2), the foreigner-outsider-inside demonstrates transgression of the norm, whether this be a cosmopolitan norm or otherwise statist-citizenship norm. Through Kant, 'irregular' 'migrant' workers may well represent moral digression and anarchy since they exist beyond or in spite of the state (Axinn 1971, 425). Without the state, according to Kant, the individual is an irrational being and lives in anarchy, which Kant equates with evil (i.e. chaos, disorder). This extends further to include those who circumvent or subvert the state (Axinn 1971, 424). The hospitality that is fundamental to Kant's *Perpetual Peace* (1795) under the claim that 'The Law of World Citizenship Shall Be Limited to Conditions of Universal Hospitality,' is mediated through the state and reinforces the prerogative of civil society and civil law of that state. This paradigm, dedicated to statist hospitality, is fundamental to our present-day conception of the nation-state and the responsibility-obligation citizens bear towards immigrants, visitors and other migrants. Those who lay claim to the nation-state suggest that the nation-state provides a home, envied by all who travel from distant shores. But it remains the prerogative of those who lay claim to the nation to mediate whose arrival is to be welcomed and who is to be refused entrance, denied a welcome, and deemed illegal. For example, the UK Home Secretary in August 2019, Priti Patel, made clear that the priorities of the UK Home Office were to reserve immigration rights and pathways for the 'best and the brightest' while cracking down on 'criminals' facilitating 'illegal crossings' (Gov.UK 2019b). The UK tactic for addressing this infraction included providing money for France's border patrol. The move raised concerns not only about the financial priorities of the British government, but also for the post-Brexit maintenance of immigration provisions such as family reunification and children seeking asylum (LeConte 2019). The actions of the UK Home Office, as well as other EU countries (Italy, Malta and Greece have all refused to allow boats to dock in their ports) and the collective EU border enforcement responses via organisations such as Frontex, as mentioned earlier, illustrate that the nation-state is not a meeting point. There is no mediation. The official reception of migrants to the UK and Europe is not an encounter but a threshold preceded by hospitality or hostility.

Home implies a site, or grounding, for economic practices: practices that are relational, creative and productive. As the site of relation, Irigaray writes, 'at the base of relating to others is the imperative, or the pursuit of home: place and belonging – a ground from which to stand' (2013, 47). Home also implies ownership, employment and property, which – like the classic model of labour discussed in the previous chapters as the standard employment model – is a profoundly gendered notion of market economic participation and property ownership (Still 2010). The woman, in contrast to the property-owning male, is charged with maintaining the home and its privacy. 'Women's work' is to provide the ground of home, the site of relation. However, as a material experience, the home is rarely a settled, singular, place. Neither is it clearly distinguishable from the so-called public political sphere. Not only does the home ostensibly provide the base from which one participates in the world (is fed, cared for, sleeps and so on), it can also be the site of violence, disruption and dislocation. Assuming that a 'home' is one's own, and a physical space, presumes a stability and ownership that is not widely experienced. Neither is it within the Western-colonial modern tradition an ownership afforded to women. The distinction between 'guest' and 'host' is not always clear. The host is assumed to be the one who is recognised as a participant in the community of value, and the guest the one permitted entrance. Nevertheless, the 'guest' when not welcomed is always at risk of slipping into being an intruder, while the 'host' is in danger of losing her 'home' once the guest enters and makes herself 'at home' (Tataryn 2013).

The 'community of value' (see Chapter 2), illustrates how persons considered citizens risk slipping from 'host' to 'guest', or to 'not-quite-good-enough' (Anderson 2013, 6) merely 'tolerated' citizen (Anderson 2013, 89 and 93). The same groundlessness can happen in the relationship of being singular plural. The proto-political community (as cosmopolitanism), exclusive citizenship and the market economic system obscure this precarity, necessarily in order for the Western, modern-colonial liberal ideology and economic market system to continue. Quijano (2010) refers to this as part of the colonial matrix of power. Thus, seeing home as a pursuit rather than a place, the theme of the foreigner, the stranger, intrudes not only on epistemic categories, but intrudes at the very core of moral correctness (Nancy 2008). The stranger, disruptively, enacts being singular plural. While Good Citizens are *meant* to be welcoming, according to liberal democratic humanitarian values, this moral correctness cannot address the irregular. The 'irregular migrant' or the 'precarious irregular labourer' is not a guest; the irregular is already 'within' being in the plural. The irregular is a defamiliarisation that is always already happening. Meanwhile, the illusion that home is attainable suggests that the foreigner, or the relationship formed, can and will become familiar, or un-strange. But there is no ground or stability. Home is a pursuit, not a place.

Homes exist only as destroyed

Home is not a singular, individual concept but is realised only in relation to the plurality of what is (what *exists*) outside of home. Home is constituted in multiple instances and in multiple ways, whereas a sense of home is experienced as a singularity always in the plurality. Rather than the traditional notion of home being a physical house or structure, or belonging to a particular territory, 'home' is an *infinite plurality of singular instances of home*. Home is experienced, created and recreated, each time that there is an encounter at the threshold of intimacy and foreignness or difference. Home, realised via hospitality, is where the limit of our security is exceeded. Home is the sense of our being singular plural in one of its most intimate manifestations. Home is *eco*technical.

Is home only known when it is threatened? When it is lost? Why do children, or any people, cry when they leave home? This mourning is not for home as a place, but perhaps for home as a past that is being left behind, never to have or to regain, even if that past is an idea of the past that never existed. Or is it mourning home as a *feeling* that can be known in fragments, never as a cohesive experience or memory? Maybe the sadness of longing for home is not because we need a stable-nuclear-paternal-house that is home but because home is never known until it is absent, cut, or broken. Home is never lost just as it is never possessed. Rather, home is endlessly reconstituted and redefined, or reaffirmed. Home is always home as something different, but guided by a familiar, yet unsettled, sense of yearning. Yearning for some*thing*, or some *feeling* that is home, an uncanny familiarity that can creep up at the strangest thresholds, only to disappear as un-homely, yet be known. It is sensed as an experiencing of dwelling; eco.

If an unsettled home, whose threshold itself is under question or doubt, is the only 'home' from which we can offer hospitality, what is the use of a concept such as hospitality? The idea of a home from which to offer hospitality suggests that there is an achievable form that gives shape to 'home', not as an experience, but as a place. This ideal is a yearning, powerful enough to fuel the philosophical and social, political, pursuit of grounding, of origin. In other words, of home through nation-state, citizenship and law, including the ethnonationalism of current political rhetoric in Europe discussed earlier. However, this pursuit reveals that every concept is at its foundation uncanny. The question that is always asked at the threshold, the question that constitutes the threshold, like the one asked of the stranger at the threshold of hospitality (Derrida and Dufourmantelle 2000), disturbs the pursuit of grounding by reflecting back onto it its own un-groundedness and its un-homliness. If there is 'nothing other than the passage to the limit, not its attainment: it is the being-exposed at, on and as the limit' (Nancy 1993, 29), then home and hospitality is called into question and is named at such a limit, before concretisation. Therefore, the question of home is the exposure to the excess and restraint at the limit. Home is *eco*.

Hospitality understood in this way embodies a sense that is manifest as yearning. Yearning involves a limit from which one yearns while at the same time is intrinsically aware of the inadequacy of its constitution and its changing nature. Yearning is the sense (of the world) exceeding itself, experienced as groundlessness, reflected back as no single locus and no fixed threshold. The unhomely, the threshold unravelling itself as it is encountered, is the only threshold that we can ever know. Yet we crave the limit that gives us finitude; we crave the same limit that gives us identity, difference and law, i.e. the nation-state; citizenship; legal status. Our sense of need for security, for comfort, for boundaries, drives us to relentlessly search for the threshold, and moreover to constitute a threshold by reaffirming (fundamentally unquestioned) categories such as citizen, national, migrant, foreigner. These categories, porous and unsatisfactory as they are, make us all the hungrier for home, compelling us to retreat from the excess of the limit to cling desperately onto categories and distinctions, ultimately arriving at nationalism, protectionism, xenophobia.

The attempt to define and condition the limit, for instance the attempt to fix and 'find' home, is an attempt to define and fix sense as some*thing* that can be named, hence turning to the techne of law. Once it is fixed, home – as property, territory, a gendered, racialised sphere – has to continue justifying its imagined existence through modern law, the nation-state and a neoliberal ideology of progress and growth ('attainment'), for fear of losing the ground that has been constructed. We experience a denial of the 'uncanniness of imperatives' which comes 'out of a profound contempt for the condition of insecurity and groundlessness it announces' (Nancy 1993, xxvii). While there is no 'interiority' without being 'entirely in exteriority', likewise there is no exteriority without being entirely in interiority. All we have, all we can know, is what exists, which means what is expressed and experienced, external of a singularity, but not proscribed by a detached other or externality. The participation of the singularity with the external, which is likewise constituted by the internal, is an uncanny, unsettled, existence. It is at once immanent and present, but also 'indistinguishable from its transcendence' (Nancy 1993, 30). This immanent transcendence is not

> a 'passage out of' – . . . it is the insistence of a burst; transcendence takes place on the spot, here and now, as a presence that would be the singular presence of a strike, of a spring, of a free leap in existence and of existence.
> (Nancy 1993, 58)

Thus, home, or rather un-home, is neither a fixed known home nor a wandering homelessness that lacks home. For postcolonial scholars, this can be 'homelessness-as-home' (JanMohamed 1992). It is eco-technical.

The infinite yearning for home, or home *as unhomliness*, is obscured by the overwhelming technologies of home that constitute our subjectivity as if home were attainable. As mentioned previously: property, territory, ownership, citizenship, nation, belonging, sovereignty. Such ideals, taken to their limit, speak to fixed, predetermined, concretisation of being. They reinforce modernity's prison of the domestic sphere, where culturally and historically specific hierarchies violently render gendered difference and legitimate male participation and superiority while sanctioning female oppression and inferiority. They reinforce colonialism's racial difference, where Anglo-American-European epistemologies render racial, ethnic, linguistic difference, and legitimate colonial superiority, sanctioning the polluting, denigration, resource extraction and dumping of *other* foreign countries and peoples. They reinforce economic market hegemony, attributing value to 'profitable' (capital accumulating) work rendering non-conformist bodies malfunctioning, diseased and unworthy of participation. The nation-state, where Good Citizens are meant to have a home, promises security. The nation-state, where persons are made irregular, exploited and denied legal subjectivity, delivers unhomliness. This is the experience of existing in the world.

Defamiliarising home

Ecotechnics, when considered through attention to bodily materiality in a groundless home, renders not the body of the stranger (the 'migrant') as the intrusion, but the ecotechnical nature of capital, embodied in the economic market, intrudes as capital alone comes into relief as the stranger inside. The market model and processes of neoliberalisation capitalise and commodify bodies producing and reproducing. Categories that claim to frame being (i.e.

identity) attempt to seize 'eco' but of course fail to ever capture existence. Moreover, the frame is determined by the dominance of those whose personhood is inscribed in modernity's image of the citizen subject and claim authorship over a universal, 'global', sphere. Because the neoliberalising market prioritises capital and economic growth, embedded in the state, it sets free eco*sociality* and abandons us (being) to the incommensurability of being within the limited onto-epistemic frame. Abandoned to groundlessness we are not without relationship. But we are abandoned to embrace the strange/r as our homeless being (singular plural) and faced with the need to seek other knowledges and pluriversal vocabularies in order to gather all that we are.

In the previous chapter, law was discussed as uncanny in that it is impossible to fix a law; the law here understood as the law that traces the limit (Nancy 1993, 30). The existence that exists at the limit reflects back an inability to locate or distinguish ground or home – thus the limit is pushed or reached. Hospitality, as a concept and/or an act, obscures an indistinguishable home. This obfuscation is important, because without threshold and without a sense of home, the ideas of security and citizenship-belonging that form the parameters of society, economy and politics unravel. Unravelling the concepts underlying the nation-state in pursuit of the *eco* is my aim.

As seen in Chapter 1, *eco-nomics* originally refers to the regulation, or logic, of the 'home': *eco* – the environment or the household (*οικος*) and *nomos* – law (*νόμος*, *nómos*). The law of the environment was narrowed to a focus on the household and private ownership of the home, which was fundamental to the structure of society resting on a patriarchal family structure. The household was the foundation enabling the man – the original 'good' citizen – to participate in the public sphere (the *polis*). Women, children, domestic workers and slaves, in contrast, were contained in the so-called private space of the home, where the foundation of eco-nomos was established and nurtured but denigrated. Thus, eco-nomics, on the one hand, harkens back to the traditional racialised and gendered structure where the citizen emerged from the private to the public; *his* economic activity upheld both the home and the public, i.e. the state. On the other hand, economics, the logic of a household, does not necessarily need to reaffirm the singular, historically specific interpretation of the household. The 'household' and the 'home' could be the basic relation of the singular plural, embracing 'continuous material and conceptual movement' (Philippopoulos-Mihalopoulos 2011, 2). Economic understanding can be pluriversal.

Redefining eco-nomos would entail uprooting the concept of eco- from the ideologically weighted, historically specific contingency of the household, property and -nomos. Eco must be dislocated from the nation-state, citizenship and modernity's embedded assumptions about home. Eco- as a household of ecology (home-as-homelessness) and nomos as originary sociality would posit household as a shared space, bounded by an ethical relationality to the singular plural beings that rely not only on each other (*nomos*) but on the environment and ecology of life (*eco*). This relationality is 'continuous material and conceptual movement.' Eco-nomos, uprooted from the predominant (neo) liberal market ideology upholding our onto-epistemological structures of law and economics, maintains and sustains not only human, animal relationship, but that within nature, ecosystems and biodiversity.

The ostensibly most familiar subject, the Good Citizen, is intrinsically unknown. For who is the Good Citizen? Where is s/he? Strangely, in spite of seemingly setting the goal for all others, how does this Good Citizen maintain the global economic system, save occupying a hegemonic position over the subjectivity of all others who are not-quite-Citizen? These questions unsettle the fantasy of citizenship. Thinking about the 'eco' activates what critical theorist Rosi Braidotti has termed *defamiliarization* (2013). A foreigner is an intruder imposing on hospitality and the nation-state, who acts to defamiliarise the rights-bearing, autonomous individual citizen-subject. The intruder, for instance the irregular migrant labourer, disrupts the notion that 'I' am the realisation of 'my' own self, in the stability of a fixed home-space where 'I' belong: be it home as private property, owned and inhabited, or a domestic national market economy. In either case, the home has within it, intrinsic to itself in stereotypical assumptions, the disruptive 'working' woman and the disruptive 'settled' migrant. Far from being a settled, stable space, the home as a space for the 'I' is nothing but a site of technologies that can be replaced, operated on, and fixed in order to prolong 'my' life. For the person considered 'migrant', the nation-state promises a home to those who participate as Good Citizens; that is, those who participate in the neoliberal economic system in 'high valued' work. In practice, the market system is a technique of production and reproduction where neoliberalisation engulfs the work of bodies into an insatiable capitalist system. Even the Good Citizen can be 'irregular' in the market. A shifted focus on irregular migration and labour highlights the limit of legal recognition and subjectivity in and of itself. Home is nothing but a confrontation with homeless-ness, with precarity and groundlessness. For this reason, sociability and the relation that occurs at the level of the encounter of plurality of singular beings *is* originary, disruptive and intrusive every time.

Terms of law and togetherness

As we have seen in the previous chapter, originary sociality, as singular plural, can be seen as being the reason for, and limit of, law. Such a theorisation of law resists the governance power of predetermined categories because it enables thinking to give credence to the material possibility of our being 'with'. Here, relationality is key. The relationship that we, as beings, have with each other before determination or signification is what forms the element of sociality and society. The coming together of persons has also been extensively discussed in terms of community. Nancy (1991) explored the coming together of persons as unravelling predetermined, programme-oriented frameworks through material lived experience. Community rethought in this way was intended to resist determination; coming together cannot be accounted for within common signification (May 1997, 31). Community as unravelling, or inoperative (*désoeuvrement*), provides an antidote to calls for 'authentic community' (i.e. belonging in the nation) that enforce exclusive boundaries, ignoring the movement and happening of sociality.[4] Inoperative, unravelling, community, therefore, is neither a bond nor a production of unity, but is the 'condition of our existence.'[5]

Invoking words such as community, sense and creation has been discredited as harkening to a transcendent form and thereby undermining a deconstructive process (James 2014, 125). As an additional concern, neoliberal society has a tendency to 'immediately ruin whatever new chances a renewal of the concept of community could provide to our political discourse today' (Lambert 2014, 57).[6] Accordingly, 'the theme of "community" now run[s] the risk of becoming, yet again, "excessive" and "inappropriate" as a philosopheme or as an element in our current political discourse' (Lambert 2014, 57). Since the early 1990s, with the fall of the Soviet Union, objections to conventional uses of the term community, where 'community' is used to describe a collective of individuals that *should* be formed, have been discussed and debated.[7] The constructive definition of community is one where people are made to fit and conform to a group. Such an approach underlies nationalism and citizenship, where people are expected to conform to the community as either excluded or included and are subjected to a self-affirming totality. This totality identifies its members according to an overarching governance programme (nationalism)

4 Thirteen years after writing *Inoperative Community*, Nancy's 2001 (original publication) 'Confronted Community' was written in response to Blanchot's *Unavowable Community*. In response to Blanchot, Nancy indicates that he is in favour of substituting 'being-together', 'being-in-common' and 'being with' for the term 'community', preferring the 'with' to the 'co-' (Nancy 2003, 31). According to Blanchot, community is the 'sharing of "something" which precisely, seems always already to have eluded the possibility of being considered as part of sharing' (Blanchot 1988, 8). It is an unavowable experience, a presentation of the mortal truth, a presentation of finitude and excess without return (Blanchot 1988, 11). Unlike the term *désoeuvrement*, translated as 'inoperative' or 'unworking', the term 'unavowable' is work that cannot let itself be communicated, but its work is no more a fact than the fact of 'being in common' (Nancy 2003, 33). Nancy concludes his response in 'Confronted Community' by asking, 'without god or master, without common substance, what is the secret "community" or "being-with"?' (Nancy 2003, 34).

5 Devisch 2013, 30. Community, 'being with' or the 'being together' is elemental to the ethical-political stakes of deconstruction (Devisch 2013, 22). For Nancy, the bodily, present and material singular plural being-in-common *is*. We are always in relation within the world where a being is not total onto itself (Nancy 2000, 48). Further, being-with happens because we *are* in the world, not because we have determined a particular foundation or definition through which to speak of ourselves. Therefore, attention is given to what happens under, above or beyond false contingency, rather than what may be possible to change.

6 The best example of this is how news outlets such as the *New York Times* can be condemned for being 'racist' when they call out the Trump administration (Schwab 2019; Meister 2019).

7 Community, when used in discussions of social or legal phenomena, is a term used to represent communitarian and socially prescriptive ideologies. For a discussion of communitarianism versus liberalism, particularism versus universalism see Devisch 2013, 11.

that envisions a particular form for individuals in-common. Such an enforced collective can, in the extreme, result in the uniformity and repression of difference experienced in totalitarian regimes. In ostensibly more benign or democratic contexts, the identifying members in a collective similarly enact violence through enforcing hierarchies and selective exclusions – based on citizenship as belonging, for example. As a result, such communities – of the 'nation' and of 'value' – are not open to the material presence (action, labour) of all persons, nor to the relationships happening to sustain or maintain life.

Relationality and dwelling: eco before techne

To be in common is elemental to relationship. It is the happening of the singular plural. Feminist, decolonial and ecological writing mobilises discussions of relationality towards a relational-ontology: lived, experienced, socially environmentally dynamic ethical being. Rosi Braidotti writes of 'ethics of affirmation' as an 'eco-philosophy of multiple belongings for subjects constituted in and by multiplicity' (Braidotti 2013, 144). While the terminology and entry into discussing ethics is different from my approach through ecotechnics, Braidotti is similarly concerned with that which is experienced together, in an affirmative (another word for 'productive' without the connotations of market productivity and quantification) ecology of experience (i.e. what is happening). Braidotti writes towards an ethical relation that looks to joint projects and activities to affirm a positive becoming (2013, 190). Her approach to critical theory affirms a non-essential vitalism concerning multiple ecologies of belonging, similar to being singular plural. Braidotti refers to a subject that is post-anthropocentric, a subject that is relational and non-unitary but also distanced from assumptions of universal value (2013, 188).

Importantly, Braidotti's explication of the PostHuman, and its redefinition of critical thought, projects an aspirational affirmative community, 'combining ethical values with the well-being of an enlarged sense of community' (2013, 190). Unlike the originary possibility of 'eco', experienced each and every time in the singular plural, Braidotti prescribes an ideal form for the future: a *better* affirmative future in ethical community. While I do not discredit this as an important project in its pursuit of a different way of relating from within a system of forms, ecotechnics does not proffer an alternative form to which we can aspire. Ecotechnics has only the irrefutable present, happening. Thus, any suggestion stemming from ecotechnics concerns our onto-epistemological perspective: modes of thought concerning our being singular plural and from this, the world. Ecotechnical being is not in itself a self-fulfilling entity. Rather this term, with my approach, tries to access being singular plural as that which is happening in circulation with techne (capital) and ecologies of belonging and becoming. Being is paradoxically within itself as a singular being yet opposed to the individuality of being that denies interdependence with a plurality of other beings. In other words, this being is what other theorists have identified as an ongoing condition of life where the experience of becoming is an actual praxis, embodied and embedded but 'firmly located somewhere according to the radical immanence of the politics of location' (Braidotti 2013, 188). Being is relational, through and through.

Within this relationality a dwelling is *happening:* eco. The law of the home is uncanny, unhomely or homeless, insofar as it is tracing (in motion) the limit of our being in relation (singular plural) with the entirety of socio-ecology that sustains and maintains where we, beings, dwell. Ecology, economy and ecosociality share dwelling – *oikos* – where ecology nurtures possibility and economy determines dwelling. Ecosociality involves 'world creation' as the totality of resonance in lived experience in the circulation of sense. This world creation is happening whether we pay attention to it or not. Yet to pay attention to ecology and environmental change (i.e. crisis) is to pay attention to the crisis of our sociality. Thus, to draw out ecosociality undermines formed, defined categories in law and nationhood. Ecosociality is therefore not democratisation or counter-cultural organisation because it is not about adhering to, or using, the institutions of politics and government either to join or oppose. Equally, ecosociality is not ecological conservationism. Conserving an ecology 'out there' or an environment 'there' suggests that we are external to ecological circulation, able to protect 'it' as if it were distinct from 'us'. The being singular plural is everything, including and not limited to, nature.

The politics of ecotechnics are radically different from politics understood as 'management of production, exchange and growth' (Morin 2012, 104). Ecotechnics defamiliarises the normative vision of self and others. The defamiliarisation works to shatter 'the flat repetition of the protocols of institutional reason' (Braidotti 2013, 169), where 'institutional reason' is what conditions exclusive categories of belonging and filters experiences of precarious work through discourses of migration. Institutional reason relegates individuals into an ambiguous category of 'migrant' that functions in support of a neoliberal market economic model. According to the dominant model, guided by this institutional reason, capitalism – capital accumulation and economic growth – is proliferated through its power to define value. Value is understood as proliferating an infinity of ends (i.e. accumulation). Accordingly, the end to be reached is an endless increase imagined through uninhibited market growth. Economic growth of this kind, and the economic market model, espouses capital as the end in and of itself. As such, capital is reinforced as if it were the only way to participate in the economy. Yet economy (not *the* economy) can be much more than capital accumulation.

Rethinking work and movement (citizenship) from 'the law of the home' or *eco-nomos* involves disentangling labour from the 'legal conception of work' (Routh 2018, 31; Supiot 1996, 605). According to Routh, this means recognising the socio-ecological context of work. Currently, labour law functions within a system that understands work as a 'market-based exchange relationship aimed at economic productivity' (Routh 2018, 31), or, a 'private market productivity framework' (Routh 2018, 32).[8] However work can be equally understood for its activity that is part of the ecology sustaining human life and nonhuman nature as human labour contributes to the ecological circulation of the world (Routh 2018, 31). Zbyszewska calls this the 'socio-ecological scope for labour law' (2018, 11). As the law of the home, economy surpasses discussions of work and labour within a capitalist market economy. The 'home', deconstructed as a home-as-unhomeliness, leads us to question (as many feminist scholars have argued for years, see Zbyszewska 2018; Federici 2012; Salleh 2009; Gibson-Graham 1996; Picchio 1992): what is valued? How do 'we' attribute and assign value? In order for labour to be disentangled from its legal conception, what 'we' value must be carefully interrogated.

Over 20 years ago, Sandra Fredman argued that an 'ethic of responsibility' was needed to change the way law and economy privilege male workers (and their jobs) over traditionally 'women's work' and women's labour (Fredman 1998). An ethic of responsibility, however, will never circulate within a system that aspires towards progress, capital accumulation and market growth. Substituting women's labour into the market economic system, i.e. commodifying domestic work and care work, will not cause this work to be equally valued or of market worth to traditional, ego-logical, productivity-based labour. In fact, rather than care work increasing in value, other traditional labour sectors have become increasingly precarious and devalued. For example, skills-based trades acquired through apprenticeships and long-term relationships of knowledge exchange and learning (Standing 2011). The systemic logic of capitalism (primitive accumulation) has reinforced difference through gender oppression, environmental destruction and colonial (racial, ethnic) violence (Oksala 2018, 220, see also Chapter 3). As Mies (2014) emphasises, capitalist exploitation of waged labour is the tip of the iceberg. The iceberg for Mies is women's unpaid work, reproduction, 'work in the colonies' and resource extraction from the earth: labour and *being* that cannot be fully incorporated into the capital circulation of the market because it cannot be fully calculated. Their non-incorporation is why they continue to be undervalued (Oksala 2018, 230; see Mies 2014). Salleh elaborates,

> what is rarely understood, even by thinking people, is how the entire edifice of international capital ultimately rests on the material regeneration of global thermodynamic cycles by reproductive labor power. Child-care, elder care, forest nurture – by such functions, housewives or indigenes catalyse not exchange value, not use value, but a 'metabolic

8 Labour law – seen as regulatory tool in market-based exchange relation (Routh 2018, 44). The exclusion of 'responsible' labour of workers such as waste pickers, care workers leads Routh to conclude that ecological and social contributions not picked up by 'legal apparatus' (Routh 2018, 46).

> value form' that flows into and sustains the essential bio-infrastructure of the capitalist system.
>
> (Salleh 2019)

In the 1970s, the 'Wages for Housework' campaign (1972) sought to illustrate the 'immense amount of unpaid labor' that although 'not built exclusively or primarily on contractual relations' has been obscured by the focus on the wage relation in labour/employment law, policies and labour movements. Federici illuminated how 'the wage relation hides the unpaid, slave-like nature of so much of the work upon which capital accumulation is premised' (Federici 2008). By demanding wages and attributing monetary value to housework, the Wages for Housework campaign sought to speak the language of capitalism back to capitalism. This is not dissimilar to the economic argument against climate change, which demonstrates the economic costs and losses incurred by climate change (see Routh 2018, 38; Stern 2006). However, as explored in Chapter 3, Federici herself acknowledges that 'there are serious limits to the extent to which reproductive work can be reduced or reorganised on a market basis' (Federici 2009, 110). Similarly, there are serious limitations to the extent to which ecology and the environment can be reduced to market, and entirely anthropocentric, calculations. Tactics of commodifying care, environment and ecology are an attempt to fit these experiences and existence into a pre-existing form. A form that, by its very nature of technologising being into capital, excludes and undercuts the value of unwaged labour or ecological stewardship.

The Enlightenment roots of modern liberal thought and modern law attempted to make nature calculable, a 'calculable technics' (Fritsch et al. 2018, 262). Thus, it is no surprise that an anthropocentric view of nature and climate crisis looks for human solutions to remedy human-made problems within an epistemology where the market economic system is assumed to be the solution to any problem. The 'assumption of the naturalness of markets is crucial to the insistence that There is No Alternative' (Massey 2013, 16). The notion that there is no alternative to the market, and thus to the status quo, shares similarities not only with gender and women's work, but more broadly with the paradoxical incommensurability found within law as explored in Chapter 4. That the law does not hold the ground that we expect it to is hidden by a systematic, institutionalised and epistemologically affirmed insistence that law 'is' some-*thing*. Our environment and ecological circulation are likewise incommensurable. 'It' (eco – ecology, environment) does not exist somewhere. Any attempts to 'save the environment' already miss the point, and confuse the relationship between human and beings: 'can we condemn anthropocentrism and human exceptionalism on the one hand – the human is the ultimate culprit – while embracing and reaffirming these centrisms with the other – the human is the only one who can save the day?' (Kirby in Fritsch et al. 2018, 134–135). By attending to ecology and 'eco', we cannot 'restore a lost purity' (Fritsch et al.

2018, 13). The idea of purity in ego-logical modern epistemology technologises rather than releases sense.

Instead, ecology is a 'bundling of forces and appearances with neither beginning nor end – an enfolding genesis were in every ending is an inventive reiteration, a beginning' (Kirby in Fritsch et al. 2018, 129). Beings are not external to ecology: our sense is the only sense of the world and its ecosystem. But this sense is disruptive and relational. As ecotechnics illuminates, the relation within the world of ecology is a relation of interruption: the eco interrupts, disrupts and transgresses techne. By paying attention to sense, rather than the technologised action of 'saving' or 'preserving' which aspires to a purity found in something or some form, our relationship to environment becomes one that nurtures the singular plural as ecology itself. The ecosociality of sense cannot but create a relationality, a sociality, where ecological environment is life and being. Following from this, I suggest that an 'ethic of responsibility', like relational ethics, can only function with a recognition of ecotechnics. With recognition of the sense that exceeds technological seizure and capital but circulates as the dwelling for all beings, singular plural still exists within techne. The techne is undeniable, but not total. Neither is the eco total. The ethical condition is precisely this movement, which is an interruption of any narrative of totality or completion (Lynes in Fritsch et al. 2018, 115). Modernity's claim and stronghold rests on the idea that modern myths – law, nation-state, the autonomous individual – have the power to gain control and contain freedom, nature and truth. For instance, the human stepping in in the absence of divinity (see Latour 1991, 41). If, as I am exploring here, we instead are doing the opposite of containing, in other words are abandoned to freedom (Nancy 1993b, 37) in pluriversality, then this eco that we open onto can only bring disorder to the current standard of modern thinking and law. In Marder's words, ecology is the 'harbinger of crisis' for the dominant onto-epistemology (Marder in Fritsch et al. 2018, 142).

Crisis evokes negativity; it is bad, undesirable and immanent. For instance, the migration crisis, the labour/employment crisis, the climate crisis.[9] But these 'crises', while irrefutably shedding light on suffering, and physical as well as normative violence (see Oksala 2018, 219), also force us to consider what is valued. These crises force us to ask, 'what is the life worth living?' (Kothari 2018, xxviii). The 'phantasm of the world's destruction [ecological, nuclear war] serves precisely to bolster a pretence of a common and shared world [*nation*]' (Wood in Fritsch 2018, 55), reinforcing the 'ground' or 'home' of the nation-state and citizenship. Released from yearning for this as a possible resolution to crisis as if resolution, or restoration, were ever possible, we have a response-ability to respond. This response-ability is not to constructs and categories, but to the

9 It should not be surprising then, that any radical attempt to deal with the ecological crisis is condemned as inevitably leading to economic disaster.

being singular plural: present, living, experience (as well as, arguably, to ghosts not yet born and dead see Derrida 1994, 15–16). It is a response-ability that is 'as empty as it is absolute' (Nancy 2003b, 296). The barrage of information through media highlighting political, migration and ecological crisis has an 'anesthetising effect' that, through techne, diverts questions of responsibility (Barad in Fritsch et al. 2018, 208). The eco brings us back to basics. What are we able to respond to? What do we value? What are 'we'? Abandoned, as we are in an ecosociality that offers no ground and no fixed home, we can only respond to the plural that is how, why, we *are* being.

Pluriversality

As discussed through the previous chapters, the nation-state offers a ground for identity, belonging and sentiments of home. However, the idea that there is security or stability through citizenship in a nation-state is challenged by practices of law, privilege and power, whereby legally recognised citizens easily slip into categories of sub-citizenship, precarity and insecurity. The practice of law as both juridical and existential further demonstrates the lack of stability, order and consistency in law (Chapter 4). The nation-state as a contained space and identity is a fallacy. This fallacy generates a fantasy of home as if it were something that can and must be enclosed and possessed. Moreover, this fantasy fuels the securitisation of borders, the exclusion of foreigners and the privileging of waged labour as valued participation in a 'globalised' economic system. The circulation of techne as capital accumulation, the circulation of categories, the technologisation and calculation of life, is not the total experience of existence. The pursuit of home, together with the yearning for a secure identity and belonging, is undeniably seized by capital, but it is not defined by capital circulation.

Pluriversality emphasises activities that already exist in our world. Importantly, thinking pluriversally sees alternatives that are already happening. I am not suggesting a project or seizure of movement to be harnessed towards a project or goal. Scholars and practitioners of decoloniality 'envision a world confluence of alternatives, provoking strategies for transition, including small everyday actions, towards a great transformation' (Kothari 2018, xxviii). Importantly, this 'great transformation' is not predetermined and neither is it singular. Rather, thinking epistemologically plural, pluriversality moves thought away from the 'colonial matrix of power' and the epistemological hegemony of European modernity that depends on silencing the knowledges (epistemologies) of the rest of the world (Castro-Gómez 2010, 287, 288).[10] Pluriversality illuminates manifestations of ecosociality. From questioning, problematising,

10 Coloniality of power managed to seize control over epistemological plurality – 'the scientific-technical rationality of the Occident, has been postulated as the only valid episteme, that is to say the only *episteme* capable of generating real knowledge about nature, the economy, society, morality and people's happiness' (Castro-Gómez 2010, 282).

deconstructing and challenging existing 'structures of enunciation' (Mignolo 2010, 45), the world as ecotechnical is illuminated with possibilities for pluriversal thinking and being.

For example, often out of necessity, such as in response to austerity measures in the UK or the unprecedented lockdowns of 2020, lives are being 'reclaimed from the control of dominant political and financial systems' (Newman 2015, 61). Non-capitalist activities (Conill et al. 2012) include activities that, not necessarily formalised, constitute many peoples' lives and local economies. Alternative economic activities such as borrowing and lending items (books, music, tools, appliances) without cost to non-family members, such as co-workers or neighbours; repairing clothes, appliances, homes, cars, bicycles; downloading and using free software; planting vegetables for consumption (Conill et al. 2012, 240) may not be the totality of people's economic participation, but does play a key part in daily relational economics. Additionally, activities such as taking care of neighbours or friends, sharing food, offering transportation or child-care, checking in on people when they are ill – these are all non-capitalist activities, unglamorous and understated, that are part of life. These activities join a multitude of actions and activities that define how beings (human, animal, nature) are in the world, around the world, away from or beyond the technologisation (and calculation, commodification) of life (see Gibson-Graham and Dombroski 2020).

Looking specifically at the UK, European and North American contexts, some of these alternate economic activities have been technologised and corporatised, most vividly through corporate apps and sites. For instance, neighbourhood apps such as NextDoor or Gumtree which claim to cultivate 'local' community and exchanges are owned by eBay. So-called 'online communities' have been marketed and technologised through website and apps, boasting profits in the billions of dollars for their corporate owners and shareholders. Online communities such as Mumsnet, LinkedIn, Reddit, and of course, Google (including YouTube – listed under the holding company Alphabet Inc), Facebook (Whatsapp, Instagram) and Twitter profit from advertising and product placement to, and user data from, 'community members' (notably, Facebook and the Cambridge Analytica Scandal, see Dance 2018; Cadwalladr and Graham-Harrison 2018). Yet in spite of the seemingly totalising presence of these online community empires, sites such as Freecycle (U.S.), Freegle (UK), MySkip (U.S.) and Trash Nothing (a site inclusive of the previous three) maintain a mandate to facilitate non-capitalist exchange of goods.[11]

11 'The Freecycle Network™ is made up of 5,317 groups with 9,224,903 members around the world, and next door to you. It's a grassroots and entirely nonprofit movement of people who are giving (and getting) stuff for free in their own towns and neighborhoods. It's all about reuse and keeping good stuff out of landfills. Each local group is moderated by local volunteers. Membership is free.'

(freecycle.org)

When considering activities of pluriversality and alternative epistemologies, we often think of non-capitalist alternative economies. Non-capitalist economies are framed in different ways, and thus are circulated back into a technologisation. Although any seizure or concretisation of the eco is techne, what is known for example as the 'solidarity economy' or 'community economy' actively resists capitalisation and capital accumulation. Eco districts are another emerging example of localised activities or 'urban experiments' (Flurin 2017, 35) that aim to address the needs and sustainable function of urban areas. The fact that there is no direct definition of what an eco-district is (see Flurin 2017, 34) but nevertheless a shared aim is to tackle 'urban design, community building, and social and economic welfare' suggests that there is scope within these emerging projects to think of ecotechnics beyond capital accumulation, towards a more originary sociality. Such alternative economies aspire towards ethically negotiated, diverse practices that support the livelihoods of humans and non-humans (Gibson-Graham et al. 2013; Gibson-Graham 2008), coming from our shared ecology (Ahmed 2015, 429–432). Indeed, this is similar to the effort of drawing attention to ecosociality and the coming together (relationality) that forms originary sociality.

Inevitably, circulating eco into techne and techne into eco is why the world is ecotechnical. Ecotechnics, as explained in Chapter 1, *is simultaneously*. However, what these technologised alternative economies and pluriversal epistemologies offer, emerging as they are from an opening onto eco, is non-capitalist forms of being that maintain openness and groundlessness as their starting point.

The authors of Radical Ecological Democracy (2019) have outlined '8 principles of a new economics of the people of a living earth.' This exemplifies an attempt to remain open and ungrounded within an intrinsically pluriversal ecosociality:

> *Principle #1: Indicators.* Evaluate the economy's performance by indicators of the well-being of people and planet; not the growth of GDP.
>
> *Principle #2: Beneficial Use.* Use resources only to support life's capacity to regenerate.
>
> *Principle #3: Use Rights.* Put use rights and responsibilities in the hands of those who provide the labour on which the well-being of the community depends, not in the hands of those who exploit life's labour to grow personal financial assets.
>
> *Principle #4: Money.* Create society's money supply through transparent public processes that advance the common good; not through secret processes that grow the unearned profits of for-profit banks and financiers.
>
> *Principle #5: Education.* Organize and manage education to support lifetime learning in service to life-seeking communities; not preparing for standardized tests on the way to obedient service to profit-maximizing corporations.

Principle #6: Technology. Create and apply technology only in ways that serve and augment the processes of natural regeneration.

Principle #7: Community. Make living communities that strive for self-reliance while sharing technology and resources to that end, the defining units of societal organization.

Principle #8: Population. Seek a stable and mutually beneficial human population size and distribution to achieve optimal balance between humans, Earth's other species, and the generative systems of a finite living Earth.

(www. radicalecologicaldemocracy.org)

There is a techne at play in these eight principles – a craft, a technique that concretises experience and effort into action. But this techne is not capital accumulation. Indeed, the techne is not uniform, but rather aims to circulate back to sense in an ongoing circulation. Pluriversal thinking is crucial in its emphasis on plurality as opposed to universality. Consequently, that ecosocialities emerge and disrupt technologised (concretised, institutionalised) forms and structures is the happening of originary sociality – unique and original every time, in spite of and because of technique concretising the sociality as it forms. The plurality of possibility comes not from careful conditioning, but from being open to what is happening before it is seized and signified, without denying that seizure and signification will happen. Moreover, signification is most commonly guided by the normative categories of modern institutional reason: modern law, the nation-state paradigm enforced through the colonial matrix of power. Any attempt at grounding, any seizure of *eco* to contain, define and categorise 'it', loses the sense that exists as ecosociality or the sense unravels. In spite of this, and notwithstanding the inevitability of not being able to contain sense, there is no reason why we should have only one onto-epistemological lens through which to signify being. Indeed, significations of being are pluriversal.

Viveiros de Castro explains that modern thought has simplified ontological questions and understandings into questions of representation via epistemological questions. As such, 'the simplification of ontology has led to the enormous complication of epistemology' (Viveiros de Castro 2004, 483). He suggests that 'materialist ontologies' that seek to understand form, relation, through cosmologies of being, including animist frames of understanding interwoven being, may 'offer cures for epistemological hypochondria' (Viveiros de Castro 2004, 484). The radical, seemingly anarchic, pluriversality of 'other knowledges' silenced by modernity and neoliberalisation, through the nation-state and modern law, would still enact techne by concretising sense, but the concretisation would take a different form and lead to different signification. While undeniably ecotechnical, the potential of the pluriversal form would remain open.

As a further example of a shift in onto-epistemic paradigms, Newman illustrates a difference between the traditional anarchist political project and an anarchist ethos (2015, xi). In the latter, the 'purpose' of struggle is not social revolution per se. Achieving or fulfilling a metanarrative is not the goal (Newman 2015, 6). He is careful to emphasise that this does not mean that the 'social bond is dissolving altogether – merely that there is no longer one dominant, coherent understanding of society but, rather, a plurality of different narratives or perspectives' (Newman 2015, 8). Thus, the anarchist ethos or *thinking anarchically* is 'anarchic' action 'that is to say, groundless and without predetermined ends' (Newman 2015, 10). Thinking anarchically can therefore be seen as the groundlessness of the eco in ecotechnics; 'a way of acting and thinking *anarchistically* in the here and now, seeking to transform the immediate situation and relationships that one finds oneself in' (Newman 2015, 12).[12] Relating to social movements and uprisings, thinking anarchically shifts how such resistance and street protests are identified and remembered. Since 2008, in response to the global financial crisis, people have come together around the world in opposition to austerity, corruption, global finance and capital: Arab Spring (Tunisia, Libya, Egypt, Yemen, Syria, Bahrain); Indignados, 15-M Movement (Spain); the Indignant Citizens Movement (Greece); Gezi Park (Turkey); Black Lives Matter, Occupy Wall Street (U.S.); Umbrella Movement, anti-extradition protests (Hong Kong); Maidan (Ukraine); Red Shirts (Thailand); Venezuela (Byrnes 2014). These uprisings share a demonstration of opposition to the state and its status quo. In response to state violence – violence that in many of these instances was ongoing before, throughout and after the uprisings –

> the people who gather in the squares and public places of our metropolises look towards one another rather than towards the state. They embody the desire for autonomous and sustainable life which no longer bears the imprint of the state.
>
> (Newman 2015, x)

While most of these movements eventually shifted into various forms of new or old governance, regime changes and/or escalated repression, the movements themselves reoriented being towards an originary sociality of plural thinking and plural possibility embedded in the pluriversal potential of the very word, revolution (Weil 1973, 136). The movements exemplify potentiality, rather than a predetermined sociality (see Tataryn 2019; Mulqueen and Tataryn 2012). Similarly, people moving across borders and engaging in work is an originary sociality, happening, in spite of / as well as / because of,

12 I do not, however agree with Newman's adherence to the individual as the centre of post-anarchist thought. In drawing on Stirner (Newman 2015, 44–46), Newman continues an ego-logical way of thinking by focusing anarchic thinking as thinking about the self, the ego, and then the relationship with other bodies. Ecosociality, conversely, considers the singular as impossible without the plural: there is no being but for a being in relationship.

predetermined sociality within politics, economy, law. What comes from this sociality is unknown, but this sociality, rather than the concrete form already circulating as techne, is what forms the basis for law, when it is, inevitably, signified. In other words, recognising manifestations of ecosociality in various occasions and various contexts involves an energy of undoing the world at the same time that we reveal the world as an energy 'to distort the present on behalf of what the present can become' (Berlant 2011, 263). The world and its law is *happening* ecotechnically, but undoing the sociality reveals an unknown possibility for the happening of/as law.

Material sense embodied ('to give material or concrete character' 'to draw together, solidify') is not concretised. Yes, bodies are technologised, used as mechanisms of capital circulation, yet they are not totally techne. Capitalism justifies materialism, as if beings were all solely products of the market. This totalising, universal presence of capital is shared between capitalist, neoliberal thought and Marxist thought. In capitalism, man controls capital. In Marxism, the state controls capital. In both, the market economic system forms the totality of the social world and relationship, as if the concretisation of sense was totalising in and as capital. But what escapes this, even on a very simple level, is that 'society considered in its relationship to the individual cannot be defined simply by the methods of production' (Weil 1973, 142). The eco and techne are simultaneous but not consumed by one another. Ecology does not, cannot, become technology; it forever escapes seizure. We can sense this by thinking of material embodiment. Embodiment (human, animal, nature) is an experience of how we are affected, but not consumed by market forces. We are part of the market, as circulating in/as capital, but we cannot lose our embodiment as singular beings in the plural. Creativity as creation is the intrinsic connection of the singular plural, as opposed to liberal autonomy which reifies the separation (individuation) of the singular from the plural.[13]

Ecotechnical labour, migration and law

This book has explored the movement of persons across territorial borders (migration), and the need to engage in work – work valued as waged labour and work that persists as lower waged, lower value even, or especially, when it is vital to the circulation of beings in sociality (labour) – as ecotechnics. The legal (political, economic) regulation of work and movement reveals the tenacity of a specific (modern, Western, European, neoliberal) onto-epistemological frame that posits the technological seizure of life into capital circulation as if it

13 This reification is illustrated in social uprisings and movements when attention is fixed on a leader who somehow embodies the movement of the people. As such, without a shift in onto-epistemology, revolutions and revolutionary organisations can 'reflect to a large extent the faults that they denounce in the society in which they are evolving' (Weil 1973, 136).

were the only possibility for our being in the world. Ecotechnics offers a shift in attention not to deny the technological seizure, but to see the sense of being through eco as happening simultaneously. The eco challenges universal claims over the economy and value. Notions of value and the 'law of the home' (eco-nomos) have been embedded in the idea of the nation-state, which harnesses our yearning for relationality and grounding. The fantasy of achieving ground is mobilised by the fantasy of law and the fantasy of the nation-state. But, as fantasies, they fail to provide stability, security and ground. The ecotechnics of labour migration law or seeing our world as ecotechnical through labour migration law suggests that we can only ever be epistemologically grounded in an ecological pluriversality. A pluriversality happening in the movement of our being singular plural.

Discourses of irregular migrant labour (Chapter 2) shed light on how persons are reduced to work in low-waged, low-skilled, devalued labour sectors. This is a condition most commonly experienced by persons who do not hold citizenship in their country of residence and work. However, the experience is not limited to formal legal categories. Indeed, citizens can be relegated to situations of 'irregularity' and identified as 'migrant labourers' or otherwise, sub-citizens. As the nation-state is reconsolidated, neoliberalism diffuses the responsibility of governance for the sake of bolstering the constructed, ostensibly global, economic market. Individual responsibility is emphasised, as is the commodification of relationships and disciplinary social policy. Yet sociality is always in movement, 'we' exist through pluriversal knowledges whether acknowledged by the mainstream 'institutional reason' or not. This is something even neoliberalism cannot universally, totally, concretise. As part of this eco-techne, labour and work happen in spite of normative categories that ascribe value according to wages and a hierarchy of valued participation in an ostensibly global market economy. In spite of widespread movements of nationalism, nationalism is not global. The people who are often considered to be 'subaltern' ('those from below') do not conform to 'the fraternal imagined community of 'those from above' (Sanjinés 2010, 160). Neither do persons who are 'migrant', either literally or discursively, necessarily share the pursuit of attaining a stable, fixed home to occupy.

Eco-technical analysis, through attention to ecosociality, radically challenges ego-logical thought, which is individualist, atomised thinking of the 'self'. The techne, the structural, systemic motion that capitalises on the movement of beings as capital across the world – legal/illegal, regular/irregular, waged/unwaged, citizen/noncitizen – is only part of the circulation. The other part is 'eco': dwelling, environment and home (*as homelessness*). Ecotechne, simultaneously, is the world. The point I am pursuing here is not to change ecotechne, but to be able to resist the technological seizure of life into, and as, capital accumulation we have to somehow cohabitate differently. At the same time, we already are cohabitating differently. Otherwise there would be no school strikes, there would be no concern for the rapid disappearance of biodiversity (UN report

2019; Global Climate Strikes 2019). There would be no gestures in case law to support Miss Hounga or Miss Onu, no opposition to precarious work and the conditions of labour, no opposition to ghost workers in the shadows of formal and informal economies, no concern for unpaid carers (Chapters 2 and 3). There would be no ongoing 'crisis' in labour law, as labour lawyers grapple with their purpose and mission (Chapter 3). There would be no Sea Watch 3 rescues (Chapter 4). There would be no uprisings, no spontaneous acts of kindness, no care, no empathy, no generosity, no support of interdependence and no calls to respect and learn within ecosystems and ecologies.

As I write this (early 2020), people in the world have been united in a day of climate crisis strikes, which saw millions of school children, young adults and adults leave their classrooms and places of work to protest against the inaction of governments around the world to respond to scientifically identified rapid climate change and destruction. This movement, these climate strikes, have aligned with existing local environmental movements and groups such as Extinction Rebellion, Greenpeace, and political campaigns such as The Green New Deal. Yes, these alignments demonstrate that there is a concretisation of a programme, an agenda, a goal (techne) behind these campaigns. But this does not discount or undermine that in and of itself the climate strikes are a strike, an interruption. They exceed techne as eco. The power of this movement comes not from its output, but in its interruption of daily life. The strikes pause the myth or the fantasy that the day is of use, or of value, as it is normalised. The strikes, 'school children' not going to school, in and of themselves, embody the 'eco' that escapes – but not denies – technologisation. Even further, the recognition within these strikes happening in different cities and regions around the world is that environmental action and attention is linked to action for decolonisation. They are calling on previously subjugated voices and knowledges to be heard and listened to, illustrating movement beyond capital.

We do not have to search for a new way of being: the world as ecotechnics exists in all possibility.

References

Ahmed, Pepita Ould. 2015, 'What does solidarity economy mean? Contours and feasibility of a theoretical and political project' *Business Ethics: A European Review* vol. 24, no. 4.

Anderson, Bridget. 2013, *Us & Them: The Dangerous Politics of Immigration Control*. Cambridge: Cambridge University Press.

Anghie, Antony. 2005, *Imperialism, Sovereignty and the Making of International Law*. Cambridge: Cambridge University Press.

Axinn, Sidney. 1971, 'Kant, authority, and the French revolution' *Journal of the History of Ideas* vol. 32, no. 3, pp. 423–432.

Barnard, Helen. 2018, 'UK poverty 2018' Joseph Rowantree Foundation www.jrf.org.uk/report/uk-poverty-2018

Benhabib, Seyla. 2006, *Another Cosmopolitanism: Hospitality, Sovereignty, and Democratic Iterations* (with essays by Bonnie Honig, Will Kymlicka and Jeremy Waldron). Oxford: Oxford University Press.

Berlant, Lauren. 2011, *Cruel Optimism*. Durham, London: Duke University Press.

Bhaba, Jacqueline. 1998, 'Enforcing the human rights of citizens and non-citizens in the era of maastricht: Some reflections on the importance of states' *Development and Change* vol. 29, no. 4, pp. 697–724.

Bix, Brian. 2006, 'Legal positivism and "Explaining" normativity and authority' *American Philosophical Association Newsletter on Philosophy and Law* vol. 5, no. 2, Minnesota Legal Studies Research Paper No. 09–05.

Blanchot, Maurice. 1988, *The Unavowable Community*. trans., Pierre Joris. New York: Station Hill Press.

Braidotti, Rosi. 2013, *The Posthuman*. Cambridge: Polity Press.

Butler, Judith and Chakravorty Spivak. 2007, *Who Sings the Nation-State?* Chicago: Chicago University Press.

Byrnes, Mark. 2014, 'The remarkable year in protests' *City Lab* 24 December 2014, viewed 29 September 2019 www.citylab.com/equity/2014/12/the-remarkable-year-in-protests/384012/

Cadwalladr, Carole and Emma Graham-Harrison. 2018, 'Revealed: 50 million Facebook profiles harvested for Cambridge Analytic in major data breach' *The Guardian* 17 March 2018, viewed 28 September 2019 www.theguardian.com/news/series/cambridge-analytica-files

Cahn, Claude and Elspeth Guild. 2010, 'Recent migration of Roma in Europe' (2nd edition). Organisation for Security and Cooperation in Europe (OSCE), viewed 28 September 2019 www.osce.org/hcnm/78034?download=true

Castro-Gómez, Santiago. 2010, 'The missing chapter of empire: Postmodern reorganisation of coloniality and post-Fordist capitalism' in *Globalisation and the Decolonial Option*. Walter Mignolo and Arturo Escobar (eds), pp. 282–302. New York: Routledge.

Cheah, Peng. 2009, 'The untimely secret of democracy' in *Derrida and the Time of the Political*. Peng Cheah and Suzanne Gerlac (eds), pp. 74–96. Durham: Duke University Press.

Cholewinski, Ryzard. 2009, *Irregular Migration in Europe*. Oslo: Institute for Social Research.

Clarisse, Yves. 2018, 'French farmer who helped migrants showed "fraternity," court rules' *Reuters* 6 July 2018, viewed 15 December 2019 www.reuters.com/

Columb, Seán. 2020, *Trading Life: Organ Trafficking, Illicit Networks and Exploitation*. Stanford: Stanford University Press.

Conill, Joana et al. 2012, 'Beyond the crisis: The emergence of alternative economic practices' in *Aftermath: The Cultures of the Economic Crisis*. Manuel Castells, João Caraça and Gustavo Cardoso (eds), pp. 210–250. Oxford: Oxford University Press.

Dance, Gabriel et al. 2018, 'As Facebook raised a privacy wall, it carved an opening for tech giants' *New York Times* 18 December 2019, viewed 28 September 2019 www.nytimes.com/

Darian-Smith, Eve. 2013, *Laws and Societies in Global Contexts: Contemporary Approaches*. Cambridge: Cambridge University Press.

Dauvergne, Catherine. 2008, *Making People Illegal*. Cambridge: Cambridge University Press.

Davies, Margaret. 2017, *Law Unlimited*. Abington: Routledge.

de Sousa Santos, Boaventura. 2014, *Epistemologies of the South*. Colorado: Paradigm Publishers.

Derrida, Jacques. 1994, *Spectres of Marx*. trans., Peggy Kamuf. New York, London: Routledge.

Derrida, Jacques and Anne Dufourmantelle. 2000, *Of Hospitality: Anne Dufourmantelle Invites Jacques Derrida to Respond*. trans., Rachel Bowlby. Stanford: Stanford University Press.

Devisch, Ignaas. 2013, *Jean-Luc Nancy and the Question of Community*. London: Bloomsbury.

Douzinas, Costas. 2007, *Human Rights and Empire: The Political Economy of Cosmopolitanism*. Abington: Routledge.

Dussel, Enrique. 2014, 'Anti-cartesian meditations: On the origin of the philosophical anti-discourse of modernity' *Journal for Culture and Religious Theory* vol. 13, no. 1, pp. 11–52.

European Council of Refugees and Exiles, 'Mare nostrum to end: New Frontex operation will not ensure rescue of migrants in international waters' *Weekly Bulletin* 10 October 2014, viewed 9 April 2015 www.ecre.org/operation-mare-nostrum-to-end-frontex-triton-operation-will-not-ensure-rescue-at-sea-of-migrants-in-international-waters/

European Court of Human Rights (ECHR). 2010, 'Convention for the protection of human rights and fundamental freedoms' as amended by Protocols Nos. 11 & 14, Registry of the European Court of Human Rights, June 2010.

European Parliament and Council Directive 2004/38/EC 'The right of citizens of the Union and their family members to move and reside freely within the territory of the Member States'.

Fanon, Frantz. 2008, *Black Skin, White Masks*. trans., Richard Philcox. New York: Grove Books.

Federici, Silvia. 2012, *Revolution at Point Zero*. Oxford: PM Press.

Federici, Silvia. 2009, 'The reproduction of labour-power in the global economy, Marxist theory and the unfinished feminist revolution' Paper for UC Santa Cruz seminar, 7 January 2009, viewed 28 September 2019 https://caringlabor.wordpress.com/2010/10/25/silvia-federici-the-reproduction-of-labour-power-in-the-global-economy-marxist-theory-and-the-unfinished-feminist-revolution/

Federici, Silvia. 2008, *Precarious Labor: A Feminist Viewpoint*, viewed 28 September 2019 http://inthemiddleofthewhirlwind.wordpress.com/precarious-labor-a-feminist-viewpoint/

Fitzpatrick, Peter. 2008, *Law as Resistance: Modernism, Imperialism, Legalism*. Aldershot: Ashgate.

Flurin, Claire. 2017, 'Eco-districts: Development and evaluation. A European case study' *Procedia Environmental Sciences* vol 37, pp. 34–45.

Fredman, Sandra. 1998, *Women and the Law*. Oxford: Oxford University Press.

Fritsch, Michael, Phillipe Lynes and David Wood. 2018, *Eco-Deconstruction: Derrida and Environmental Philosophy*. New York: Fordham University Press.

Gibson-Graham, J. K. 2008, 'Diverse economies: Performative practices for "Other worlds"' *Progress in Human Geography* vol 32, no. 5, pp. 613–632.

Gibson-Graham J. K. 1996, *The End of Capitalism (As We Knew It): A Feminist Critique of Political Economy*. Oxford: Blackwell.

Gibson-Graham, J. K., Jenny Cameron and Stephen Healey. 2013, *Take Back the Economy*. Minneapolis: University of Minnesota Press.

Gibson-Graham, J. K. and Kelly Dombroski (eds). 2020, *The Handbook of Diverse Economies*. Cheltenham, UK: Edward Elgar Publishing.

Gilroy, Paul. 2004, *After Empire: Melancholia or Convivial Culture?* London: Routledge.
Gilroy, Paul. 2019, 'Agonistic belonging: The banality of good, the "Alt Right" and the need for sympathy' *Open Cultural Studies* vol. 3, no. 1, pp. 1–14.
Global Climate Strikes. 2019. viewed 16 December 2019 https://globalclimatestrike.net/
Gov.uk. 2019b, 'Britain and France to strengthen joint action against small boats' *News Story*, viewed 28 September 2019 www.gov.uk/government/news/britain-and-france-to-strengthen-joint-action-against-small-boats
Guild, Elspeth and Leonie Ansems de Vries. 2018, 'Seeing refuge in Europe: Spaces of transit and the violence of migration management' *Journal of Ethnic and Migration Studies* vol. 45, no. 12, pp. 2156–2166. doi:10.1080/1369183X.2018.1468308
Hall, Stuart. 1998, 'The Windrush issue, postscript' *Soundings* no. 10, pp. 188–191.
Irigaray, Luce. 2013, 'Toward a mutual hospitality' in *The Conditions of Hospitality: Ethics, Politics, and Aesthetics on the Threshold of the Possible*. Tomas Claviez (ed), pp. 42–55. New York: Fordham University Press.
James, Ian. 2014, 'Differing on difference' in *Nancy Now (Theory Now)*. Verena Conely and Irving Goh (eds), pp. 110–126. Cambridge: Polity Press.
JanMohamed, Abdul R. 1992, 'Worldliness-without-world, homelessness-as-home: Toward a definition of the specular border intellectual' in *Edward Said: A Critical Reader*. Michael Sprinker (ed), pp. 96–120. Oxford: Blackwell.
Jordan, Miriam. 2019a, 'An Arizona teacher helped migrants. Jurors couldn't decide if it was a crime' *The New York Times* 11 July 2019, viewed 15 December 2019 www.nytimes.com
Jordan, Miriam. 2019b, 'Reporting on the retirees making migrants' journeys a little easier' *The New York Times* 29 May 2019, viewed 15 December 2019 www.nytimes.com
Joseph Rowantree Foundation. 2019, 'In-work poverty' viewed 15 December 2019 www.jrf.org.uk/work/in-work-poverty
Kallis, Aristotle. 2018, 'The radical right and islamophobia' in *The Oxford Handbook of the Radical Right*. Jens Redgern (ed), pp. 44–46. Oxford: Oxford University Press.
Kant, Immanuel. 1795, 'Containing the Definitive Articles for Perpetual Peace Among States' *Perpetual Peace: A Philosophical Sketch* section II, viewed 15 December 2019 www.mtholyoke.edu/acad/intrel/kant/kant1.htm
Kothari, Ashish et al. 2018, *Pluriverse: A Post-Development Dictionary*. New Delhi: Tulika Books.
Krastev, Ivan. 2017, *After Europe*. Pennsylvania: University of Pennsylvania Press.
Lambert, Gregg. 2014, 'Literary Communism' in *Nancy Now*. Verena Conley and Irving Goh (eds), pp. 37–58. Cambridge: Polity Press.
Latour, Bruno. 1991, *We Have Never Been Modern*. London: Simon and Schuster.
LeConte, Marie. 2019, 'Being an EU citizen in the UK was hard enough. Now Priti Patel has made it worse.' *The Guardian* 20 August 2019 viewed 28 September 2019 www.theguardian.com/commentisfree/
Lindahl, Hans. 2009, 'In between: Immigration, distributive justice, and political dialogue' *Contemporary Political Theory* vol. 8, no. 4, pp. 415–434. https://doi.org/10.1057/cpt.2008.50
Macklin, Audrey. 2007, 'Who is the citizen's other? Considering the heft of citizenship' *Theoretical Inquires in Law* vol. 8, no. 2.
Marks, Susan. 2009, 'False contingency' *Current Legal Problems* vol. 62, no. 1, pp. 1–21.
Massey, Doreen. 2013, 'After neoliberalism? Introduction to the Kilburn Manifesto' *Open Democracy UK* 21 June 2013, viewed 15 December 2019 www.opendemocracy.net/en/opendemocracyuk/after-neoliberalism-introduction-to-kilburn-manifesto/

May, Todd. 1997, *Reconsidering Difference: Nancy, Derrida, Levinas, and Deleuze*. Pennsylvania: The Pennsylvania State University Press.

Meister, Jason. 2019, 'To smear Trump the New York Times pivots from Russiagate to hoax to racism' *Fox News* 26 August 2019, viewed 28 September 2019 www.foxnews.com/

Mies, Maria. 2014, *Patriarchy and Accumulation on a World Scale: Women in the International Division of Labour* (3rd edition) London: Zed Books.

Mignolo, Walter and Arturo Escobar (eds). 2010, *Globalisation and the Decolonial Option*. New York: Routledge.

Morin, Marie-Eve. 2012, *Jean-Luc Nancy*. Cambridge: Polity Press.

Mulqueen, Tara and Anastasia Tataryn. 2012, 'Don't occupy this movement: Thinking law in social movements' *Law and Critique* vol. 23, no. 3, pp. 283–298.

Nancy, Jean-Luc. 2008, *Corpus*. trans., Richard Rand. New York: Fordham University Press.

Nancy, Jean-Luc. 2003a, 'The confronted community' trans., Amanda Macdonald *Post-Colonial Studies* vol. 6, no. 1, pp. 23–36.

Nancy, Jean-Luc. 2003b, *A Finite Thinking*. Simon Sparks (ed). Stanford: Stanford University Press.

Nancy, Jean-Luc. 2000, *Being Singular Plural*. trans., Robert Richardson and Anne O'Byrne. Stanford: Stanford University Press.

Nancy, Jean-Luc. 1993, *The Experience of Freedom*. trans., Bridget McDonald. Stanford: Stanford University Press.

Nancy, Jean-Luc. 1991, *The Inoperative Community*. trans., Peter Connor. Minnesota: University of Minnesota Press.

Newman, Saul. 2015, *Postanarchism*. Cambridge: Polity Press.

Oksala, Joanna. 2018, 'Feminism, capitalism, and ecology' *Hypatia* vol. 33, pp. 216–234. doi:10.1111/hypa.12395

Olusoga, David. 2019, 'The cult of optimism got us into this mess. It's time to embrace pessimism' *The Guardian* 14 July 2019, viewed 28 September 2019 www.theguardian.com/commentisfree/

Peck, Jamie. 2013, 'Explaining (with) neoliberalism' *Territory, Politics, Governance* vol. 1, no. 2, pp. 132–157. doi: 10.1080/21622671.2013.785365

Peck, Jaime and Nik Theodore 2019, 'Still neoliberalism?' *The South Atlantic Quarterly* vol. 118, no. 2, pp. 245–265.

Philippopoulos-Mihalopoulos, Andreas. 2014, *Spatial Justice: Body, Lawscape, Atmosphere*. Abington: Routledge.

Philippopoulos-Mihalopoulos, Andreas (ed). 2011, *Law and Ecology: New Environmental Foundations*. Abington: Routledge.

Picchio, Antonella. 1992, *Social Reproduction: The Political Economy of the Labour Market*. Cambridge: Cambridge University Press.

Quijano, Aníbal. 2010, 'Coloniality and modernity/rationality' in *Globalization and the Decolonial Option*. Walter D. Mignolo and Arturo Escobar (eds), pp. 22–32. New York: Routledge.

Radical Ecological Democracy. 2019, viewed 15 December 2019 www. radicalecological-democracy.org

Roslofsen, Maartje and Claudio Minca. 2018, 'The superhost. Biopolitics, home and the community in the *Airbnb* dream world of global hospitality' *Geoforum* vol. 91, pp. 170–181.

Routh, Supriya. 2018, 'Embedding work in nature: The anthropocene and legal imagination of work as human activity' *Comparative Labor Law & Policy Journal* vol. 40, no. 1, pp. 29–60.

Rydgern, Jens (ed). 2018, *The Oxford Handbook of the Radical Right*. Oxford: Oxford University Press.

Salleh, Ariel. 2019, 'Planetizing the labor movement' *Great Transition Initiative*, viewed 15 September 2019 www.greattransition.org/roundtable/wokers-world-ariel-salleh

Salleh, Ariel (ed). 2009, *Eco-Sufficiency and Global Justice: Women Write Political Ecology*. London: Pluto Press.

Sanjinés, Javier. 2010, 'The nation: An imagined community?' in *Globalisation and the Decolonial Option*. Walter Mignolo and Arturo Escobar (eds), pp. 149–162. New York: Routledge.

Sassen, Saskia. 2008, *Territory, Authority, Rights* (updated edition). Princeton: Princeton University Press.

Schwab, Nikki. 2019, 'Trump accuses New York Times of going on a racism witch hunt' *New York Times* 18 August 2019, viewed 15 December 2019 https://nypost.com/

Soysal, Yasemin. 1994, *Limits of Citizenship: Migrants and Postnational Citizenship in Europe*. Chicago: University of Chicago Press.

Standing, Guy. 2011, *The Precariat: The New Dangerous Class*. London, New York: Bloomsbury Academic.

Statewatch Observatory. 2019, 'The refugee crisis in the Med and inside the EU: A humanitarian emergency' viewed 23 November 2019 www.statewatch.org/eu-med-crisis.htm

Stern, Nicolas. 2006, *The Economics of Climate Change: The Stern Review* 30 October 2006, viewed 28 September 2019 www.lse.ac.uk/GranthamInstitute/publication/the-economics-of-climate-change-the-stern-review/

Still, Judith. 2010, *Derrida and Hospitality: Theory and Practice*. Edinburgh: Edinburgh University Press.

Supiot, Alain. 1996, 'Perspectives on work: Introduction' *International Labour Review* vol. 135, no. 603.

Tataryn, Anastasia. 2019, 'From social uprising to legal form' *Law and Critique* vol. 30, no. 1, pp. 41–65.

Tataryn, Anastasia. 2013, 'Revisiting hospitality: Opening doors beyond Derrida towards Nancy's inoperativity' *Law Text Culture* vol. 17, pp. 187–213.

Tondo, Lorenzo. 2019, 'Sicilian fishermen risk prison to rescue migrants: "No human would turn away"' *The Guardian* 3 August 2019, viewed 15 December 2019 ww.guardian.com

Trilling, Daniel. 2018, *Lights in the Distance: Exile and Refuge at the Borders of Europe*. London: Palgrave Macmillan.

UN report. 2019, 'UN report: Nature's dangerous decline "Unprecedented"; Species extinction rates "Accelerating"' *Sustainable Development Goals* 6 May 2019, viewed 15 December 2019 www.un.org/sustainabledevelopment/blog/2019/05/nature-decline-unprecedented-report/

Viveiros de Castro, Eduardo. 2004, 'Exchanging perspectives: The transformation of objects into subjects in Amerindian ontologies' *Common Knowledge* vol. 10, no. 3.

Von der Burchard, Hans. 2019, 'MSF to resume Mediterranean migrant rescue operations' 21 July 2019, viewed 15 December 2019 www.politico.eu/article/msf-to-resume-mediterranean-migrant-rescue-operations/

Weil, Simone. 1973 original 1955, *Oppression and Liberty*. trans., Arthur Wills and John Petries. Amherst: University of Massachusetts Press.

Westmoreland, Mark W. 2008, 'Interruptions: Derrida and hospitality' *Kritike* vol. 2, no. 1, pp. 1–10.

Zbyszewska, Ania. 2018, 'Labor law for a warming world? Exploring the intersections of work regulation and environmental sustainability: An introduction' *Comparative Labor Law and Policy Journal* vol 40, no. 1.

Case Law

Ajayi v (1) Abu (2) Abu [2017] EWHC 1946
CN v The United Kingdom [2012] Application no. 4239/08
Hounga v Allen [2014] UKSC 47
Mruke v Khan [2018] EWCA Civ 280
Nambalat v Taher & Anor: Udin v Pasha & Ors [2012] EWCA Civ 1249
Pimlico Plumbers Ltd and Another v Smith [2018] UKSC 29
Siliadin v France, App No. 73316/91, Judgment of 26 July 2005
Taiwo v Olaigbe and another; Onu v Akwiwu and another [2016] UKSC 31

Index

For Product Safety Concerns and Information please contact our EU representative GPSR@taylorandfrancis.com
Taylor & Francis Verlag GmbH, Kaufingerstraße 24, 80331 München, Germany

www.ingramcontent.com/pod-product-compliance
Ingram Content Group UK Ltd.
Pitfield, Milton Keynes, MK11 3LW, UK
UKHW011013180926
475701UK00004B/715

* 9 7 8 0 3 6 7 6 2 1 6 6 7 *